D1582338

Possible Scotlands

POSSIBLE SCOTLANDS

WALTER SCOTT AND
THE STORY OF TOMORROW

Caroline McCracken-Flesher

OXFORD

UNIVERSITY PRESS

2005

OXFORD
UNIVERSITY PRESS

Oxford University Press, Inc., publishes works that further
Oxford University's objective of excellence
in research, scholarship, and education.

Oxford   New York
Auckland   Cape Town   Dar es Salaam   Hong Kong   Karachi
Kuala Lumpur   Madrid   Melbourne   Mexico City   Nairobi
New Delhi   Shanghai   Taipei   Toronto

With offices in
Argentina   Austria   Brazil   Chile   Czech Republic   France   Greece
Guatemala   Hungary   Italy   Japan   Poland   Portugal   Singapore
South Korea   Switzerland   Thailand   Turkey   Ukraine   Vietnam

Library of Congress Cataloging-in-Publication Data
McCracken-Flesher, Caroline.
Possible Scotlands : Walter Scott and the story of tomorrow /
Caroline McCracken-Flesher. — 1st ed.
p. cm.
Includes bibliographical references and index.
ISBN-13 978-0-19-516967-6
ISBN 0-19-516967-0
1. Scott, Walter, Sir, 1771–1832—Knowledge—Scotland.
2. Historical fiction, Scottish—History and criticism. 3. National characteristics,
Scottish, in literature. 4. Literature and history—Scotland.
5. Scotland—In literature. I. Title.
PR5343.S3M33 2005
823'.7—dc22   2005015446

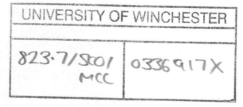
1 3 5 7 9 8 6 4 2

Printed in the United States of America
on acid-free paper

For

PAUL

and

CONOR

conditions of my possibility

and for

JILL RUBENSTEIN, *d. 2002*

who saw all things possible

in her junior colleagues

ACKNOWLEDGMENTS

Acknowledgments for *Possible Scotlands* threaten to outrun the book. So I must note that my thanks here can only hint at my debt, and cannot approach the level of my gratitude.

My thanks to all those who have encouraged this project: the generous scholarship of Robert Crawford and Cairns Craig opened a space for my argument; Suzanne Gilbert and Douglas Mack (University of Stirling), and Murray Pittock (in 1999 at the University of Strathclyde) invited me to give talks at their institutions; Ian Duncan, Susan Manning, and James Chandler commented upon arguments in progress; Jane Millgate, Ian Alexander, Peter Garside, Graham Tulloch, and David Hewitt helped with details; Ina Ferris, Jeff Smitten, Marilyn Orr, Penny Fielding, and Aileen Christianson lifted my spirits; students in novel and theory classes tolerated my obsessions; Elissa Morris smoothed my path at Oxford University Press. Jill Rubenstein, who died in 2002, celebrated the excitement and pushed the assumptions of my developing argument. She should have lived to debate this book.

Many librarians and archivists also deserve my gratitude. Both Iain Brown and the staff at the National Library of Scotland, and the University of Wyoming's research and interlibrary loan librarians, proved unfailingly willing and resourceful. Peter Henderson of The King's School, Canterbury; Jane Anderson at Blair Castle; Greg Giuliano at the Rosenbach Museum; the librarians of the New York Society Library; and the National Archives of Scotland (formerly Scottish Record Office) helped fill in many gaps.

Generous administrators have speeded research by sharing their funds. At the University of Wyoming, I thank Dean Oliver Walter and the College of Arts and Sciences, the Alumni Association and Vice President Bill Gern and his Research Office. I also thank the American Council of Learned Societies.

Thanks, too, to colleagues and friends at the University of Wyoming. Mark Booth, Janice Harris, Ric Reverand, and Paul Flesher read drafts of

VIII   ACKNOWLEDGMENTS

the manuscript. Susan Aronstein, Christine Stebbins, and Susan Frye have shared their optimism and good humor.

And continued thanks to Fiona, Pete, Peter, and Andrea Ritchie, Don McCracken, Val, Ollie, and Aileen Ludlow.

Then Paul and Conor, the conditions of *my* possibility.

PERMISSIONS

CONTENTS

ABBREVIATIONS

ACR	Atholl Charter Room, Blair Castle, Perthshire
EEWN	Edinburgh Edition of the Waverley Novels
Journal	*The Journal of Sir Walter Scott*, ed. W. E. K. Anderson
Letters	*The Letters of Sir Walter Scott*, ed. H. J. C. Grierson, 12 vols.
Lockhart	*Memoirs of the Life of Sir Walter Scott, Bart.*, 7 vols.
Magnum	Waverley Novels, New Edition, 1829–33
NAS	National Archives of Scotland, formerly Scottish Record Office, Edinburgh
NLS	National Library of Scotland, Edinburgh

Possible Scotlands

1

The Problem of Walter Scott

Waverley, Guy Mannering, and a Scot(t)ish Theory of Worth

> Before their eyes the Wizard lay,
>
> As if he had not been dead a day.

[In] the temporary home of the Scottish Parliament. . . . The builders were hard at work.

    [Inspector Rebus interviews an MP whose MSP brother has been murdered at the site of the new Parliament:]

    "What can you smell?" Rebus asked. . . .

    Grieve sniffed the air. "Sawdust."

    "One man's sawdust is another's new wood. That's what I smell."

    "Where I see portents, you see a fresh start?" Grieve looked appraisingly at Rebus, who just shrugged. "Point taken. Sometimes it's too easy to read meanings into things." (Ian Rankin, *Set in Darkness*)

In 1999, after nearly three hundred years, Scotland regained its Parliament. Is it "set in darkness"? In Ian Rankin's novel by that name, two bodies are found where the new Parliament's buildings will arise. A desiccated corpse looms from a walled-up fireplace; a Member of the Scottish Parliament sprawls dead outside. But neither body belongs to the servant supposedly murdered, roasted, and eaten in this same space by the son of a Scottish architect of Union on the night the Act was signed in 1707.[1] Despite audience expectations, these bodies play out no tale of a Scotland dead at the moment of her incorporating Union with England, now walking again.

    This book contends that either body might have belonged to Walter Scott—the architect of cultural Scottishness who still walks. He seems the uncanny presence ever producing yet bringing into question the nation in formation. His were the words invoked by First Minister Donald Dewar at the opening of the new Parliament: "only a man with a soul so dead could have no sense, no feel for his native land."[2] They were featured on the hoardings that surrounded the rising Parliament building, site of a nation both newly symbolic and real. These are also the words, however, that erupt and are resisted when Glaswegian comedian and world citizen, Billy Connolly, gazes across a highland lake in his 1994 *World Tour of Scottish History*. "Makes you come over all patriotic and Sir Walter Scottish," he jokes: "You have to fight these feelings."[3] It was Scott's portrait that the Edinburgh-educated Tony Blair moved to his new digs at Downing Street, his *Ivanhoe* that the British prime minister chose as his one book should he ever be cast away on a desert island.[4] Yet it was Scott who most challenged the new Parliament's minister for tourism, culture, and sport. Mike Watson acknowledged "Scott's success in putting Scotland on the international map. . . . I do recognize too, however, that the cultural images and identity created by Scott have, in a sense, been too successful."[5] The author serves as the cultural bump in the road for modern Scottishness. A television interviewer actually tracked down Scott scholars at their 1991 conference to ask "why should anyone read Scott these days?" And Scott's perplexed role within Scotland's cultural and political matrix is so pervasive it was reflected by a Scottish friend when my research turned northward. Oblivious to William McIlvanney's claims as a fiction writer, she presented me with *Docherty* as "some of the *real* Scotland," and encouraged me to ditch the romantic twaddle of Sir Walter. Scotland is haunted by the corpus of Walter Scott. So much so, that even in a new millennium we must look to the productive body of Scott's novels to understand some of the complexities that motivate Scottish identity.

   Possible Scotlands: Walter Scott and the Story of Tomorrow investigates how the author stands central to the cultural work that is Scotland. This is no uncontested position. After all, today's Scotland is a product of economics and politics (to name but two of the relevant forces) transformed by the efforts of generations into laws and acts.[6] Obviously, too, many Scots deride Walter Scott's influence. Still, Paul Henderson Scott, diplomat and nationalist politician, while sure that Scotland's survival as "more than a geographical expression is due to the determination of the Scottish people as a whole," stresses its "impulse, definition and sense of direction has been given by the writers" (32–33). James Mitchell, director of the Politics Research Centre at the University of Strathclyde, admits: "Throughout the history of the modern Scottish national movement some of the most significant developments have occurred in the field of affirmative politics, that is, in affirming that Scotland exists as a distinct political entity. The very nature of identity, tapping into subliminal consciousness, makes symbolic actions politically important" (25). If Scott's relevance is admitted, however, must it be appreciated? Tom Nairn claims "negative, even profoundly negative, emotions have been . . . important in generating nationalism. Not so much 'love of country,' in fact"—and I might here substitute "Scott"—"as detestation of it, sheer inability to stand it" (*After Britain*, 103). Just like Scotland's politicians and authors, cultural critics often have been simultaneously fascinated and appalled by the author's constructions of his native land. Scott is either the great historian or great romanticizer of Scotland, and in both cases he has defined the nation and pushed it into the past. But by careful attention to the modes of nationalism and the processes of literature, I will argue that precisely because his influence is both admitted and resisted Scott is in fact a site of contestation producing the nation today.

How can Scott constitute a problem undermining modern Scotland? Or how can an author dead one hundred and sixty-seven years (in 1999) continue to energize the nation? We need only map the responses to Scott's novels. For the earliest critics of Scott's first novel, *Waverley* (1814), the book straddled the boundary between supposedly unrelated genres: the romance and the "real" (or history). The *Scots Magazine* made the case clearly: "Romance . . . readers . . . desire to have some instruction blended with their amusement. . . . [R]easoning and information have been alike attempted. . . . [No novels] are more pleasing than those which . . . delineate the peculiarities of national manners. . . . Of late, Scottish manners have been undertaken. . . . The picture . . . is drawn with a very masterly hand. And . . . it is characterized by the strictest truth, though presenting features which almost surpass the wildness of romance."[7] Scott's novel manages to be "wild" yet "true"; it is at once romantic and real.

At first, this appeared an advantage, a double determination making visible a Scotland that had begun to fade into Union. Ina Ferris points out how critics applauded "the fact and accuracy of the novel" (Ferris, 83–84). At the same time, foreigners and Scots alike appreciated the seductions of Scott's vision. Theodore Fontane enthused, "What would we know of Scotland without Scott!"[8] But the very strength of Scott's characterization, later cultural critics have thought, trapped Scotland in its past. So heavily coded as "national," Scott's generic vision distracted nineteenth- and twentieth-century Scots from the political tasks of their moment.

Cairns Craig argues that, on the one hand, Scott's historical writing gave pattern and voice to nationalism: "Insofar as the nation itself is primarily a narrative that unites the past to the present, Scott's novels provided the generic means by which the nation could be narrated as a product of history and history could be seen as the expression of a national identity" (*Modern*, 117). On the other hand, Scott's patterns proved delimiting for Scotland, pushing the nation "out of history": "Those same Scott novels which initiate the engagement with history in the name of the rest of the world have, however, been seen in Scotland as disengaging Scotland from the processes of history. . . . No issue has been more debated in Scotland over the past thirty years [from the 1970s push for devolution to the new Parliament], in terms of its political and cultural consequences, than the falsification of Scotland's history initiated by Walter Scott." Examples are not far to seek. Criticism of Scott and Scotland is replete with the accusation that the author foregrounded the past, but thereby romanticized Scotland and set her aside from the narratives of progress. Scott's son-in-law characterized the King's Visit of 1822 as "Sir Walter's Celtified Pageantry" (Lockhart, 5:204). Murray Pittock argues the case with regard to Jacobitism: Scott "invented Scotland as a museum of history and culture, denuded of the political dynamic which must keep such culture alive and developing. Scott loved his country, but denied its contemporaneity" (*Invention*, 87).

Ian Duncan recognizes the creative tension between romance, the novel, and the real. It marks "a fruitful trouble and division at the core of national cultural identity" (Duncan, 6). But while "[r]omance reproduces itself as the figure of mediation and synthesis by turning contradiction into ambiguity," in the Waverley novels "[t]he final image of domestic and political reconciliation is the most fantastic, artful and labyrinthine of all evasions. . . . Scott had historicized romance as the form of a difference from modern life" (15). In this context, "[r]omance . . . signifies . . . illusion sustained in self-knowledge: a play of sensibility that marks off a private space at the limits of real history" (92). The romance and history that the *Scots Magazine* considers to energize the novel as national repeatedly appear, for Scottish critics, to work in a conjunctive opposition producing, at best, an anxious stasis.

Such criticism at times becomes impassioned. In 1970, Tom Nairn lamented the prevalence of what Scots have come to see as Sir Walter's signs in these same terms of romance versus the real:

> Elsewhere, the revelation of the romantic past and the soul of the people informed some real future—in the Scottish limbo, they *were* the nation's reality. Romanticism provided—as the Enlightenment could not, for all its brilliance—a surrogate identity. . . .
>
> . . . .
>
> Sporranry, alcoholism, and the ludicrous appropriation of the remains of Scotland's Celtic fringe as a national symbol. . . . sickening militarism. . . . these are the pathetic symbols of an inarticulate people unable to forge valid correlates of their different experience. . . .
>
> . . . .
>
> Nationalist politics are built upon this web of accreted myth-consciousness.
>
> ("Three Dreams," 34–35)

Both romance and history seem opportunities lost.

As recently as 1996–98, argument ripped through the *Herald* (Glasgow), with readers and scholars, locals and exiles hectoring one another over whether Burns was the true representative of Scottishness and liberty, and Scott a British collaborator. Mark Calney extended the argument to the Internet, where it is headed by his own "Controversy in Scotland: Sir Walter Scott Was British Intelligence Agent." This article overwhelms debate with the declaration: "Though Sir Walter Scott has been granted a certain literary sainthood by the British establishment, especially for what that London-centered oligarchy considers 'proper Scottish culture,' and his Romantic novels about the alleged glories of feudal society (such as *Ivanhoe*) are still required read [sic] in many American and British schools today [where, we might wonder?], not all Scots are enamored with his life and works."[9] Scott is the pro-British romanticist—as opposed to Burns, the Scottish real!

Would Leith Davis's analyses change the perspectives of participants in the *Herald* debate? Davis sees Burns as a canny subject speaking Scottishness within Union (Davis, chapter 4). Or would the combatants benefit from reading Robert Crawford, who links Burns and Scott "Writing in a culture under pressure [and seeking] to bind that culture together, to preserve it and celebrate it" (*Devolving*, 113)? Could they be challenged by Katie Trumpener, who stresses that "To explore the ways in which the romantic novel takes up and reworks the nationalist debates of the late eighteenth century is to watch a process through which ideology takes on generic flesh" (Trumpener, xv)? Probably not. Calney and his disputants seem caught in an argument that requires romance and history to produce one another as opposites, rather than to work symbiotically to offer a site for national identity. A more productive critical strategy might be to consider why Scott produces such critical angst, such extreme popular investments of a like and dislike posited as national and strangely distributed across literary genres. We might also ask whether such responsive resistance is itself an eruption of Scottishness that we owe to Walter Scott.

Critics such as Pittock, Craig, and Duncan temper their conclusions. Yes, Scott may have prevented Jacobitism from completing its role as an oppositional politics in Scottish history, Pittock notes, "Yet there lurks a revolutionary instinct in Scott. There is a sense that the happy and comforting conclusions he provides are forced endings" (*Invention*, 87). For Craig: "[Scott's] characters end with their faces turned bravely towards a progressive (and apparently narrativeless) future, but at the opening of each new novel the future turns out to have acquired again the features of a barbaric past which, once more, has to be expunged from the kingdom of historical progress" (*Out of History*, 46). In Scott's novels, as Duncan has suggested, there is both less and more to the disjunction between the romantic and the real. Oppositions that seem fixed hint at collapse.

Modern analysis suspects that such binary oppositions, whether between romance and history, Scotland and Britishness, past and present, try to limit the play of less precise and more dangerous alternatives. What could be of more concern in Scott's works than the suggestion (identified by critics) that the nation is over; that all is genre; that genre is necessarily restrictive; that Scotland no longer generates itself? What dangerous possibility could need so insistently to be shut down into evidently unsatisfying terms?

Scott's works provide no easy meanings separating worlds, times, genres. Quite the contrary, for Scott himself abjures history and romance both. In *Waverley*, the "Introductory" chapter offers the reader a sequence of generic approaches to the text through literary signs. Each one marks the text not for what it is, but for what it is not:

> Had I, for example, announced in my frontispiece, 'Waverley, a Tale of other Days,' must not every novel-reader have anticipated a castle scarce less than that of Udolpho . . . ? Again, had my title borne, 'Waverley, a Romance from the German,' what head so obtuse as not to image forth a profligate abbot, an oppressive duke . . . ? Or if I had rather chosen to call my work a 'Sentimental Tale,' would it not have been a sufficient presage of a heroine . . . ? Or again, if my Waverley had been entitled 'A Tale of the Times,' wouldst thou not, gentle reader, have demanded from me a dashing sketch of the fashionable world . . . ?[10]

The text, thus negatively overdetermined, never becomes clear. What genre is *Waverley*? All critical certainties to the contrary, Scott places it within neither history nor romance—nor a host of other options. Rather, he strives to keep text and reader in the space where generic meaning is made, constantly circulating between alternatives and across fashions located but not contained within place and time.

Later, however, in the introduction to *Tales of the Crusaders*, Scott seems to make an investment in history.[11] The Author of Waverley, negotiating with his joint stock company to produce novels by steam power, finds his colleagues resistant. "I am tired of supporting on my wing such a set of ungrateful gulls," he complains: "I will discard you—I will unbeget you . . . I will leave you and your whole hacked stock in trade—your caverns and your castles—your modern antiques, and your antiquated moderns—your confusions of times, manners, and circumstances. . . . in a word, I will write HISTORY." But this passage provides no solace for those who would read Scott as historian. One of the company retorts: "The old gentleman forgets that he is the greatest liar since Sir John Mandeville," but Oldbuck, the Antiquary, corrects him: "Not the worse historian for that, . . . since history, you know, is half fiction." When the Author then goes on to assert he will write (as Scott did), "the LIFE OF NAPOLEON BUONAPARTE," even the invocation of history within living memory fails to stabilize the form. The Author has already pointed out: "I intend to write the most wonderful book which the world ever read—a book in which every incident shall be incredible, yet strictly true—a work recalling recollections with which the ears of this generation once tingled, and which shall be read by our children with an admiration approaching to incredulity." History, the more accurate it is, resides the more within the marvelous. It is undone by a telling that the nature of events requires to be romantic.

Scott, then, denies readers the luxury of fixed generic systems. Rather, he reveals the ways in which genres are constructed and reconstructed against and through one another, across time and shifting literary space. He privileges the constant negotiation between terms that gives the impression of meaning but can never assure its presence. And *Possible Scotlands* will argue that this is the case throughout his works. Where critics sought to link "the Author of Waverley" to Walter Scott, in his prefaces Scott posited not one author, but many. He multiplies personae, drawing some, like Oldbuck (*The Antiquary*), from their novels and into narrative frames. None seems reliable. Indeed, all circulate together, contesting their recognition by the Author of Waverley, himself a mere Eidolon (*The Fortunes of Nigel*), and perhaps only a dream vision of Dr. Johnson (*Peveril of the Peak*). Where critics sought to denominate the novels as Scottish, English, or British, Scott provided many and contesting visions of each. He locates the boundaries between Scotland and England as shifting across centuries and winding from the north of England (*Rob Roy*) to Palestine (*The Talisman*) and various points in between. Most importantly, where critics look for a past, and bemoan the lack of a present, Scott constructs tales and modes of telling that refuse to be locked in time. They are not this, not here, not then. They require their continued writing in the future through the persistence of an undetermined author and the resistances of Scott's ever-anxious reader.

The tale of Thomas the Rhymer reveals what is at stake. This one story Scott returns to again and again. It implies, however, no limited author telling and retelling one version of Scotland from and as the past. The recurrences of Thomas the Rhymer make clear Scott's emphasis on the movement that allows meaning by differential play across place, plot, time, teller, and reluctant reader. Scott informs us that around 1799 he toyed with a romance "Which was to have been entitled, *Thomas the Rhymer*" (*Waverley*, "General Preface" and appendix 1 [1829], 351 and 361). Then in 1802, "Thomas the Rhymer" appears as Scott's signature piece for the *Minstrelsy of the Scottish Border*. Here, weaving together traditional materials with Thomas's prophecies and Scott's own words, Scott gives the tale of the Rhymer's sojourn with the fairies, his return to the world, and his call again to fairyland, from whence he may yet return.[12] He notes the fairies' prohibition to the Rhymer against speech among them, but their gift to him of prophecy. *The Lay of the Last*

Minstrel (1805) recalls Thomas through the person of the minstrel who has outlived his moment yet continues to sing, and tells a tale of return concerning a further prophet, the Wizard Michael Scott. Finally, in *Castle Dangerous* (1832), Thomas makes a spectral visit to a minstrel in the story's past to direct that his prophecy be kept hidden until another era when his book predicts a national future enacted in the tale's present by yet a third minstrel. If there is a type for the Author of Waverley/Peter Pattieson/Chrystal Croftangry/ and the host of Scott's slipping tellers of differential tales, it is surely True Thomas with his unpredictable gift of prophecy that is always capable of erupting in the future and requiring voicing through an unsuspecting other. The Rhymer, an ever-circulating, speaking, non-subject implies that Scott subsists not as a conventional source for meaning or a mere teller of tales gone by, but as the site of an ongoing literary and national differing between terms, and deferring of meanings. He implies, too, that through Scott we stand constantly subject to the tale not as told, but as telling differently, in a new place and time, and because of us, the resistant readers.

Scott preemptively deconstructs the restrictive terms on which readers of narrative and nation often rely. He foregrounds meaning as the indeterminate result of constant movement. And he himself embraces that movement. Thus, readers looking to him for literary or national truths find themselves struggling to constrict his tales within the known parameters of narration and nation: genre and time. Scott's tales, we insist, are either romantic or historical, and in both cases, thoroughly past. But our resistance to the slipping tale being told, and our efforts to avoid being implicated in its never-ending formation, involve us in it further, and activate it more. We must read against the grain—persistently, anxiously. So precisely where we fear the collapse of nation and narration, they arise through us. The definition of nation through narrative becomes an energetic process to which there is no location and no end. Reluctant readers are pitched toward the future, themselves possessed by the narrative potentiality that is Walter Scott.

David McCrone points out that in our reductive reading of Scotland's signs (such as those encoded by Walter Scott), we have fixed not Scotland, but ourselves. Yet neither signs nor selves ever can be stable, and instability can serve to our advantage. He suggests: "It has become an *idée fixe* . . . that Scotland suffers from a deformation of its culture; that it has sold out its political birthright for a mess of cultural pottage. . . . However . . . most Scots are ambivalent about Scottish heritage icons like tartan. . . . The heritage icons are malleable. They take on radical as well as conservative meanings" (*Scotland*, 5). Scott teaches us how such icons are constructed, how to construct them ourselves, and how not to fear their reconstruction in other times and places, or by other Scottish subjects. As Robert Crawford remarks, and I stress in the case of Scott: "[Rather] than something to be eschewed, the invention or construction of traditions is a key activity in a healthy culture, one whose view of itself and of its own development is constantly altering and under review" (*Devolving*, 14–15).

How successful are we at imagining Scotland through Scott's signs and despite ourselves? At the moment of the new Parliament, Scott's coining of multiple Scotlands, many pasts, and diverse subjects all projected into the future forced Tom Nairn to reconsider his critique: "From the time of Walter Scott onwards, [the] roots of statehood were endowed with the glamour of a lost kingdom, and the tantalizing sense of redemption which always informs nostalgia. Although mocked from the outset as wilful and unreasonable, this display-identity has in truth proved incomparably stronger than every one of its philistine adversaries. . . . the eclipsed state-land of the Scots has run beneath . . . until ready to resume its interrupted existence" (*After Britain*, 12–13). *Possible Scotlands* suggests that by disliking, fighting with, and resisting the apparent but constantly shifting "display-identity" offered by Walter Scott, Scotland has maintained a sense of self as difference. Now it moves energetically into a future that will ever be "Scotland," but can never be the same.

Scott, Scotland, Theory

Then Deloraine, in terror, took
From the cold hand the Mighty Book
(C2. XXI)

Scott haunts the nation and disturbs his readers because he writes Scotland across the elements of narrative *as a process*. Rather than situating the what or the where of a nation or its tale, Scott challenges us to consider and forces us to participate in the how, why, and when of its differential construction. Scott's novels do not stay contained within the bounds of genre—romance/history—or the reductive and often binary assumptions of nationhood—England/Scotland, progress/past. Instead, they play through time and reconstruct Scotland by unbalancing readers who would rather cling to the certainties of time, place, and tale, and whose resistance produces and energizes nation and narration.

Scott, too, is part of this differential construction. Like Thomas the Rhymer, not here, not now, the author seems nonetheless to be everywhere, and involved in everything. In Scott's own time, his strategies spilled over to activate texts and moments more political than literary. Thus, Scott erupted as national author in the middle of banking crises and monarchical visits, further breaking the bounds and revealing the intensely productive relationship between nation and narration. Moreover, as Author of Waverley but also national authority, Scott constitutes a political event. In Scotland, at times it still appears that nation and narration are problems founded in the construction and valuation of Walter Scott himself. Scott enacts the problems of telling his nation, and the opportunities residing within those difficulties of coherent narration, across tales, characters, narrators—and in his own person—through time, annoyed readers, and irritated compatriots. Scott disturbs and produces Scotland into this twenty-first century.

An anxious Scott reader myself, I have struggled for ways to articulate textual and authorial complexities against my own critical assumptions. I have thus found myself becoming an engaged, often perplexed, and sometimes oblique reader of literary, national, and cultural perspectives. Nonetheless, this book hopes to carry its theory lightly. So to relieve the burden within the text, I here explain those approaches most helpful to me and that underpin *Possible Scotlands*. Readers will find that, like Walter Scott, I have been guided by the past, but have reconstructed it for myself, often forging through the gaps in one theory to make connections with an unlikely alternative and accomplish a disturbing, but perhaps enlightening, theoretical romance.

Possible Scotlands received its first theoretical impetus through postcolonial considerations. It has become commonplace in nation theory and Scottish analysis alike to argue that Scotland has been akin to a postcolonial nation, subject to the same strains in its self-narration. David McCrone, however, finds the assertion problematic, noting "there is limited analytical value and not much empirical evidence for treating Scotland as a colony of England" (*Understanding*, 36). Nevertheless, in understanding the use to which Scott has put his various narratives, and the ways in which they are constructed as national, I have found it invaluable to think in terms set out by Frantz Fanon and Edward Said. Predominantly, it is in the context of England that Scotland has found it necessary to define herself. Here Scotland often has seen herself as grotesque. Given this construction she has struggled—or Walter Scott has struggled on her behalf—to achieve modes of narration that could make her visible, inoffensive, and yet nationally effective. Scott works so disturbingly and successfully because, like a Saidian critic, he remains extremely conscious of, and writes to make obvious, the situatedness of the national and narrational subject—whether anonymous Author, persona, or uncomfortable reader.

To understand how Scotland can speak for herself, and at the same time speak in many different, mutually disturbing voices across Scott's novels, within his texts, and sometimes against those texts and the author himself, I have turned to Homi Bhabha. For Bhabha, the nation is a narrative (*Nation*, 2). It expresses a shared story of itself—the "pedagogical" tale that teaches subjects what the nation "is," and how it subsists in a larger context. But the tale of the nation takes place through language. At the same time, it must be enacted through the variety of the people (297). For these reasons, even the simple restatement of the nation through its pedagogical signs (such as flags, loyal songs, etc.) never produces it as "the same" (312). Bhabha posits the nation not as a certainty containable (as critics might suggest of Scott) in a tale (romance), or a time (the past). Rather, the nation is constantly fracturing and reforming at the moment of its utterance. The nation, as a narrative "performed" by many tellers, expresses "the otherness of the people-as-one" (301). From their points of otherness, the people can disrupt but also energize and, Bhabha even allows, direct the nation. Their included difference opens a rift within culture, reforming the nation along the lines of popular practice (299, 306, 312). So Scott, writing within a Scotland situated in relation to England but played across by the power differentials of class, gender, ethnicity, and so on, deploys multiple resistances in his texts through the persons and words of his performers. Powerlessness, in Scott and in line with Homi Bhabha, can offer a site of articulation for cultural challenge.

I also deploy nation theory. From this perspective, the discomforts we sense in Scott's novels arise from his work, in Benedict Anderson's terms, to "imagine" a community. McCrone points out that usually, we imagine nations to be coherent: "The 'narrative' of the nation is told and retold through national histories, literatures, the media and popular culture, which together provide a set of stories, images, landscapes, scenarios, historical events, national symbols and rituals. Through these stories national identity is presented as primordial, essential, unified and continuous" (*Sociology*, 52). But reality is far different. Anthony Smith notes: "The idea that nations are real entities, grounded in history and social life, that they are homogeneous and united . . . no longer seems as true as it did" (Smith, 2). The Scott who sought to express nation through narrative met public expectation in defining a Scotland that could be posited against England and as past against present. But simultaneously, when he made visible the nation's multiplicity Scott manifested its disruptions and discontinuities—and made unavoidable Scotland's disturbing energies.

Nation theorists who have turned their attention to Scotland express Scott's difficulties with some precision. Beveridge and Turnbull argue that Scots see themselves in the English context, and thus as "inferiorised" (*Eclipse*, 17). Given this perspective, McCrone adds, they obsess over "a unified Scottish national culture" that must be distinct from England's (*Understanding*, 194). This culture looks backwards: "for much of the past three hundred years Scotland was deemed to be 'over.' . . . its elites came to believe that the future belonged to the political entity of 'Britain,' whereas the past was Scottish" (60). At the same time, today's Scotland requires a more dynamic theory. Jonathan Hearn observes: "[Identities] are multiple and situational. Scottish national identity hangs in a constellation of overlapping and interpenetrating identities . . . which can be variously combined and emphasised according to the goals and demands of the moment. Not only is identity a 'pick-and-mix' business to a degree, but the choices shift over time.

Identity is processual, what it means to be Scottish not only varies between individuals, but also historically, as do the larger bundles of identifications with which it becomes associated" (Hearn, 11). Such thoroughgoing reconsiderations of Scottishness helpfully situate Scott within the discourse of an ongoing national difficulty.

Yet Scotland's nation theorists too can fall subject to the limiting systems of romance (the past) and the real (the political). Stranger still, they often identify Scott as the pivot on which Scotland turns its narrative over to Britain and twists itself toward days gone by. McCrone, for instance, traces the nation's backwards dynamic to Scott and his remark that "the 'heart' was Scottish, but the 'head' British," even though Scott's strategies confirm McCrone's further comment that "history can be reconnected to the concerns of the present and future, and be made to 'live' again."[13] Scott demonstrates that McCrone's connectedness occurs not through the supposed sequences of history and determinacies of national tales, but through the imprecisions and inadequacies of their telling across the people who (broadly considered) constitute Scotland. So Scottish nation theory explains many of Scott's complexities but resists his energies. In fact, it too points to Scott as the site of a cultural anxiety, and challenges this book to foreground the mobile, strategic, contingent play that is Walter Scott and that could invigorate Scottish culture of tomorrow.

To such an end, I turn to the deconstructive economics of Jean-Joseph Goux. The nation exists only in its narration, and stands constantly in play through the unpredictabilities of language. At the same time, narrative deploys power. Bhabha theorizes both the determinative power of nationhood and the contestatory power of the national subject through the performance of the nation in language. But how is power negotiated within the linguistic shifts that unmake and make a nation? How to make that visible within Scottish and other nation theories? In *Symbolic Economies*, Goux considers that all negotiations of value—all determinations of power—take place in language, through the exchange of signs—what he calls the circulation of "equivalents" (4). Indeed, the circulation of signs is inherently the negotiation of value, for: "the notion of value . . . is implied in every replacement" (9). Scott, with his many tales, voices and times, none of which is certain but all of which are strategic, plays the market of valuation through its raw material—the shifting, shaping sign.

But the sign can shape and be shifted through the play of equivalence because of its instability. Within the discourses of the nation, this poses a problem, for value never will be fixed. Given that the sign points ultimately to lack and the impossibility of determinate meaning, the nation may rise but certainly will fall with the negotiation of its signification through equivalent terms. Yet Goux notes how the need for valuation produces terms to dominate and restrict the play of signification, and thus imply meaning and worth. All signs point to lack, but persistent invocation of one term in the context of others converts its fundamental absence into excess, constituting the ineffability of Derrida's "transcendent Sign," or Goux's "general equivalent." Walter Scott somehow understood that embracing and even insisting upon lack appropriates the function and at least temporarily eludes the effect of the endless differing and deferring that allows but calls into question the illusion of meaning. By repeatedly positing his texts and himself as lack—*Waverley* is not a romance; the Author of Waverley is other than Walter Scott; Jedidiah Cleishbotham (I use the EEWN spelling) is not Peter Pattieson—Scott removed himself from the cycle of equivalence, the mere circulation of signs. He became a lack requiring obsessional substitution. So paradoxically, the absent Author of Waverley and his works, determined through what they are not, figure as excessive. They can hoard meaning and operate as the law, giving value to the systems required to give value to Walter Scott and his narration of the nation.

How does Scott as absence become a presence that troubles critics and Scots right through to the Scottish Parliament? How can Scott exceed time— especially given that he stands forth as transcendent sign, an excessive lack, and thus visibly and inevitably subject to collapse? Derrida offers a possibility. In *Given Time: 1. Counterfeit Money*, Derrida deconstructs the notion of exchange as it is posited by Marcel Mauss in *The Gift* (1950). For Derrida, the effect of meaning appears through the linguistic movement of *différance*. By circulating through what is not, we gain the impression of what "is." However, our idea of what is remains haunted by the trace of what it is not. For Derrida, in every exchange that appears to indicate value (Goux's circulation of equivalents), the trace is actually the "gift." The idea of the "gift," impossibly requiring no return, undoes the illusion of valuation by the petty calculations of equivalent terms. More, if valuation aims to establish presence and persistence, the gift is "Time." Time undermines all notions of giving, all the precisions of exchange. The play of time may allow and produce, but also prevents and unravels the construction of contingent value.

It is by playing on literature as a gift of lack, from we know not whom or when, and the nation as elsewhere than we expect it in place and in time, that Scott gives to us the gift we are unwilling to receive and that—because out of time—he surely cannot give: the unstable and thus energetic making of modern Scotland. By constantly deconstructing himself and his tales of Scotland, Walter Scott situates both in the movement that is outside of time and that makes valuation a dynamic literary process. This is how Scott can persist disruptively in the time of the new Scottish Parliament.

As I have struggled with Scott's complexities, I have proceeded alongside others whose insights have informed mine. Cairns Craig's 1996 ideas of a Scotland "out of history," operating "beyond history" and through "simultaneity" have challenged me to articulate why I think Scott is never outside history, but rather caught up in the web of words to which there is no outside. Craig's concern that Scotland seems stuck in cycles of repetition has forced me to determine, with Bhabha, that repetition never returns as the same— even for a land so supposedly caught in/out of history as Walter Scott's Scotland. Robert Crawford's willingness to read from Scottish literary history across international boundaries in *Devolving English Literature* (1992) has taught me to beware of constraining my notions of Scotland too narrowly in place or time. And Susan Manning's *Fragments of Union* (2002) has encouraged me to see precedents and thus authorities for a Scott interested not so much in meanings as in their making in a Scotland of greater possibility and in earlier times than I had hitherto imagined.

From all these textual problems, theoretical opportunities, and scholarly debts, I have tooled a syncretic argument. *Possible Scotlands* situates itself among theories and texts to understand the productive inconsistencies of an author we insist upon as consistent and limited. It hopes to encourage thought beyond the where or what of narration or nation, and toward the when, the how, the why, of the nation as narrated. It offers layered, sometimes contentious readings of texts, tellings, and cultural moments. In so doing, it seeks to engage established criticism of Scott, and theories of the nation. Perhaps it will help to shift the direction of Scott and Scottish criticism away from genre studies, and a focus on the past, toward the generation of meaning, both narrative and national.

Telling Scot(t)ish Worth: Waverley, Guy Mannering, and "the Author"

> Loud sobs, and laughter louder, ran . . .
> Because these spells were brought to day.
> (C 2.XXII)

We can best understand the dynamic of Scott's work through example. Critics consider Scott's first novel, *Waverley* (1814), historic, but prefer to read through the discourse of romance. The wavering English hero takes a tour to Scotland that implicates him in the 1745 rebellion yet accomplishes the past as a romance of domesticity (see Duncan). *Guy Mannering*, Scott's second novel (1815), receives less attention—perhaps because of the ways it foregrounds but resists being read as romance, and dwells upon the problems of telling a coherent tale. Told into the romance of exile by an astrologer and a fortune teller, young Harry Bertram re-enters history against competing tales and at the moment of his tellers' expulsion from life (Meg dies and Mannering retires). Together, *Waverley* and *Guy Mannering* pose the problem of what national tale to tell, to whom, how, why, and of course, when?

Scholars often read Edward Waverley as a determining and delimiting force in the narrative that is Scotland. The tartan-clad Englishman who looms from his portrait in the novel's last chapter is held to figure Scott's British-oriented nostalgia and prefigure a Scotland locked in the romance of the past through England's cultural and economic dominance. Cairns Craig outlines the problem:

> [The] end of *Waverley* finds the . . . hero looking at a painting of himself and his [already executed] Jacobite companion [Fergus Mac-Ivor] . . . 'in highland dress' . . . his life in history has been . . . 'framed' and removed from the flow of events. . . . By the very power of the model of history which they purveyed to the rest of Europe, the Enlightenment philosophers and Scott reduced Scottish history to a series of isolated narratives which could not be integrated into the fundamental dynamic of history . . . the order of progress could only be narrated from somewhere else. (*Out of History*, 39)

Scott's narrative serves to keep Scotland "out of history." Waverley is a sort of tailor's dummy barring the ingress of modernity into the process of narration through which the nation should subsist in the present.

Of course, Craig recognizes Scott's manipulations of the narrated past to disrupt the unself-critical story of progress that writes out Scotland. He praises the author for inaugurating a tradition of literary resistance over successive novels. This, he says, "confronted the historical in radical ways—by challenging it with what it had left out of its ideological conception of social life, by reminding it of what it had excluded but could not forget, by pointing forwards to the barbarity which would turn out to be waiting around every corner of the progress of civilization" (*Out of History*, 46). He goes on to offer a compelling model of multiple and simultaneous narrativity "beyond" history for Scotland in the matrix of Britain (chapter 7). But with Waverley in the breach (though not unbreeched, despite popular imagination) it is hard to imagine Scott and his inheritors mounting anything more than exotically dressed raids on the fashion system. Reading history oppositely through Scott's signs may expose the knees and proclivities of the current scion of the House of Windsor, who seems afflicted with Scottish dress, but may not otherwise intervene in British politics. Within Craig's argument, Edward Waverley's naïve historicism, his posture before the romanticizing mirror of his portrait in his home-sweet-Tullyveolan, still sets Scotland apart from the activity that is history making—that forges into the future.

This, however, is a lot of responsibility to hang on a self-conscious clothes horse who Scott himself termed "a sneaking piece of imbecility."[14] I suggest that, dazzled by the vision of Waverley in his tourist tartan, critics have read Scott's window-dressing as his stock-in-trade—the focus of his critique as his last word. We have privileged the tale over its telling and locked ourselves out of the lively process of negotiation by which Scott narrates a nation's future. In fact, in his first two novels, Scott begins to establish narration as a space within which Scotland stands always in production. Through a narrativity whose posture is potentiality, constantly leaving behind the tale already told, Scott initiates an expansionist trade in possible Scotlands. He projects the nation toward a future wherein it can achieve valuation as worth in the market of ideas that is the ever-becoming space of history.

By 1810 (which following Peter Garside I take as the date of *Waverley*'s first significant composition), Scott was beginning to understand narration as an act of national valuation situated between peoples and places, authors and audiences, past and future. As he composed his opening chapters, Edgar Johnson tells us, *"The Lady of the Lake* . . . shattered all records for the sale of poetry"* (Johnson, 1:335–36). Critics, the general public, Scots, English, and other foreigners snapped up the poem and then "set out to overrun the once lonely scenery of Loch Katrine." "The lake had formerly been visited by fifty or sixty carriages a year; within the first six months after the publication of *The Lady of the Lake* the number rose to 297! . . . Traffic so increased that 'the post-horse duty in Scotland rose to an extraordinary degree.'" Scott later joked: "I had at last fixed a nail in the proverbially inconstant wheel of Fortune."[15] Through an act of Scottish narration projected across national boundaries by means of nineteenth-century commerce, Scott had redirected the flow of cash and credit north of the border. He had located authorship as a point of negotiation between nation and valuation.

Yet Scott was equally aware that through authorship he, his tales, and thus his nation teetered on the brink of devaluation. Already, Byron had sneered that Scott debased himself by writing for money: "when the sons of song descend to trade, / Their bays are sear, their former laurels fade. / . . . For this we spurn Apollo's venal son, / And bid a long 'good night' to Marmion."[16] As recently as 1813, the affairs of both the publishing company and printing office in which Scott was embroiled fell into such dire straits he contemplated leaving Scotland, for: "I will not live where I must necessarily be lookd down upon by those who once lookd up to me."[17] It was not until 1825–26 that Scott's profits and his productivity would be bound in the great, public tussle over his monetary credit and his authority as a voice of the nation. Nonetheless, the intertwined relationship between Scott's finances, his status, and national reputation, disturbed the novelist himself as early as mid-1813—almost a year before *Waverley*'s completion.

This relationship was constantly negotiated even in good times. In August 1813 Scott consulted the Duke of Buccleuch regarding two matters of "credit."[18] He was concerned to purchase back his copyrights from the failing Ballantynes (his printers and partners), and required the Duke's "sanction to my credit as a good man for £4000." In particular, he needed the Duke's countenance to outface "the London Shylocks"—moral credit to support his financial dealings in the British market. But he also asked for advice concerning "a very flattering offer from the Prince Regent of his own free motion to make me poet laureate." He remarked (somewhat disingenuously): "I am very much embarassd by it." Subsequent comments indicate that although Scott appreciated this sign of his cultural worth, he recognized that it could redound to his discredit as narrator of a living tale. In a flurry of letter writing, Scott confidentially informed his friends, relatives, business acquaintances of the offer, and carefully massaged his reasons for rejecting it.[19] Most often, he cited the apparent greediness of appropriating yet another governmental salary, but his true concern peeped out. To Buccleuch he admitted: "the office is a ridiculous one somehow or other." He told his mother: "I was convinced I should have lost credit by the necessity of writing birth day odes & so forth & after all could not reconcile myself to a situation which obliged me officially to praise the Court twice a year whether I thought they deserved it or no" (*Letters*, 3:354). To his brother-in-law Charles Carpenter he declared: "I wish to be altogether independent of Kings and Courts" (3:341). Scott resisted installation as laureate because he recognized the offer established him as an object of worth but subjected him to another's valuation and thus served to devalue. It would fix him in time and place—perhaps away from the developing narrative that was Scotland. Moreover, most interestingly for our purposes, in refusing to become the object of valuation Scott became its invisible yet ineffable site. Walter Scott, who is not the laureate, and may shortly lack funds, through his whispering campaign determines and exceeds the worth of the office and its supposedly transcendent, notably English source. His own value is yet to be "realized," and remains fully possible.

Even as Scott writes *Waverley*, then, he appreciates the conjunction between nation and valuation across narration. Further, having established the inherent delimitation of any tale once told—specifically, the tale of authorship—he recognizes how a tale ever in formation through its telling inevitably gestures toward realization in the future; it beseeches the margin between the present of its narration and the moment of its completion. Occulted telling stands as the site of a valuation in process, projecting the narrative—and in this case the nation—into a tomorrow that allows the possibility of worth. Consequently, through the gap that will figure as "the Author of Waverley," Scott begins to position the nation so that it can always intersect with the future and enter the domain of "real history."[20]

Which is to say that Scott both manifests and manipulates the phenomena of narrative construction in the field of differential power that was nineteenth-century Scotland. While Scotland's circumstance was not simply "postcolonial," Scott's novels yield to this discourse. Across *The Lady of the Lake* and the laureateship the author learned that in Scotland's British context, to tell is to risk being told. Although he had seized a Saidian permission to narrate, he flirted with a Fanonesque renarration as grotesque within the ambit of English literary and social politics and economics. Although he might, in Bhabha's terms, open a Scottish margin within the British cultural middle, he needed to remain unnarrated and unnarratable himself if he were to maintain story telling as a site of valuation capable of projecting the nation toward the future we call "history." In this circumstance, he anticipated the theories of Jean-Joseph Goux. The anonymous author, within yet beyond and constantly invoked by the text, Scott looms as the ineffable Sign that can tell a tale and imply worth but that gestures ever to the tale still untold and value still to be determined. His Scotland lies immanent within the telling, not limited by the tale. It is always at the moment of entry into history, and standing against all history as it is told. History—at least in Hayden White's sense—belongs to Scotland.

Scott manifests this perplex in *Waverley*. Lacking that easy site of valuation, a king, Scotland is a land of signifiers circulating in hope of meaning—each depending on but being undermined by the others. Tullyveolan depends on the Baron of Bradwardine, but he seeks his relevance in the Stuart past, leaving the village to "the incessant yelping of a score of idle useless curs, which followed, snarling, barking, howling, and snapping at the horses' heels" (chapter 8). Because he seeks his valuation in all the wrong places, the Baron in turn is constituted by Fergus—only a putative clan chief—and even Donald Bean Lean, the Jacobite cattle-thief, as one term moving among many. Fergus colludes in stealing Bradwardine's cattle, and despite his own problematic origins, demands recognition as an equal from the Baron.[21] Evan Dhu Maccombich, negotiating to return the cows, conveys Fergus's prayer "that things may be as they have been heretofore between the clan Ivor and the house of Bradwardine. . . . And he expects you will also say, you are sorry" (chapter 16). Donald Bean Lean, who should be a step further from the Baron's power, tells Waverley: "You might as well have confided in me; I am as much worthy of trust as either the Baron of Bradwardine or Vich Ian Vohr [Fergus]" (chapter 17). Moreover, through an excessive troping of movement, Scott implies that such circulation is the Scottish condition. Whether in Flora's romantic promenade across the high beam, the Baron's "swift and long strides, which reminded Waverley of the seven-league boots of the nursery fable," or Davie Gellatley's fractured dance, Scots are caught in a frenzy of action that can never achieve the progress of valuation (chapters 22; 10; 9).

In this arguably postcolonial situation, Scott notes that his compatriots look south to the site of assumed worth for a more powerful figure to make them meaningful. They find Edward Waverley. Scot after Scot assumes Waverley to be the locus of valuation. Fergus, Donald Bean Lean, obliquely Flora, even Prince Charles Edward Stuart, bring themselves into circulation with a Waverley who is presumed able to lend value to their cause and their reputation within it. Evan Dhu, who expresses Fergus's circulation through his own perambulations in search of the Baron's cows, "was obviously flattered with the attention of Waverley" (chapter 16). Donald Bean Lean assumes Waverley's centrality and his ability to establish Scottish worth: he "was so sanguine as to hope that his own talents were to be employed in some intrigue of consequence, under the auspices of this wealthy young Englishman" (chapter 51). Fergus comports himself on first meeting Waverley in ways that assume the newcomer's power of valuation: "He was well aware that . . . unnecessary attendance would seem to Edward rather ludicrous than respectable" (chapter 18). Even Flora, in her rejection of Waverley, implies his centrality to her cause (Valente, 254–55).

Scott stresses, however, that Waverley enjoys all the lack yet none of the excess required in a sign that operates as a site of valuation. No romantic hero, he nurses an undeclared passion for "Miss Sissly, or . . . Miss Caecilia Stubbs." This he promptly forgets when made a captain, for "[t]here is no better antidote against entertaining too high an opinion of others, than having an excellent one of ourselves at the very same time. . . . [Alas]! hoop, patches, frizzled locks, and a new mantua of genuine French silk, were lost upon a young officer of dragoons who wore for the first time his gold-laced hat, boots, and broad sword" (chapter 5). And ironically, Waverley never has a chance to fill out his clothes with the achievement of rank—his commission is bought, and recalled before any military engagement. More, we know from the novel's earliest pages that his learning is quick, not deep, and that he has lost forever "the art of controuling, directing, and concentrating the powers of his . . . mind for earnest investigation" (chapter 3), so we are not surprised when Waverley's fortunes shift through his father's political maneuverings. This center for Scottish valuation has always been an inadequate substitute in a system that can hold him as cheap as any other. It is not surprising, then, that as the Scots head south, few English aristocrats rise to the banner. Waverley lacks the power to hoard and communicate value upon which the Scots depend.

In fact, Scott insists that Waverley is a confidence trick practiced by needy Scots against themselves. Consider Edward's debatable valor at the Battle of Prestonpans. Fergus exhorts after the event: "your behaviour is praised by every living mortal to the skies; and the Prince is eager to thank you in person" (chapter 49), thus leading John Sutherland to suppose Waverley must have killed a number of "uncommissioned, unregarded, private soldiers and NCOs."[22] But the text gives no evidence for remarkable heroics. Waverley is Fergus's invention. Indeed, Scott later emphasizes that the Scots knowingly construct Waverley as the illusion of power. When the Prince detains Edward in talk to which the latter is clearly inadequate, the narrator remarks: "It is probable that this long audience was partly meant to further the idea . . . that Waverley was a character of political influence" (chapter 43). Waverley himself never understands the Scots' need and characterization of him. In his first encounter with highland culture, he recognizes his own name in the bard's exhortation, but has no idea of its context and thus of its significance (chapter 20). The Englishman is what he appears in the mirror before which he endlessly postures—an absence that by a trick of imagination reflects as substance. Still, as our final image of Fergus and Waverley together should imply, this is an absence that, once constructed as the site of Scottish valuation, has deformative strength. Forget the portrait, however, which deforms primarily Waverley, and recall instead Fergus on his way to his execution and his installation as past history, grotesquely "supporting Edward by the arm" (chapter 69).

Given Scott's precise critique of Waverley's construction, it is ironic that we subject ourselves to the character's image and find it the end point of Scotland's life in the narrative that is history. It is particularly so since the dynamic of the text refuses to leave Waverley as a barrier to Scotland's future, rather suggesting a lively alternative. In chapter 1, "Introductory," the supposed author characterizes Waverley from the start as an absence that finds its meaning in us: "I have . . . assumed for my hero, WAVERLEY, an uncontaminated name, bearing with its sound little of good or evil, excepting what the reader shall be hereafter pleased to affix to it." When the novel then shows that no amount of effort can make Waverley a presence, and that such maneuvers deform the reader as well as Waverley's constitutive Scots, it situates us within the critique of Scottish narration and forces us to look for meaning in the tale. Yet here, too, Scott has anticipated us. His first chapter imagines various constructions for the text: "Had I, for example, announced in my frontispiece, 'Waverley, a Tale of other Days,' must not every novel-reader have anticipated a castle . . . ? Would not the owl have shrieked and the cricket cried in my very title page?" Every possibility projects a lack through which no presence looms—we are already through the first page; there is no owl and no cricket cries. So there is only the act of telling.

Telling also seems unpromising, given that the novel lacks any figure of authority. Even as Scott appropriates the narrative voice, he denies its force: "I am too diffident of my own merit," he offers as an excuse for his strategy of non-characterization. He is "a maiden knight," incapable of lending value to that which he tells. Through the novel Scott will indicate the difficulty of establishing national value by the circulation of persons and stories. Here, he denies merit yet asserts himself as a maiden knight; he figures authorship as absence yet immanence. The tale not yet begun stands ever in process; the maiden knight's battle is ever to be won. The act of telling looks toward a future where value shall be realized. It persistently undoes the tale that is told and opens the possibility for significant history.

But read even from this perspective, *Waverley* constitutes a problem. How to maintain the posture of potentiality that Scott so carefully initiates? Although occulted acts of telling project toward the future construction of history, they yet beg the question of the tale in which value may be realized. Further, because the role to determine value depends on repeated substitution to maintain the absence that functions as excess and casts a lure in the direction of ultimate valuation, the tale of telling itself must be repeated and risk becoming a tale that is told. *Guy Mannering*, Scott's second novel, testifies to Scott's awareness of such concerns and develops a strategy.

In *Guy Mannering*, too, those who should serve to fix the worth of a region have fallen into decline. By making a fetish of money and law—reductive terms that short circuit the negotiation of worth—the Bertram family has lost property and now place. It has unfixed its dependents and joined them in the circulation that always resolves in the direction of devaluation (Goux, 38, 18, 15). Into this circumstance comes the English Mannering. In parallel, he as astrologer and Meg Merrilies as spey-wife tell a tale that expresses and perhaps creates a representative loss in the space that should be the site of valuation. Mannering charts and Meg weaves a doom for the heir of Ellangowan. And in time, young Harry Bertram indeed falls from his role to fix local values as the hopeful heir of a significant family: he is kidnapped and possibly killed by smugglers. Actually thrown into circulation across place and time, Bertram becomes a tale told awry in English and Scottish mouths. As Vanbeest Brown, latterly Captain Brown, his value slips and slides. He is Dutch, Scottish, a clerk, a Captain, a lover, a murderer, a corpse, depending on the context within which he negotiates at a given moment. The upstart Gilbert Glossin, trying to move into Harry's rightful place, insinuates that "Brown" is a smuggler of the same name, and at best an illegitimate offshoot of Ellangowan (254, 345). Perhaps most notably, Mannering himself risibly yet tragically misrecognizes Brown, who is courting his daughter, as a wife-stealer. Thus, in *Guy Mannering*, Scott confirms his earlier suggestion that a Scotland seeking valuation stands deformed both north and south of the border.

If in *Waverley*, however, there was no true tale to tell, here Scott suggests that although Harry Bertram, as a tale, risks being untold, he demonstrates Scotland always will tell true. Bertram tells as himself through mind and body. Before we meet him, his innate goodness forces an eruption of poetry within the narrative voice: "With prospects bright upon the world he came, / Pure love of virtue, strong desire of fame; / Men watched the way his lofty mind would take, / And all foretold the progress he would make" (96). To strangers, he manifests truth. He has "a fund of principle and honest pride" that renders him instantly recognizable as value to stalwarts such as Dandie Dinmont (96). Then, when the time foretold is past, Bertram's body speaks his reality. Lawyer Pleydell has only to see him to declare "the very image of old Ellangowan" (304). Dominie Sampson exclaims: "If the grave can give up the dead, that is my dear and honoured master!" (305). Bertram figures as an absence that is excess, a repetition that is preternaturally the same and thus breaks the cycle of circulation to achieve meaning in the future that is now the present. He enters the moment and achieves history.

Yet if Bertram's body speaks for itself, it becomes true through a telling that, as in *Waverley,* permeates and escapes the text. Bertram is foretold by Guy Mannering and Meg Merrilies, both of whom labor to allow the tale to tell itself as truth in the future. Nevertheless, like Waverley, Mannering fails to recognize his own, English story in Bertram's tale. The result is great personal loss—his wife dies and his daughter is estranged—and a consequent inability to understand and participate in the tale that is Harry Bertram. Then, when the child stolen from the text enters the present, Mannering effectively disappears from the novel, becoming thoroughly subject to the Scottish tale that has been told. He limits his participation to "ballast . . . of Sicca rupees"—thus fulfilling the Scottish dream of England as confined within the narrative of the sugar daddy—and declares "Here ends THE ASTROLOGER" (355). The Scottish Meg, who has ever told Bertram true, also exits the text at the moment he enters history. Her story, too, always has been implicated in his, for it was she who enunciated the curse that symbolically forced the inadequate Bertrams into circulation. Now she declares the story's fulfillment: "*the Hour's come, and the Man*"—and promptly receives her death blow (334). She is shot by that dealer in illicit circulation, Dirk Hattaraick the smuggler. Twenty years before, Hattaraick sustained Meg's prophecy by stealing away Harry Bertram (332). But all those long years ago that same smuggler first interrupted and ended her prophetic declamation, foreshadowing her subjection as teller to the tale once told (24–25). Indeed, the only figure remaining from Harry's first enunciation is Dominie Sampson, the stickit minister who lacks the gift of pulpit speech. The speaker who cannot pronounce alone remains to tell Harry Bertram true. Thus, although Bertram's telling implies that Scotland's tale in process will enter the future that is history as truth, through the collapse of its fictional tellers it simultaneously gestures outside the novel toward an interested but hidden act of telling yet ongoing.

The novel describes the space that is, by 1815, the "Author of Waverley." *Guy Mannering* is unusual in the Scott corpus for its lack of an introduction. When the removal of Bertram's tellers draws us behind his tale we can find no locus for an author in a prefatory chapter. But the act of telling looms from Scott's epigraph:.

> 'Tis said that words and signs have power
> O'er sprites in planetary hour;
> But scarce I praise their venturous part
> Who tamper with such dangerous art.

Taken from the *Lay of the Last Minstrel* because it should point away from his pen (Scott was imagined not to reference himself), this quotation exacerbates authorial absence to the point of presence. The lines admit the potential of signification ("'Tis said that words and signs have power"), but they suggest its dangers. They leave such signification as a negotiation between teller and tale—tampering—and that resides again somewhere else: "scarce I praise *their* venturous part / Who tamper with such dangerous art" (emphasis added). The verse sets the text apart from Scott and the speaker sets the telling apart from himself. Moreover, "scarce I praise [those] who tamper" constructs tampering as ongoing and projected into the future. In fact the reference to *The Lay of the Last Minstrel* invokes once more the Wizard Michael Scott, who continues to speak in the future through his mystic book, as well as the "last" minstrel who is thereby "latest." It figures Thomas the Rhymer, who through his persistent returns signifies the unremitting modernity inscribed in "telling" Scotland. So in this second novel, Scott asserts the truth of Scotland's tale through and despite the precise Englishman Mannering and the ever mobile gypsy, Meg. He accomplishes the telling of Scotland's hidden truth, but he again constitutes the act of telling as oriented toward the future—like Bertram it is smuggled out of the present and into the always-opening moment when tale meets history and becomes reality. Yet even then, neither author nor tale will be fixed as "told."

Across *Waverley* and *Guy Mannering*, Scott suggests that history will happen and value stand evident—only tomorrow, and through the ever-renewed power of anonymous authorship. By careful circulation through the differential gaps of meaning, Scott begins to steal his way into the time yet to come of the Scottish nation.

Scott's Tales

> Some saw an arm, and some a hand,
>   And some the waving of a gown. . . .
> And knew—but how it matter'd not—
> It was the wizard, Michael Scott.
> (C. 6.XXVI)

This book tracks the many possibilities of place, person, time, and telling through which Scott construes a living Scotland. Given the vastness of Scott's oeuvre, scholars seeking to grapple with his multiplicity generally have produced sequenced readings that support unifying theories. Invaluable in this context is Jane Millgate's *Walter Scott: The Making of the Novelist*, which argues that "[t]he entire career of the Author of *Waverley* took its shape and direction from the achievements of 1814–19. . . . The sequence of novels became its own flexible but coherent category" (*Walter Scott*, x). Equally important, Nancy Goslee's *Scott the Rhymer*, Ian Duncan's *Mod-

ern Romance and Transformations of the Novel, Ina Ferris's *The Achievement of Literary Authority*, and Fiona Robertson's *Legitimate Histories*, focus on Scott within the aesthetic sequences of genre. This book, however, will produce no such unity. *Possible Scotlands* traces Scott's engagements with the problems of narration and of nation. Because Scott's linked national and authorial challenges are necessarily contingent, unpredictable, and arose in no particular order, this book will encounter them as they erupted through narrative gaps, cultural moments, personal difficulties.

Possible Scotlands will find itself privileging not Scott's coherences, but his tales' multiple meanings; their inconclusive valuations; Scott's strategic but often stuttering efforts to tell them. It will be concerned with the constant and mutual encroachments of life and literature, and see both as circulating uncertainly in a marketplace of ideas that is aesthetic and national. The book will therefore establish no unbroken sequences of novelistic development or Scottish concern. Rather, it will consider constellations of events, novels, and social interventions as they arose under pressure from the politics and economics of Scotland's richly textured daily life. It will necessarily leave gaps for, and actively invites, further and differing critical engagements with Walter Scott's national tale telling.

In this introduction, I have already considered how Scott's entry into fiction precipitated narrative as a site of national valuation. *Waverley* (1814) and *Guy Mannering* (1815) manifest Scott's developing strategies for how to tell a Scottish tale that exceeds the text in which it is contained. In these novels, Scott works through a telling that can persist beyond the tale.

A second section will focus on *The Antiquary* (1816), *The Tale of Old Mortality* (1816), and *The Heart of Mid-Lothian* (1818). Often linked in an historical sequence with the prior two novels, *The Antiquary* now appears important for its overt considerations about the difficulties of telling a complete or coherent tale. Even the material proofs of the past militate against the inclusiveness of narration. Now, too, *Old Mortality* and *The Heart of Mid-Lothian* appear as distinct tales of a varied Scotland, each of which is internally subject to different telling, and each of which finally offers but also resists resolution into the past—the one through the aberrations of extreme but foundational Scottish religion, the other through the uncanniness that is gender.

The Fortunes of Nigel, completed by May 1822, and George IV's visit to Edinburgh in August that year, constitute another cluster. Having initiated the circulation of Scottish signs south of the border in exchange for financial and social status, Scott began to ponder the implications of his strategy. In *Nigel*, he begins to articulate the risks involved. The King's visit, however, offered him an opportunity to work the system of exchange, and gamble possible loss against personal and national gain. It is here that Scott himself becomes figured as the site of valuation for signs in circulation beyond his texts and both north and south of the border. The King comes to Scotland to see . . . Walter Scott.

But the group of texts from June 1825 to March 1826 demonstrates again the risks of Scottish narration within the orbit of England. I focus on *The Talisman* (1825) and *Woodstock* (1826), both often critiqued within the discourses of English and imperial composition. In each case, the text reveals considerable anxiety about the complicity of cross-cultural storytelling. If Nigel risked devaluation in England, Sir Kenneth risks voicelessness—stepping beyond the processes of valuation—and *Woodstock* hints that there is nothing but circulation. All is posturing, performing. Here, Scott digs deep into the ethics of his national narration.

A financial and cultural crisis disrupted Scott's final composition of *Woodstock* and determined the next set of texts. From November 1825 to January 1826, Scott labored under the imminent collapse of his business investments, and agonized over his probable loss of literary and national reputation. In the same few months, his wife died. Yet the "Malachi Malagrowther" letters spewed rapidly from his pen through February and March 1826.[23] In addition, as a kind of therapy, Scott produced the fractured tales that make up *The Chronicles of the Canongate* (1827). For both compositions the Author of Waverley spoke as Walter Scott. Here we will consider how, through images of a Scotland suddenly grotesque, and a telling more fractured than ever before, Scott took back to himself an even more problematic—but therefore productive—narration of the nation.

Yet what is the possibility of Scotland with the Author dead? The final section of *Possible Scotlands* sees Scott negotiating for his continued value against that ultimate devaluation. Standing in opposition to his publisher and his editor son-in-law, both of whom wished him to stop writing and thereby maintain the monetary value of his works published so far, Scott continued to write novels (*Castle Dangerous*, 1832), letters, and prefaces. He continues to speak, to tell, to move, to value, when he should be silent and still. Building on the theories and practices established over a long career where he constructed an author-ity immanent through absence, Scott opens up a route to the future for an author who should be locked in the past. It is here that Scott steps out of time, and haunts the time even of the Scottish Parliament.

These moments and cases should help us come to a nuanced understanding of Walter Scott as a mover and player in national culture, and of Scotland as read, but also as written—by us. Criticism typically has seen Scott's works as generically cohesive and culturally limiting. By viewing Scott's negotiations with cultural pressures through his texts, and with narrative possibilities through the shifts of culture, we may see the nation as narrated, multiple, contentious, unfinished, erupting in the future through the anxious reader.

   Scottish critics and nation theorists are inclining toward Scott's conclusions. McCrone contends that "Scotland is a society with an 'unmade' history insofar as its history seems incomplete and thereby unpredictable"; the nation is "an idea, an aspiration. It should be considered not simply as 'place' but as 'process'" (*Understanding*, 13, 30). Cairns Craig now recognizes "The nation, like the self, [as] a space of dialogue." It is "a place of dissonant voices, a dialectic of relationships: it consists not of undivided individuals but of persons in relation, and it is constituted . . . by its inner debates and by the dialectic of its dialects (*Modern*, 116). Nevertheless, we remain more invested in describing the present than embracing the future. McCrone oddly insists that signs like tartanry (often brought home to Scott) are "less dominant than is made out" and concludes "the variety and eclecticism of Scottish culture today corresponds to world conditions in the late twentieth century rather than the distorting legacy of these 'mythic structures'" (175). The future must only happen within acceptable parameters. Craig's post Scott-ish novel privileges dissonance, but operates apart from history: "The modern Scottish novel . . . rests on a fundamental paradox: the forms of history that it charts in its narratives are what it seeks to negate through its creation of narrative forms which will defy and deny the primacy of the historical" (166). Simultaneity may run beside, but risks being disconnected from, the here and now. We have yet to accept Scott's extensive vision that pitches the present toward a multiple, unpredictable, and thus creative future. Scott insists on no pasts, and threatens no futures; he promulgates no reductive histories, and he delimits no current narratives. Instead, he has always invited the Scots to think of themselves as floating signifiers capable of making meaning through, and in places and times beyond, his tales.

   Walter Scott makes us uncomfortable because he worked to throw Scotland not into a state of "noisy inaction," as N. T. Phillipson notoriously suggested, rather into a state of energetic disagreement that impels the nation into the future ("Nationalism," 186). McCrone has posited "When was Scotland?" (*Understanding*, 30). Scotland *is* whenever Walter Scott's many tales, his shifting politics, his invisible narrative self, erupt within and disturb the complacency of a Scotland that would be a modern nation/state. *The Lay of the Last Minstrel* makes clear that what is "last," is also "latest." Scott is ever up-to-date. Through a tale telling that is strategic and playful, he exceeds the past and disturbs the becoming-space that is Scotland. It is time for Scotland to play along.

2

Circulating Scotlands

Telling, Tellers, and Tales in
The Antiquary, *The Tale of Old Mortality*,
and *The Heart of Mid-Lothian*

Who shall tell us a story?

Sir Walter Scott of course.

—*E. M. Forster*

For E. M. Forster, Walter Scott's one redeeming quality was that he could tell a story (44). But Scott does not "tell a story" in Forster's reductive terms. In fact, Forster's statement deconstructs in each of its aspects. "Who" presumes a singular answer, but implies other possibilities; "tell," assumes a simple communication, but splits along the fault lines of telling as production or evaluation: someone produces this tale, and the tale is told down like current coin that shifts the value of the listener; "a story" begs the question of what constitutes such an artifact, whether a story is ever singular, and how that story might be multiplied according to "who"—and how many—tell(s) it. Finally, who "shall" tell us a story? Walter Scott *will* tell us a story because that is his limitation? He *shall* tell us a story because we will make him? Or in the future, whatever our desires or deserts, Scott's stories still shall "tell"— through us?

This chapter traces how Scott explores the limits and activates the possibilities of the story that is Scotland. Through *The Antiquary* (1816), *Tales of My Landlord*, First Series (*The Black Dwarf* and *The Tale of Old Mortality*, 1816), and *Tales of My Landlord*, Second Series (*The Heart of Mid-Lothian*, 1818), Scott ponders the complexities of telling, the variability of tales—the lively, insistent nationality that can be evoked when the circulation of equivalent Scotlands forces conjunctions and disruptions between tellers, tales, and readers.[1] This chapter will consider a Scott actively multiplying the voices, modes, and stories of Scottishness so that Scotland becomes a state of many margins reperforming the nation and constantly making available its multiplicity to new readers situated at the opening edge of history.

The Antiquary may seem an unlikely site for such explorations, for Scott formulated it as a backward-looking tale in his own oeuvre. The "Advertisement" that prefaces the novel declares: "THE PRESENT Work completes a series of fictitious narratives, intended to illustrate the manners of Scotland at three different periods" (Antiquary, 3). It goes on to claim a Wordsworthian tradition, representing an intensity of manners in the lower orders, and to assert that the writer has "been more solicitous to describe manners minutely, than to arrange in any case an artificial and combined narration." Scott regrets "that I felt myself unable to unite these two requisites of a good Novel." Then the "Author of 'Waverley' and 'Guy Mannering'" concludes with gratitude to the public "for the distinguished reception which they have given to works, that have little more than some truth of colouring to recommend them," and "[takes] my respectful leave, as one who is not likely again to solicit their favour." Scott implies that his tale constitutes an end: the end of a series; the end of a project; the end of a literary career.

The Monthly Review objected: "We suspect . . . that such a classification as this, by which the three parts constitute a whole, never entered into the writer's mind until after all the portions were fairly and honestly written."[2] John Wilson Croker critiqued Scott's historicism and wrote acerbically in the Quarterly: "the able and ingenious author, after having written these three very amusing romances, has indulged himself in a fanciful classification of them, and, waiving his higher claims, prefers the humbler one of writing on a system, which he never thought of, and in which, if he had designed it, we should have no hesitation in saying that he has, by his own confession, failed."[3] The reviewers raise two issues: these novels do not feel historical, nor do they seem a logical historical sequence. Scott, however, was ahead of them. While he may invoke "different periods" and imply history, in the "Advertisement," history already subsists under the sign of "fictitious narratives." Although Scott declares a sequence of novels, he stresses his failures in coherence—his inability to "unite these two requisites [manners and structure] of a good Novel." Again, what Scott claims with regard to history is not what he does. Bringing an end to history, he opens it up.

During the period when Scott produced The Antiquary and the first two sets of Tales of My Landlord, he also produced "Harold the Dauntless" and began to work on a history of Scotland (Johnson, 1:507, 512, 562–63). These two projects, one avowedly the last of Scott's romances, the other apparently a straightforward history, clarify Scott's processes.[4] Begun in 1815, but completed and published in January 1817, "Harold" implies Scott's ongoing commitment to romance. A narrator, subject to ennui, claims as his refuge to "con right vacantly some idle tale" ("Introduction"). He finds "to cheat the time, a powerful spell / In old romaunts of errantry . . . / Though taste may blush and frown, and sober reason mock." Subsequently, he produces such a spell, set beyond the bounds not just of reason, but of criticism. His rhymes "Court not the critic's smile, nor dread his frown; / They well may serve to wile an hour away, / Nor does the volume ask for more renown, / Than Ennui's yawning smile, what time she drops it down." At the end, in confirmation of a task accomplished, he exhorts:

And now, Ennui, what ails thee, weary maid? . . .
Be cheer'd—'tis ended—and I will not borrow,
To try thy patience more, one anecdote. . . .
Then pardon thou thy minstrel, who hath wrote
A Tale six cantos long, yet scorn'd to add a note.
("Conclusion")

The poem asserts romance only to mock its processes in writer and reader both. Its joke turns on Scott's punning use of "ennui," which alludes at once to the indolence that requires a text like "Harold," and "the tale fair Edgeworth wrote, / That bears thy name, and is thine antidote" ("Introduction"). Scott's romance tips over into its critique.

As for the history of Scotland, Scott and his publishers talked about it a lot—for years. In 1816, Johnson tells us, Scott proposed to Constable "a three-volume *History of Scotland* . . . which he believed he could revise and have ready for publication by the following Christmas" (1:549). However in 1820, "as soon as [*Ivanhoe*] was finished, Constable thought, Scott should have set to work on the *History of Scotland*" (1:698). In 1823, Cadell anxiously suggested that Scott should "give your time to the *History of Scotland*, which will give you no trouble" (2:845). What did Scott write of this history, and when? Lockhart ingenuously remarks: "if he ever wrote any part [of the *History of Scotland*], the M.S. has not been discovered. It is probable that he may have worked some detached fragments into his long subsequent [in production from 1826] 'Tales of a Grandfather'" (Lockhart, 4:27). So this was the history that wasn't. Scott presented it to Constable as such from the first, refusing to attach his name "at full length" to the project for "When a man puts his name to so grave a matter as a History, it should be something very different from the rapid and, I trust, animated sketch which I intend to furnish."[5] Perhaps most importantly, he wrote to Lady Louisa Stuart: "My ostensible employment is a view of the history of Scotland long since written & on which I set so much value that I shall revise it with great care. Such therefore is your answer my dear Lady Louisa when any one asks what your friend W.S. is about."[6] Scott vaunts the specificity of history as a reason for its extended production, but intends to produce an "animated sketch," not history, and uses the project as a red herring to distract attention from what he actually is writing.

When Scott produces—or claims to produce—romance or history during this period, even in their most unadulterated forms, each brings its own form into question and serves as a shield for something else. Scott was getting into the business not of closing down genres, his career, or the past by inscribing them authoritatively; rather, he was beginning to bring into conjunction the "ends" of history and romance as the "odds" that make meaning through their disjunctive circulation. His pedagogy—the limited genre of romance; the precise data of history—he deployed to provoke lively performance.

The Antiquary seems to focus on the ends of history, both in Scott's "Advertisement" and through the bits and pieces the title character accumulates and reads as signs of the past. But McCrone et al. have implied a different way to read the apparently static realia that is "heritage." In *Scotland—the Brand*, they evaluate the role of national properties in identity formation. For their test subjects, heritage objects (privileged antiquities) bring "the past into the present, in such a way that the histories of ancestors or mythological events become an intimate part of [Scots'] present identity" (181). Heritage has an identity-conferring function that in a nation not yet a substantial political entity confirms Scotland as a "land of dreamtime" (209). Yet the data point also to a more forward-looking possibility that McCrone neglects. Scottish subjects emphasize that history is of the past, heritage of the present. They declare: "'History is dead; heritage is ongoing and living.' . . . 'Heritage always seems more alive. . . . History . . . is rather dry—it's books and events.'. . .'Heritage is the interest in what is; history is more the background to how things came about'" (162). Heritage, it seems, operates not simply in the past or in the present. It is "alive" (161). Constantly mis/recognized by new subjects, who read out of it a past of their own construction, its dynamic is forward. It is part of the ever-opening experience of the nation.

Further, part of heritage's unlikely momentum derives from the fact that it is inevitably multiple. Whatever the present's coherent tales of the past, the artifacts that make up heritage testify to its variety in time, provenance, and type. Antiquarianism is inevitably a site where Scottishness-es visibly circulate. And Scott cultivates this aspect of antiquarianism, stressing the variation not just in artifact, but in its telling, the tales that are told about it, and the tellers who relate it and thus project it into the future. In *The Antiquary* and then the first and second series of *Tales of My Landlord*, Scott throws up terms, modes, perspectives, times, tales, and tellings of Scottishness. He forces them into an agitated movement that refuses the illusory coherences of history or romance in favor of the contestations that project a living nation.

Twisted Telling in The Antiquary

"she may come to wind us a' a pirn"

The Antiquary often is thought to display Scott's limitations, not his venturesome possibilities. Early critics took Scott at the word of his "Advertisement." The *Augustine Review* regretted that "the careless and hurried manner in which the work has been prepared, has given birth to so many imperfections," and went on to deride "the ridicule of antiquarianism [as] a beaten path"—though in the *Quarterly*, Croker recognized it had been trodden first by Scott's Baron Bradwardine.[7] In fact, antiquarianism became the focus of negative criticism for a novel otherwise admired. Part of the ongoing problem we can trace to Lockhart. In 1837, he confirmed the reviewers' sense that Scott and the Antiquary were cognates: "although Scott's Introduction of 1830 represents him as pleased with fancying that, in the principle personage, he had embalmed a worthy friend of his boyish days . . . he could hardly . . . have scrupled about recognising a quaint caricature of the founder of the Abbotsford Museum, in the inimitable portraiture of the Laird of Monkbarns" (Lockhart, 4:12). The process is one of embalming; the result a caricature. Surely there are echoes of Lockhart's formulation in Carlyle's reductive praise:

> The phraseology, fashion of arms, of dress and life, belonging to one age, is brought suddenly, with singular vividness, before the eyes of another. A great effect this; yet by the very nature of it, an altogether temporary one. Consider, brethren, shall not we too one day be antiques . . . ? . . . the steeple-hat will hang on the next peg to Franks and Company's patent, antiquaries deciding which is uglier. . . . Scott . . . is not to be accounted little,—among the ordinary circulating library heroes he might well pass for a demigod. Not little; yet neither is he great. (336–37)

Here, the antiquarian perspective is a thing of the eye only, and the author is damned as a "demigod" among "circulating library heroes." He is confined by data to a ridiculous literary role enacted for an intellectually feeble audience.

Yet if Scott's contemporaries found his antiquarianism, precipitated into the Antiquary, over-insistent, recent criticism has identified our obsession with the character, and this characterization of Scott, as an indication of antiquarianism's productive problematics.[8] Richard L. Stein observes that "immersion in the past is not an end in itself in Scott's writing, nor of unquestioned value" (219). He remarks of Old Mortality, "[Scott] continually parodies the triviality of merely antiquarian historians whose absorption in the data of history . . . [limits] their capacity to function in the present."

For Yoon Sun Lee, "Even when written to celebrate British unity . . . the antiquary's productions . . . draw attention to the brevity, the discontinuity, and the factitiousness of the history of the British nation" (563).

But where Lee dwells on the deconstructive tendency of antiquarianism, this chapter sees its differentiating play, its ever-productive possibilities. To Robert C. Gordon, heterogeneity in *The Antiquary* reaches beyond the material culture circulated by the title character. He reads disjunction also in plot and persons, across class and genre, through the (false) invasion of history, and in the difficulties of communication (39–42). Robin Mayhead argues that these textual oddities "engender in the book a textural 'irritation' and agitation quite incompatible . . . with any notion of stasis" (135). In fact, such deliberately cultivated irritation allows Scott's novel to become a formative text in its time, critiquing the unifying narrative of Britishness, and to act again through us in the moment of its reading.

In *Fragments of Union*, Susan Manning grounds Scott's conflictual mode. She traces Scotland's sense of a fragmented past versus an oppressively coherent British present to the Union. In Hume's *A Treatise of Human Nature*, she registers Scottish emphasis on fragmentation, a foregrounding of the impossibility of making meaning, and Hume's insistence on the mind as inhabiting a space of disjunction. "The true idea of the human mind," Manning quotes, "is to consider it as a system of different perceptions or different existences, which are link'd together by the relation of cause and effect, and mutually produce, destroy, influence, and modify each other" (35). Unity, Hume continues, "is merely a fictitious denomination which the mind may apply to any quantity of objects it collects together" (37). American modernism, Manning contends, derived its paratactic style from such Enlightenment philosophy (288). Might not Scott, too, here have discerned an alternative use for the fragments of the past than lack and lament? In a world of bits and pieces (which, in our postmodern era, we might consider any and all worlds), these imply gaps in which the mind constructs contingent but nonetheless vibrant new realities. Scott, I suggest, heir to the eighteenth century, multiplies data and foregrounds empiricism through the fiction that is *The Antiquary* to display, interrogate, and make available the process of meaning making. He offers a future of productive *différance*.

This is obvious in Scott's turn from the occulted telling of his earlier novels to telling as a site of division and deconstruction of the "real" and the "true." In *Guy Mannering*, Scott suggested that Scotland always told true through a voicing absent thus insistent. Now, Scott exposes telling as in no wise "true." Deriving from the fragments of experience, it is necessarily inaccurate, often lying, at least twisted, and certainly twisting in its effects. In his introduction to Hewitt's edition of *The Antiquary*, David Punter notes the novel's "problems concerning how information is delivered" (xiv); Sharon Ragaz remarks that the book lacks "confiden[ce] about the possibilities for unmasking or excavating truth" (32); Shawn Malley ties the difficulty of telling back to the impossibility of data: "the pluralities, limitations, and malleability of material history as narrative is a major theme" (238). Scott's positivistic antiquarianism has always precipitated the critique of its own utterances.

Scott embraces the problem in his opening chapter. Hero Lovel waits for a coach. The text stresses the prescriptive nature of this experience, surrounding it by language that implies limitation, restriction—meaning accomplished within careful confines: the coach "was calculated" to carry six "regular" passengers, who would be "legally in possession" (5). "The written hand-bill . . . announced that the Queensferry Diligence, or Hawes Fly, departed precisely at twelve o'clock on Tuesday, the fifteenth July, 17—" (5). But, the narrator tells us, it "lied upon the present occasion like a bulletin" (6). Oldbuck of Monkbarns, the Antiquary, who now arrives to take his place in the coach, at first assumes by the vehicle's absence that he is late. For him the coach exists in its description and thereby can be used to set time (7). On its continued non-appearance, he accosts the woman who keeps the coach stand: "Does [that advertisement] not set forth, that, God willing, as you hypocritically express it, the Hawes Fly, or Queensferry Diligence, would set forth to-day at twelve o'clock, and is it not, thou falsest of creatures, now a quarter past twelve, and no such fly or diligence to be seen?—doest thou know the consequence of seducing the lieges by false reports?" (8–9). "Diligence, quoth I?" he finishes; "Thou should'st have called it the Sloth" (11). Words claim to express a regulated reality, to have an unproblematic relationship with the artifacts they name, yet there is no relation between the two. Word may substitute for thing, yet thus create it as other than it is: "a lie" Even Scott's epigraph foregrounds the deconstructive inevitabilities of naming:

> Go call a coach, and let a coach be call'd,
> And let the man who calleth be the caller,
> And in his calling let him nothing call,
> But Coach! Coach! Coach! O for a coach, ye gods!
> *Chrononhotonthologos* (5)

Every naming of the coach makes it less apparent and exposes further the problems in "telling" anything true.

This is the motivating theme for Scott's novel. As Jane Millgate observes, "Much play is made in the novel with right and wrong readings" (*Walter Scott*, 97). In fact, data—disparate equivalents randomly knocking up against one another—produce readings that are inevitably wrong. The coach, as it is told in print, can only ever be a lie. Scott was well aware of this problem of history, articulating it through the contentions between Sir Arthur Wardour (the heroine's snobbish and gullible father) and Oldbuck over reading the one remaining (possibly) Pictish word (48–49). He knew the writing of Scottish history produced the problem, and kept it alive. In 1760, William Tytler both invoked the "Casket Letters" and declared them a fraud to defend Mary Queen of Scots against complicity in Darnley's murder. As Marinell Ash tells us, this argument, based on a particular evaluation of artifacts, "so incensed David Hume that he refused to be in the same room with Tytler" (89). Generations of Tytler's descendents similarly insisted upon data to produce controversial arguments—right through to Scott's friend, Patrick Fraser Tytler, who began to write his history in 1823, at Scott's suggestion (Ash, chapter 4). Nor should we forget Ossian, for Macpherson's dependence on inaccessible data is questioned once more in *The Antiquary* (243–45). The reading or evaluation of data—its telling down as cultural coin—always will shift what is told. It may even revalue it.

Scott's interest in the power of inadequate data to produce a telling that can only be twisted but may yet be vibrant is bound up in the tripartite figure of Dousterswivel (the German diviner of riches), the Antiquary, and Rudolf Erich Raspe (the first to publish Baron Munchausen's tall tales). Oldbuck usually is considered the voice of sympathetic reason, occasionally hindered by antiquarian nit-picking, but always turned toward truth. It is he who explains away Lovel's dream by invoking a remarkably prescient psychological method, resists the gothic tale told by Isabella (the heroine), argues against Ossian, and always suspects Dousterswivel (104; 146; 243–45; 101–2). His antiquarianism balanced with Edie Ochiltree's folk knowledge manifests common sense. Millgate remarks: "Every story told in the novel demands comment or explanation"—a telling "true"—"and the expository or interpretative role usually falls to Oldbuck or Edie" (*Walter Scott*, 98). But together with Dousterswivel—who notoriously as adept, miner, assayer, never "tells" true—and Raspe, Oldbuck allows an incisive critique of telling, yet also its construction as the site of cultural productivity.

Who was Raspe? The son of an accountant who worked for the Hanoverian state department of mines and forests in the Harz region gothicized through (heroine) Isabella's tale, he was well educated in geology and a precursor to Lyell. He developed eventually respected theories of vulcanology and was made a member of the Royal Society. Raspe was also a proponent of Macpherson's Ossian, reviewing it in the *Hannoverisches Magazin*, and initiating its European significance. Yet he was a scoundrel. Curator for the General Count von Walmoden (illegitimate son of George II, and monarchy's only representative in Hanover), Raspe lived outside his means and purloined the medals he was employed to catalog. His crimes were discovered in 1775 and he fled to England. There, in himself, he constituted an international incident, given the context of British/German cooperation in America's Revolutionary War. He was removed from the Royal Society, and if not thereby notorious enough, he circulated through a number of positions that might have made him known to Scott by reputation. It was while serving as assayer in Cornwall that he wrote down tales first told by a real Baron Münchhausen, embellished with others from myth (1785, dated 1786; Raspe uses the spelling "Munchausen"). Another version of the tales shortly appeared through Gottfried Bürger, whose *Lenore* Scott later translated, and in whose biography he would have found a credit to Raspe as first author/ compiler (Johnson, 1:114; Dawson 206 [see Raspe n. above]). Raspe also worked with the engineer and manufacturer Matthew Boulton, partner to James Watt and a friend of the Dumergues, with whom Charlotte Charpentier lived before she became Mrs. Walter Scott (Johnson, 1:147; *Letters*, 1:183 n). He collaborated with James Tassie, the famous Scottish medal sculptor. To crown his career, he was said to have salted a mine to cheat Sir John Sinclair, compiler of the *Statistical Account of Scotland*—who Scott through his entire life thought a great bore (*Letters*, 2:219; 419–20; 7:231; 296). Thus, for late-eighteenth-century Britain, Raspe embodied the problems of material reality and truth in telling.

David Hewitt acknowledges Robert Chambers's claim that Raspe provided the model for Dousterswivel (449). Certainly, there are echoes between Raspe and a German character who purveys tales from the Harz, and salts a mine by planting old coins. The Advertisement's assertion that although "[t]he knavery of the Adept . . . may appear forced and improbable . . . we have had very late instances of the force of superstitious credulity to a much greater extent," likely refers to the stories about Sinclair. Oldbuck possibly echoes gossip about Raspe when he complains that Dousterswivel "has enough of practical knowledge to speak scholarly and wisely to those of whose intelligence he stands in awe. . . . But I have since understood, that when he is among fools and womankind, he exhibits himself as a perfect charlatan" (101). Like many another Briton in the context of Raspe, Oldbuck has received news from foreign contacts: "My friend Heavystern . . . let me into a good deal of his real character" (101–2). And Dousterswivel's effects seem not unlike Raspe's on Sinclair: "now has this strolling blackguard and mountebank put the finishing blow to the ruin of an ancient and honourable family [the fictional Wardours]!"

Yet Raspe equally provides a model for the Antiquary. Oldbuck too derives from German stock; he replicates Raspe's antiquarian proclivities; while he has been the victim, not the thief, his reference to "my old friend and brother antiquary, Mac-Cribb" who "went off with one of my Syrian medals" puts him amidst the problematic circulation of specie that marked Raspe's career (19). He too stands implicated in Sir Arthur's mining venture. Further, he mines antiquities. If Dousterswivel salts a mine, and Raspe similarly corrupted the assays, Oldbuck is a kind of border reiver of antiquities. He boasts to Lovel: "I wheedled an old woman out of [her bundle of ballads], who loved them better than her psalm-book" (24). Oldbuck even shares Dousterswivel's occult connections. He implies the adept deserves to burn, but will not suffer under the Inquisition because he belongs in the fire, and mocks the German's story of the Harz daemon with his coals of gold. However, the Antiquary claims his own founding father's apprenticeship with the descendant of "old Fust" (Faustus) and his descent from Faustus's daughter (135; 86). In the end, too, the fire supposed to signal a French invasion—but that reveals Lovel the wanderer as the returned heir Major Neville—is conjured by Oldbuck and Sir Arthur (the subject of Dousterswivel's cheat, and father to the heroine): "'It must have been the machinery [of the mine] which we condemned to the flames in our wrath,' said the Antiquary . . . 'the devil take Dousterswivel with all my heart!—I think he has bequeathed us a legacy of blunders and mischief, as if he had lighted some train of fireworks at his departure—I wonder what cracker will go off next among our shins'" (352). There are as many similarities between Oldbuck and Raspe—though Scott interestingly and atypically claimed to have forgotten the name of Munchausen's compiler—as there are between Raspe and Dousterswivel (*Letters*, 3:198).

Scott's three-way coincidence in characterization allows him to investigate the difficulty of telling true from data that is always ruptured by language or deracinated by time. It also allows him to examine the ways in which the cultural construction based on the circulation of data is necessarily a twisted telling. It is impossible to "tell" or value data correctly, to distribute a knowledge pedagogically, because its every utterance is a deformative and reformative performance arising in a gap. Throughout *The Antiquary* Scott pushes this theme, from highest to the lowest class, across men and women, the educated and the illiterate, the comic and the tragic. Mrs. Mailsetter, whose job is to connect what is sent to its receiver, interrupts the mail to read it wrongly. She sends away Jenny Caxon without her letter from Lieutenant Taffril, while her neighbors, "like the weird sisters in Macbeth upon the pilot's thumb," make out from Jenny's mail "something about a needle and a pole," and immediately make an incorrect determination of those words' value: "'to cast up to her that her father's a barber, and has a pole at his door, and that she's but a manty-maker hersel! Fy for shame.' 'Hout, tout, leddies,' cried Mrs Mailsetter, 'ye're clean wrang—It's a line out o' ane o' his sailor's sangs . . . about being true like the needle to the pole'" (110–11). And though Lovel's package refuses to yield to their gaze, "we'se sit down and crack about it," says the postmistress (113). While Lovel's documents may tell his true worth as Major Neville, they will always circulate through deformative speculation.

Again and again in *The Antiquary*, data is twisted, misdirected, and misread in its transmission by tellers who are themselves perverse. A child mailman modeled on Wordsworth's idiot boy nearly brings the circulation of Lovel's parcel to a misdirected end (114–17); Sir Arthur's snobbery prevents him from naming Lovel aright: "I wish you a good evening—Mr. a—a—a—Shovel," he declares, prefiguring his later determination that the Wardours, despite a "bend sinister" in their own shield, cannot mix with "the illegitimate son of a man of fortune" (51; 99). Between Lovel and Hector, Oldbuck's nephew and a warlike highland soldier, "a prejudice seemed to arise . . . at the very commencement of their acquaintance" (147). Sir Arthur's lawyers behave differently according to the shifts in their client's fortune: "'Sir—[Oh! I am *dear* sir no longer; folks are only dear to Messrs Greenhorn and Grinderson when they are in adversity]" (337–38). Such telling is inevitably deformative. To it can be traced Lovel's exile from his origins, the misfortunes of those who told his story wrongly (such as the Meiklebackits and Glenallans), the Wardours' financial collapse, and a host of other disturbances in the family romances that make up Scotland as community.

At the same time, however, the deracinated data of a fractured past can be twisted into a new present. On the one hand, the Antiquary twists his telling in ways as problematic as any other character. He misrecognizes Lovel, complicating the putative lover's relationship with Isabella Wardour—Oldbuck reads Lovel's romantically overdetermined name, education, and wandering disposition as signs that he is an actor. He and Sir Arthur quibble over the supposed last Pictish word until their differences erupt in anger. On the other hand, Oldbuck brings Isabella and Lovel into conjunction: the fight produces the near-drowning that allows Lovel to save Isabella. Indeed, Oldbuck persistently shows how the detritus of the past can be forged (I use the word advisedly) into a new future. Oldbuck's insistence that the Kaim of Kinprunes is the site of the final conflict between Romans and Caledonians on one level seems ridiculous, and its silliness stands revealed by Edie Ochiltree's assertion that "I mind the bigging [building] o't"; on another level, it manifests the Antiquary's creativity with data as it is represented through persons (30–34). A twisted and twisting telling, it is nonetheless resistant in terms of class (against Sir Arthur), and celebratory in the way it links past and present through perception. Oldbuck's desire to produce the "Caledoniad" with Lovel points to the playful construction of national sensibility through the fragments of the past. "The Caledoniad; or, Invasion Repelled—Let that be the title—It will suit the present taste, and you may throw in a touch of the times." "But," Lovel objects, "the invasion of Agricola was *not* repelled." "No," Oldbuck replies, unquelled, "but you are a poet . . . and as little bound down to truth or probability as Virgil himself" (107). The Antiquary creates a new tale by unashamedly twining the remnants of the old. Value is attainable through renegotiating the past, but only in a present that is quite different.

Scott ratifies this point by contrasting the Antiquary's tale with the brutal confinement of narrative practiced by a more ancient Scottish family, the

Geraldins. Where the Antiquary represents the telling anew of Scottishness through not just the trivia of the past but the circulation of foreign blood, the re-evaluation of arcania, and the play of language, Lady Glenallan has tried to stop the making of new and different meaning. She has tried to control her children—with deathly results. She refuses to let the English Eveline Neville marry into her family; she separates Lovel/Neville's secretly married parents by the myth of incest; she makes away with their child; and she ruins the lives of those who serve her, like the complicit Elspeth Meiklebackit. But time, through which the present ever is fragmented into the artifacts of the past and the future is forged as new, eludes her. Time seems to stand still when the plots of Dousterswivel and the Geraldins intersect in the ruined graveyard of St. Ruth, yet the Countess's time has run out. As the adept, misled by Edie, delves for the treasure of Malcolm Misticot (the misbegot), Lady Glenallan herself becomes taboo: Steenie Meiklebackit and Edie stumble upon her burial. When Steenie unexpectedly drowns, this innocent grandson to Lady Glenallan's accomplice constitutes the sacrifice to the past by which the present becomes free to construct its own patterns of meaning. All the forces of the story consequently are released into a recuperative play of community that aligns the houses of Wardour and Geraldin under the sign of Lovel's legitimized illegitimacy.

What of Edie? David Punter reads in the wandering beggar "a Wordsworthian ideal personified; . . . [Edie] brings news or warning, he hoards and dispenses communal memory, he signifies continuity, he enjoins respect for age, he knits together what might otherwise fall apart" (xxi). Certainly, the memory that makes a community lies at the heart of this novel. Sir Arthur dismisses the Antiquary by privileging the recollection that is history over the disparate data that make up antiquarianism—Oldbuck's "tiresome and frivolous accuracy of memory" (40–41). And Edie first enters the text with an assertion of memory—Punter's "continuity": "I mind the bigging o't" (30). Still, we should remember Hume's caveats about how meaning is made: there is no "history" without data, and the meaning that is identity—personal, communal, national—is made in the gaps and from the clashes arising from the circulations of equivalent, fragmentary stuff.

This is as true for Edie Ochiltree as it is for the Antiquary. Edie may claim "truth"—"I never deal in mistakes, they aye bring mischances"—but this truth resides elsewhere than in the continuity of memory and the maintenance of the past (31). Edie does reconnect the message to the recipient— whether directing the idiot boy with his package to Lovel, or interrogating Elspeth with Oldbuck for the truth of Lovel's past. But he brings about unfortunate conjunctions, too. When he enlists Steenie to chastise Dousterswivel, he connects the Glenallan and Wardour pasts, and Steenie is borne away in the tide of differentiation that crests as a result. Indeed, we might say that Edie is most important for faking connections. Scott makes this clear when we meet the character. Edie informs the distressed Oldbuck:

"what profit have I for telling ye a lie . . . about twenty years syne, I, and a whin hallen-shakers [few vagabonds] like mysell, and the mason-lads that built the lang dyke . . . just set to wark, and built this bit thing here that ye ca' the—the—Praetorian, and a' just for a bield [shelter] at auld Aiken Drum's bridal. . . . [If] you howk up the bourock [mound] . . . ye'll find . . . a stane that ane o' the mason-callants cut a ladle on to have a bourd [joke] at the bridegroom, and he put four letters on't, that's A.D.L.L.—Aiken Drum's Lang Ladle—for Aiken was ane o' the kale-suppers [cabbage eaters] o' Fife." (31)

Lovel, and a host of critics, assume that Oldbuck gets his antiquarian come-uppance through Edie's folk memory. But memory plays tricks. Edie asks "what profit have I for telling ye a lie?" and given that he refuses money, he has no profit. However, one possibility does not undercut the other. Edie tells a lie that should have been obvious to Scott's readers.

Woven with the provable information of the time (there probably were masons, who did build walls), Edie invokes a well-known tall tale (463 n.31.6). Scottish children still sing the song of Aiken Drum—but it dates from before Scott's novel.[9] An eighteenth-century version, "The Piper o' Dundee," cel-ebrates misrule to the tune of "Aiken Drum":

It's some gat swords, and some gate nane,
And some were dancing mad their lane,
And mony a vow o' weir was ta'en
That night at Amulrie
(Hoggs, *Jacobite Relics*, Second Series, 43–44)

The chorus chants: "And wasna he a roguy, a roguy, a roguy / And wasna he a roguy, The piper o' Dundee?" Another old song seems named for its chorus: "Aikendrum, Aikendrum" (Second Series, 23-25). Notably, James Hogg remarks of it in 1821: "This is a most complicated business, and some parts of it to me perfectly inexplicable" (258). "But 'honour to whom hon-our is due,'" he continues. "[It] was Sir Walter Scott who first discovered the meaning of it." Perhaps not surprisingly in this context, Aiken Drum is best known through parody versions. One that should have been available to Scott's readers (see *Antiquary* 463 n.31.6) describes the eponymous hero:

An' his coat was o' the guid saut meat,   [salt]
The guid saut meat, the guid saut meat,
An' a waistcoat o' the haggis bag

Ay wore Aiken Drum.
O' the guide lang kail   [curly cabbage]
An' the Athol brose,   [stew, soup]
Ay they made his trew an' hose,
An' he lookit weel as ye may suppose,
An his name was Aiken Drum. (see fn. 9, contemplator)

Further, in different versions, Aiken plays upon a razor—or a ladle. Thus, Edie's vaunted memory transforms fiction into truth, a child's rhyme into recent history. But Edie inscribes the past in ways that should make entertainingly visible its construction through the evocation of antiquarian detail. The dance Edie "remembers" evokes "The Piper o' Dundee"; the "lang ladle" recalls Aiken Drum's fabulous ability to play any instrument, and also the need for "a lang spoon to sup wi' a Fifer" (more generally, the devil)—never mind Edie Ochiltree (463 n.31.11–12). "Aiken Drum" can only point to children's games and the fabular nature of the past when told in the present. There is no problem with Edie's memory, but it is memory that operates outwith "truth" and the directed narratives of history.

David Punter contends that "we are constantly under the apprehension that when Edie dies—or indeed when he settles down . . .—then the kind of knowledge he has will end with him" (xxi). However, far from hoarding some kind of unproblematic truth of the past, Edie remakes memory. He tells Lovel that he has "garr'd [Oldbuck] trow [made him believe] mony a queer tale mysel," and at the Kaim of Kinprunes, we see him perform another (175). He constructs another in the return to St. Ruth to fool Dousterswivel. Clearly, Edie is not reliable for the data of his memory, or its historical valence. Rather, Scott dwells on his ability to make new meanings that destabilize others. The tale of Aiken Drum throws Oldbuck into a frenzy of movement both physical and intellectual. It exacerbates the circulation of equivalents—antiquities from the past, characters and voices in the present—to produce a reality that is ever new. Perhaps this is Edie's "truth."

Raspe's Baron Munchausen, too, notoriously insisted upon the truth of his adventures. After stories of fifty brace of duck and other fowl destroyed by one shot, shooting a stag with a cherrystone and subsequently admiring the tree that sprouted on its forehead, a hound that pups while pursuing a hare that litters, and a flight to the Moon, he meets three men hanging by their heels as a punishment for "describing places they never saw, and relating things that never happened." "This gave me no concern," he declares, "*as I have ever confined myself to facts.*"[10] But "facts," as we have seen, yield something more than "truth." *The Antiquary* is not concerned with the truth or precision of the tale. That is the Glenallans' problem. Nor is the novel concerned to control its telling. Punter offers a melancholic reading of this phenomenon: "there will never be a single narrative version that will preserve the past from change and revision. . . . It is this sealed knot, this ever-pressing ambivalence of interpretation . . . that *The Antiquary* so complexly addresses" (xxx). Yet the impenetrability of the past, the fact that it subsists only in the form of dislocated data with all its strange conjunctions and clashes, allows—even requires—it to be left behind. There is always the opportunity to twist a new tale from the intersections of past and present. As the surviving literary scrap from the past assures, Sir Arthur's Knockwinnock house and land will be ever won even as they are lost—but always with a twist to the tale (328).

Indeed, there effectively is no past. For all Oldbuck's focus on antiquity, life is ever opening in the present. So the Meiklebackits make clear. Son Steenie, an energetically circulating sign who shows meaning as always in the making—fisherman, smuggler, collaborator in Edie's exploits, lover—drowns. This unexpected death in a plot not even obviously "sub-" opens a fissure in the story. Readers have long found this one of the text's compelling yet disturbing moments. Reviewers gave column inches to Steenie's sudden death and his parents' strange response.[11] The father works on at his boat: "And what would ye have me do," he gruffly asks Oldbuck, "unless I wanted to see four children starve, because ane is drowned" (267)? The mother pushes the point: "I hae some dainty caller haddies, and they sall be but three shillings the dozen, for I have na pith to drive a bargain e'enow," she tells the Antiquary. But when Hector offers her the sum she asks, she regains her humor: "Na, na, Captain; ye're ower young and ower free o' your siller—ye should never tak a fish-wife's first bode [offer], and troth I think maybe a flyte [squabble] wi' the auld housekeeper at Monkbarns, or Miss Grizzel [Oldbuck's sister], wad do me some gude" (308–9). Life, however tragic, through the circulation even of fish, and by the differing voices of those who meet through its interpretation and valuation, yields constantly to the future. With the Antiquary, we might almost look forward to the enlivening effect of "what cracker will go off next among our shins" (352).

Tales of the Landlord?

> "It's fearsome . . . when she wampishes about her arms,
> and gets to her English, and speaks as if she were a prent
> book let be an auld fisher's wife."

Scott directs us not to the tale, but its telling, as the site where Scottish meaning is made in *Waverley* and *Guy Mannering*. In *The Antiquary*, he considers the ways in which telling may be twisted and thus enliven the raw data of nation as shifting experience. *Tales of My Landlord*, First Series (1816), demonstrates how the nation may be kept new by the multiplication, too, of its tellers. If through his earliest novels Scott intensified telling as the site of Scottishness by maintaining it as an open, anonymous space, now he crams that space with characterized tellers and oppositional tales. For Bhabha, the nation subsists through what the people prescribe to themselves as national practice—but also through performance. Here, Scott throws into circulation not just the antiquarian details that are said to support national identity, but also the various voices that have articulated it. Far from making a cumulative case for a history that might be termed national, these contest that history, redirecting it this way and that through voices multiple and thus inevitably marginal.

Tales of My Landlord, First Series, appeared not through Constable, but through Blackwood. The shift in publishers required a change from "The Author of Waverley." Nevertheless, Scott did not inscribe his own name, as the publishers surely hoped. He denied that knowledge even to Blackwood's London connection, John Murray (Johnson, 1:548; 561). To Daniel Terry, his actor-manager friend, he wrote: "To give the go-by to the public, I have doubled and leaped into my form, like a hare in snow: that is, I have changed my publisher, and come forth like a maiden knight's white shield . . . with a virgin title-page."[12] However, there was more than one mark on Scott's escutcheon. It was scribbled over by numerous tellers intervening between the telling and the tale.

Through their multiplicity, these tellers compromise the singularity of telling. In The Antiquary, Scott had gestured toward the impossibility of simply telling a tale. At the core of that text resides the story of the Harz daemon, a narrative lump upsetting the progress of The Antiquary much as the daemon's lumps of gold disrupt the life of Martin Waldeck. This story proves the harder to integrate into the novel because it not only recalls that un/fortunate finder of the Harz, Rudolf Erich Raspe, in narrative terms it is Dousterswivel's tale displaced and reformed through Isabella Wardour, but given voice by Lovel, embraced by Sir Arthur, and resisted by Oldbuck (136–46). In The Antiquary, Scott often sets voices against one another. Isabella asks Oldbuck for the date of St. Ruth's Priory: "The Antiquary . . . plunged himself at once into the various arguments for and against the date of 1273. . . . the Baronet, catching at the name of one of his ancestors . . . entered upon an account of his wars . . . Dr Blattergowl was induced . . . to enter into a long explanation. . . . The orators, like three racers, each pressed forward to the goal, without much regarding how each crossed and jostled his competitors" (149). In fact, Isabella asks her question because she knows it will evoke distracting dissension.

Now, in the Tales of My Landlord, Scott pursues telling's multiplicity. The Black Dwarf (1816) sets the pattern. Here, in place of "The Author of Waverley," we encounter Jedidiah Cleishbotham. On the title page, this "Parish Clerk and Schoolmaster" figures as the tales' collector and reporter. He appears again in the dedication, offering these tales to "His Loving Country-men" from "their friend and liege fellow-subject, Jedidiah Cleishbotham." Again in the introduction, where he asserts the typicality of his tale. It arises, after all, in "*Gandercleugh*," which signifies "*the navel . . . of this our native realm of Scotland*" (5). Since this is the center of Scotland, and since Jedidiah sits by the fire in the Wallace Inn, he "*must have seen more of the manners and customs of various tribes and people than if I had sought them out by my own painful travel and bodily labour*" (5). But Jedidiah's assertion of self is always oppositional. His first sentence assumes that the title "*will secure . . . from the sedate and reflecting part of mankind . . . such attention as is due to the sedulous instructor of youth, and the careful performer of my Sabbath duties*" (5). This presumes a more critical part of mankind, already invading the reader's space and casting a jaundiced eye toward Jedidiah's chimney-nook. More-over, having claimed author-ity, Jedidiah accomplishes a twisted telling that by implication is also multiple: "*I will let these critics know, to their own eternal shame and confusion, as well as to the abashment and discomfiture of all who shall rashly take up a song against me, that I am* NOT *the writer, redacter, or com-piler of the Tales of my Landlord*" (6). Neither is "my Landlord." Rather (on page 4), Cleishbotham names his assistant, Peter Pattieson. But Pattieson compiles his tales from other sources. The opening chapter gives one such source—itself secondary. A farmer and shepherd pass through the inn on business, and tell the story that presumably is the one to appear in the body of the text.

Not only is the narrative space over-occupied by contending voices, it is a place of absences. The farmer and shepherd disappear from the text as others repeat their tale; Pattieson is already dead; my Landlord is a listener, not a teller; Jedidiah is *not* qualified to tell the tale—precisely through the terms that he invokes to support his authority (6). At the same time, however, Jedidiah disturbs the tale. Pattieson's chapter "Preliminary" is posthumously revised by a Jedidiah who inserts himself within the text, and whose disrup-tion is made worse by the publisher's explanatory notes that it requires. The schoolmaster gives himself a textual tag: "Here my [Pattieson writes] *worthy and learned* [Jedidiah adds] patron again interposed" (12). This precipitates a response from "the publisher": "*Note by the publisher.—We have . . . printed in italics some few words which the worthy editor, Mr Jedidiah Cleishbotham, seems to have interpolated upon the text of his deceased friend, Mr Pattieson. We must observe . . . that such liberties appear only to have been taken by the learned gentleman when his own character and conduct are concerned; and surely he must be the best judge of the style in which his own character and conduct should be treated of" (12). Through the prosy Jedidiah, maundering on about the text's layered provenance, Scott draws attention to the irrecuperability but also the complexity of its telling, and raises the problem not just of truly telling a tale, but of telling it once and for all. To tell, in this context, is to circulate a story through voices that ever disappear, yet nonetheless contest the textual space.

Scott repeats this gesture for *The Tale of Old Mortality* (1816) and even in *The Heart of Mid-Lothian* (1818), despite the fact that this later text returned to Constable for its publisher and thus could have figured as a novel by the Author of Waverley.[13] *Old Mortality* puts itself under Cleishbotham's ownership in title and dedicatory pages that replicate those for *The Black Dwarf*, its companion volume. Chapter 1, "Preliminary," leaps to Pattieson's narration of his meeting with a source: Old Mortality. But Old Mortality is long gone; we know already that Pattieson has died; and Jedidiah haunts the text from its opening sentence, which figures the junior schoolmaster's telling as a quotation: "'MOST READERS,' says the Manuscript of Mr Pattieson . . ." (5). And again, Cleishbotham invades through footnotes. Then in *The Heart of Mid-Lothian*, with Pattieson twice buried, Jedidiah precedes the text. In an address dated *"this 1st of April*, 1818," he invokes his "Courteous Reader," and loads the Landlord/suffering purchaser of the novel with extraneous detail about the novels' financial contribution to the architecture of his home. Once more, he sets himself against, and thereby invokes, the fracturing voices of the critics before turning to Pattieson's manuscript that, for a third time, tells a tale derived from others: the lawyers and the client who tumble from the coach into the river Gander .

Generally, critics see such layered narration as distancing readers from tellers and tales. Moreover, it pushes the tales into the past. For Francis R. Hart, we are "set, gradually, at greater and greater removes from those 'strange times'" (68; Humma, 301–15). Ina Ferris considers that Pattieson's encounter with Old Mortality "insists, almost obsessively, on the pastness of the past" (170). But Ferris goes on to note that this testifies to "anxiety about the presence of the past" (171). In this context, the narrators constitute a "dense screen that Scott constructs as he moves into a subject 'furiously alive' in popular memory" (166). Scott uses his narrators to evacuate dissension from his tale, and locate it in the past.

Ferris shows, however, that if this is his intent, Scott fails. Viewing Scott's strategy oppositely, I argue that Scott in fact succeeds. He does not distance or defuse the past. Rather, he makes it a site of contestation before he enters its textual space. The implicit arguments over literary ownership posed by Cleishbotham, the quiet Pattieson, a host of primary and secondary sources, and in the context of the Author of Waverley (as contemporary critics well knew), when articulated through that moment of inversion and play, 1 April, do not easily produce "a tale" of past or present. Rather, a host of tellers, at numerous textual levels, contend in the space where the tale insists, but is not yet told. Telling is a jostling, community activity that invites disagreement and evaluation anew, and careers headlong toward the cultural future.

The Many Tales of My Landlord

"O aye, hinnies, whisht, whisht! and I'se begin a bonnier
[tale] than that—"

If Scott's tellers multiply, they produce tales that are multiple in themselves. Scott meant each series of *Tales of My Landlord* to offer a number of disparate stories. For the first volumes, he "intended to have written four tales illustrative of the manners of Scotland in her different provinces"—as Jedidiah's dedication implies.[14] And as late as April 1818, Scott still expected his second series to include two tales.[15] He finally produced three, not the possible eight, yet the second (last) tale of the first series, and the one that took up all four volumes of the second "series," multiply internally.

Old Mortality, a tale often seen as compromising between religious and cultural extremes—establishing a "middle way" or defending the "stable order"—in fact multiplies disruptively against any attempt to contain cultural play or define Scottishness.[16] This dynamic counters a textual drive to limit the circulation of voices and tales. The novel's eponymous source manifests those forces seeking to restrict Scotland's story. Travelling between graveyards, Old Mortality labors to keep fresh the inscriptions commemorating the Covenanting dead. These inscriptions repeat the past in the present—surely a sign of Scott's tendency to force Scotland into a time gone by? Yet Old Mortality dies before we experience the telling of the tale. His teller, Pattieson, invokes John Home's tragedy, *Douglas*, to critique Old Mortality's obsession with the past: "O, rake not up the ashes of our fathers! / Implacable resentment was their crime, / And grievous has the expiation been" (14). Nevertheless, he himself has raked them up, with Old Mortality. Together, these tellers represent the restrictive voice of the past—and the multiplicity of resistant responses it invites. Indeed, since Peter Pattieson, too, is dead, and Jedidiah's domineering voice actually produces the reader's contention, Scott makes this tale ours through its very attempts to remain singular.

Within *Old Mortality*, tales likewise assert themselves as singular and nationally pedagogical, but thereby evoke alternatives and fracture into multiplicity. The novel opens by emphasizing a persistent past. Lady Margaret, despite the death of her husband and all male relatives, rapid and repeated changes in government, and the decline of familial and personal power, seeks to maintain the past as present. Once upon a time, the King "had actually breakfasted in the tower of Tillietudlem, an incident which formed, from that moment, an important aera in the life of Lady Margaret" (19). Time seems to have stopped for her. Moreover, she tries to stop it for others. She subjects her intimates to endless retellings of his majesty's "disjune" (24, 78, 103). More dangerously, she tries to make her compatriots continue in—even return to—the practices of the past. In the novel's first scene, Lady Margaret presides as a representative of government over a wappen-schaw, a "feudal [institution] which united the vassal to the liege-lord, and both to the crown" (14). Toward the end of the novel, despite the huge upheavals of the textual interval, she still strives to fold all participants into the tale of the King's visit (301). She encourages her granddaughter to marry not the rebellious, Presbyterian hero of the novel, but his aristocratic Episcopalian surrogate, and thus enact the past rather than move toward the future.

Balfour of Burley similarly tries to force others to repeat a circumscribed past. He works to limit the options for putative hero Henry Morton. Against a resistant Morton, he invokes Silas Morton, a dead father supposedly manifested through one (Covenanting) tale of the past (36; 182; 338). Burley tells that tale through one mode, the discourse of the Bible. At the start of the novel, he considers his own actions reenactments of Biblical types. A murderer of Archbishop Sharp, asleep he raves: "Thou art taken, Judas" (45). At the end, Morton meets a Burley still reenacting the murder and reviewing the consequent state of his soul in biblical cadences: "It was well done to slay him—the more ripe the corn the readier for the sickle.—Art gone?—art gone?—I have ever known thee but a coward—ha—ha! ha!" (337). And Burley seeks to inscribe Morton within his practices and terms. He obligates Morton into hosting him at Milnwood and thus inserts the younger man within his treasonable tale, and he imposes his own, supposedly spiritual language, against Morton's "carnal affections" and "carnal reason" (46; 170).

Claverhouse, Burley's opposite, serves as his cognate in this regard. Another man of the book—a little black book listing supposed malignants— he too inscribes Morton under the sign of his father: "Henry Morton, son of Silas Morton, Colonel of horse for the Scottish parliament. . . . He is . . . triply dangerous" (273). Even though Claverhouse eventually admits "now I know [Morton's] points better," he deviates not at all from his first military assessment: "His father was positively the most dangerous man in all Scotland. . . . His son seems the very model" (271; 116). It is with this determination in mind that he replicates Burley's attempt to prevent Morton's departure from his world of Biblical reenactment. Burley tosses his log bridge into a chasm, hoping to separate Morton from a fallen society. Claverhouse's monarchical tale exiles Morton across the sea, and hopes to disjoin him from alternate Scottish possibilities.

Critics often read this distribution of characters and tales as signifying Scott's preference for Jacobitism over Calvinism, the past over the present. Lockhart's story that Scott energetically asserted "no character had been so foully traduced as the Viscount of Dundee" seems to confirm this interpretation.[17] But as Daniel Whitmore points out, "Scott, contrary to the anti-Puritan tradition, also portrays the royalists . . . as literalists. The Presbyterian Left and the Cavalier Right may be . . . characterized by a fanatical adherence to the printed word" (244). That is, rather than privileging one tale over another, Scott circulates equivalent tales, resistant to one another through their rigidity. They can produce no dominant or compromising "truth," but through their clashes insist on the space between and against, where new meaning might be made.

Further, as Scott takes pains to point out, none of these confinements succeeds. The wappen-schaw unravels of itself, as Lady Margaret's anxiety for a display of loyalty folds in characters marginal not just for their politics, but their personal limitations: the goose boy upsets the authoritative performance of feudal militarism when he falls into line, but out of control of his accoutrements. "[Gibbie's] steed . . . having gambolled hither and thither to the great amusement of all spectators, set off at speed towards the huge family-coach. . . . [his] pike, escaping from its sling, had fallen to a level direction across his hands" (25). This erratic performance of national signs, shifted by age, class, and even clothing ("His casque, too, had slipped completely over his face"), stimulates further uncontrolled response. Granddaughter Edith Bellenden, remaining heir to Lady Margaret's cultural legacy, finds the situation hilarious: "so soon as Edith had heard it ascertained that the unfortunate cavalier had not suffered in his person, his disaster . . . affected her with an irresistible disposition to laugh" (52).

Indeed, the more Lady Margaret tries to define her world, the more it slips from her grasp. The famed story of his majesty's *déjeuner* constantly is interrupted. Major Bellenden, her Ladyship's brother-in-law, stops the story at its inception. "'All is to be in the same order as when'—'The king breakfasted at Tillietudlem,' said the Major, who, like all Lady Margaret's friends, dreaded the commencement of that narrative" (95). When Claverhouse arrives, and the scene is to be reenacted, others point out the impossibility that the past can persist. "'Weel, madam,' said Mysie . . . 'if every thing is to be just as his majesty left it, there should be an unco hole in the venison pasty'" (95). Moreover, at the crucial moment, the return of the past cannot be the same. Claverhouse, the third time Lady Margaret "adverted to this distinguished event . . . took advantage of the first pause to interrupt the farther progress of the narrative" (103). Subsequently Edith, exposed to her servant's simplistic/singular rehearsal of Morton's likely fate as a rebel, sinks down. "[And] she's sitting in the throne too that naebody has sate in since that weary morning the King was here!—O, what will I do? What will become o' us?" the culprit cries (196). The King's visit, from a perspective other than Lady Margaret's, yielded a "weary morning." But within pages, that moment has disappeared in the destruction of its relics when Burley invades the tower (238). The past can never return as the same; even daily life militates against it. By its very repetition, it produces difference.

This holds true for Claverhouse and Burley in their attempts to delimit the present through the supposed codes of the past. Neither maintains complete control even over those subject to their authority. Claverhouse is only one of many officers, none of whom agrees. In fact, he represents the fragmenting of a higher order. He is the Duke of Monmouth's officer, at odds with "General Thomas Dalzell . . . who executed the same violences against [the whigs] out of a detestation of their persons . . . which Grahame only resorted to on political accounts" (243). Claverhouse's subordinates are equally contentious. Evandale defies orders in a charge of vengeance against the Covenanters, and embroils the regiment in a stunning defeat (137–44). As for Burley, he too fights "the disunion implied in this virulent strife of tongues" among his religious cohort, and suffers his own internal disturbance as the religious killer of the Archbishop (178). Further, neither man controls the supposed replication of the past through Henry Morton. Morton frequently asserts his father's voice against Burley: "'I have heard my father observe,' replied Morton, 'that many who assumed power in the name of Heaven, were as severe in its exercise, and as unwilling to part with it, as if they had been solely moved by the motives of worldly ambition'" (188). Finally, if he escapes Burley's cave by a leap over the crevasse the fanatic has opened between his reality and an ever-changing world, Morton returns from the exile Claverhouse imposed at a moment that has shifted "Bloody Clavers" to the rebellious side, new-created him as "Bonnie Dundee," and already pushed him into the permanent past of death (332; 324).

What arises from this clash of tellers in contested tales? Morton resists the pressures of a Burley or a Claverhouse, and maintains a reasonable stance in the face of religious and political romance, but Morton is most importantly a shape changer, affected by—yet shifting against—circumstance. He does not subscribe to the wappen-schaw, but participates nonetheless as the "green adventurer" and wins by mounting horse to shoot down the popinjay (20–22). At home, cadet of his house and thus waiting for his avaricious uncle to cede his place, Morton seeks a gap in which to recreate himself as soldier: "I am weary of seeing nothing but violence and fury around me—now assuming the mask of lawful authority, now taking that of religious zeal"; still, "my father's sword is mine, and Europe lies open before me, as before him" (47). Civil dissension produces a movement in between the twisting, singular tales that would define a nation, and creates nationality anew. Thus Morton translates into a soldier in King William's service, returning from beyond apparent death by drowning to challenge "the same" in Scotland. The Morton who returns is almost unrecognizable, and accomplishes his narrative destination against history and as anti-romance despite and at the cost of those stories that would control him. Burley, Claverhouse, and Evandale all recede into the past; Morton moves differently in the gap.

Gaps in Tales of My Landlord

"I dinna mind the neist
verse weel"

In *The Heart of Mid-Lothian* (1818), Scott explores the principle of mobility that inhabits the gap made by excessive telling. The novel at first leaves no room for movement. Lawyers Halkit and Hardie, together with the usually self-effacing Pattieson, reduce Edinburgh's heart through wordplay. As "the Heart of Mid-Lothian," the Tolbooth prison in Edinburgh constitutes "a sad heart" (Pattieson); "a close heart, and a hard heart" (Hardie); "a wicked heart, and a poor heart" (Halkit); yet it is "a strong heart, and a high heart" to Hardie: "You see I can put you both out of heart" (14). Halkit folds: "I have played all my hearts." But Edinburgh's pre-occupied heart is thus a multiple heart. Its story is overdetermined, told differently by all those who have occupied it. As another artifact, a remnant from the Scottish past, and site of restrictive because punitive tales, the prison produces "uncertainty," the lack of which in other novels Hardie blames for the demise of the genre. In fact, every gesture of confinement produces an absence and provokes a movement. The smuggler Wilson's execution releases his accomplice Robertson/Staunton, who circulates disruptively through the rest of the text. Porteous, the over-zealous guardsman who seeks to make himself invisible within the Tolbooth and escape hanging by the mob, is contrasted against Effie, who is confined for supposed child murder and feels herself so inadequate she cannot leave even when released by her seducer Robertson. Effie's continued imprisonment stimulates movement on her behalf by a sister, Jeanie, who comes to enact the principle of mobility that underpins the construction of Scotland as future potential.

Like *Old Mortality*, this novel establishes a tension between restrictive telling of limited tales, and the twist in the tale that signifies constructive *différance*. But *Old Mortality*'s movement was motivated by an oppositional Calvinism playing within masculinized politics. Now possible tales continue to multiply as Calvinism is played through and against by gender. Davie Deans would restrict the bodily movement of the female: "'Dance!' he exclaim[s]. 'Dance?—dance, said ye? I daur ye, limmers that ye are,'" he berates his daughters, "to name sic a word at my door-cheek" (88). Robertson/Staunton, having impregnated one daughter and brought her subject to the laws against child-murder, seeks to control the other: "Do as you will, how you will, or what you will," he rants, "only promise to obey my directions" (138). This representative of aristocracy yet criminality actually invites the law to "press upon" Jeanie (165). Even Ratcliffe, the prisoner who has learned to work the system of the Tolbooth and become its keeper, strives to confine her. He seems to offer freedom of movement when he gives Jeanie a pass that will protect her from criminals as she walks to London in quest of her sister's pardon, but from his shifting, irresponsible position, he yet would determine Jeanie's words. A false declaration that Effie had confided her pregnancy to Jeanie would release her, and Ratcliffe cannot understand why Jeanie will not lie: "I must needs say . . . it's d—d hard, that when three words of your mouth would give the girl the chance to nick Moll Blood [escape hanging], that you mak such scrupling about rapping to them" (189). The Duke of Argyle himself, while conveying Jeanie to the Queen, seeks to restrict her speech. He tells her: "I am desirous that you should see her and speak for yourself," but nonetheless advises: "look at me from time to time—if I put my hand to my cravat so . . . you will stop" (328). The woman is not supposed to move within the text of masculine society.

But the confining force of a prescriptive tale evokes performative resistance. Here, it creates a gendered gap within which Scottishness achieves an unpredictable, adventurous mobility. Madge Wildfire, Effie's cognate, has been subjected by narratives of motherhood and property. Pregnant by Robertson/Staunton, she lost her child because of her socially climbing and murderous mother, and lost her wits at the same time. Now, all coercion produces her as absence. Sharpitlaw, seeking her erstwhile lover as a suspect in the lynching of Porteous, is too direct in his demands: "maybe, Madge, ye wad mind something about it, if I was to gie ye this half-crown," he bribes (150). "That might gar me laugh" says Madge, "but it couldna gar me mind." Memory, attention, caring—"mind"—all slip away under pressure of the law. The same thing happens in the eminently sane Jeanie Deans: "Your name is Jeanie Deans, and you are my prisoner . . . but if you tell me which way [Robertson] ran I will let you go," Sharpitlaw offers. But attempting to take charge of Jeanie, he extorts from her only the repeated "I dinna ken, sir" (161). Positive pressure accomplishes the woman as lack.

Jeanie cultivates movement through such absence. With Ratcliffe and Sharpitlaw distracted by the ever-present Robertson/Staunton, she flees all three of them and the law. She refuses to fill the gap in Effie's telling with words or, eventually, Effie's child—Jeanie will not tell a lie to protect Effie, and she does not tell Effie, or any other, about her part in the Whistler's escape. Rather, Jeanie gets on the road—or allows someone else to exit through the window. And travelling, she keeps herself invisible: "as she advanced, she perceived that [her bare feet and tartan screen] exposed her to sarcasm and taunts" (214). So she adjusts her dress. Her language, she cannot change, thus "she answered . . . civil salutations of chance passengers with a civil curtsy" (250). Jeanie resists signification. Indeed, where the Antiquary obsessively tried to name first the coach and then Lovel, or Burley and Claverhouse to denominate Morton as his father's son, Jeanie comes close to naming herself no one. At Dumbiedikes, in search of money to support her journey, she introduces herself as "ane wanting to speak to the Laird" (232). At Willingham, questioned by Robertson/Staunton's uninformed father, she asserts: "Sir . . . ye have an undoubted right to ask your ain son to render a reason of his conduct. But respecting me, I am but a way-faring traveller" (307). Then at court, her success hangs as much on what she does not say, as what she offers. Asked by the resentful Queen whether she had "any friends engaged in the Porteous mob?" Jeanie answers "'No, madam,' . . . happy that the question was so framed that she could, with a good conscience, answer it in the negative" (340). Instead, conversation focuses on how she has traveled, how far, and the lack that produced her movement: "'May your Leddyship never hae sae weary a heart, that ye canna be sensible of the weariness of the limbs!' said Jeanie" (339). Jeanie's evasions maintain her in circulation, allowing her to renegotiate Effie's value and thus readjust the English/Scottish relations inscribed across her sister.

Thus, Jeanie manifests the mobility, the opportunity to shift and change meanings, that opens in the clash between tellings, tellers, and tales. The "truth" of her tale is its constantly differing and deferring movement.

Returns of the Tale?

"there's unco thoughts come ower me"

Jeanie accomplishes one movement too many for the critics, however. Her travels return her not to home, but to Roseneath. Made available by the Duke of Argyle, reached by water, and inhabited by a Jeanie mysteriously made rich by her exiled sister, it seems a land of fairy tale at best, narrative failure at worst. For Judith Wilt, Jeanie now becomes "Cinderella" (141); to Claire Lamont, Scott worked too hard to "fill a four-volume novel" (xviii). Yet I suggest that in this final volume to *The Heart of Mid-Lothian*, Scott deliberately emphasizes the narrative difficulty of Jeanie's quest.

To ratify and stress his text's dynamic, Scott recreates its initial problem: Roseneath is indeed an ideal land—by the gendered standards of fairy tale. It manifests a masculine pedagogy that shocks us after the freedom of Jeanie's experiences. Davie Deans remains oppressive. His toast to Butler's ordination and forthcoming marriage reconfines Jeanie within a domestic tale: "the lad being new wedded to his spiritual bride, it was hard to threaten him with ane temporal spouse in the same day" (405). The Duke's representative, the comically manly Duncan Knockdunder, echoes this tone and function, taking advantage of Jeanie for her gendered hospitality. When Effie arrives and, as Lady Staunton, begs accommodation, Duncan officiously declares: "I have peen assuring my Lady, Mrs Putler . . . that . . . it could not discommode you to receive any of his Grace's visitors or mine" (437). In this place,

Staunton himself tries to seize control of Jeanie's voice once more. Afraid that she might let slip his alias as Robertson, he "even began to think whether there could be much difficulty in removing his wife's connections to the Rectory of Willingham. . . . then [Jeanie's] silence . . . was still more absolutely ensured" (453–54).

As Bhabha insists, however, there are no simple returns of the tale. Here we see the novel's developed concern with the differentiating possibilities produced by the clash of masculinities and overdetermination of the female. Jeanie now obviously operates as a movement in a gap. She does not return to Edinburgh; she does not travel through Glasgow; she arrives on an island that also is "not" (reached by water, the actual Roseneath lies on a peninsula across the Gareloch from Helensburgh—connected to the mainland). She does not complete the narrative trope that is Roseneath. The space may seem idyllic, yet here, she does not tell her husband about her continued relationship with her sister, despite their earlier talk that suggests there should be no gaps in marriage (107). Nor does Jeanie fall under Staunton's reasserted control. His desire to remove her to Willingham remains unspoken. Indeed, he and Deans end up dead; Knockdunder gets knocked under—capsized in the drink (411). Only Butler continues, agreeing there are some things he "must not ask" of his wife (429).

Most importantly, where Staunton would find his stolen (not murdered) child and re-establish the line of inheritance in his family, Jeanie releases the son—who unwittingly murders him. The Whistler, with a name that refuses to articulate him as subject, evades inscription in the symbolic, patriarchal, and pedagogical order.[18] Androgynous in appearance and almost without speech, he is a principle of mobility erupting in the gap opened by the text's battling masculinities. As she checks the house late at night after his capture, Jeanie pities his confinement: "Whistler," she asks, "'do the cords hurt you?' 'Very much.' . . . She cut his bonds—he stood upright, looked round him with a laugh of wild exultation, clapped his hands together, and sprung from the ground, as if in transport on finding himself at liberty" (466). He promptly escapes through the nearest window. Again a prisoner, the Whistler becomes a slave in Virginia. But, the text tells us, when Butler tries to redeem him, "this aid came too late. The young man had headed a conspiracy in which his inhuman master was put to death, and had then fled to the next tribe of wild Indians" (467).

Often this has been taken as Scott's exile of the rebellious forces released during the novel (Murphy, 197). Yet if Jeanie accomplishes a return that is not, so, potentially, does the Whistler. As A. G. Stevenson has shown, his career lies in the context of "Indian Peter," who did return. "Indian Peter" was an Aberdonian kidnapped and sold in America, freed, then captured again by natives. He escaped back to Scotland to sue the Aberdeen city fathers for their complicity in his confinement, and he eventually won. Based on his brief stay with the Indians, he made a career of exhibiting himself in native dress. He manifested the otherness constantly critiquing and recreating the nation. The Whistler, evoking Indian Peter, figures mobility in its fullest sense: in the dynamic between pedagogy and performance, the nation will always "return," but never as the same.

Telling Past the Ending

> "'Hush, hush!' said the Antiquary—'she has gotten the thread of the story again.'"

Why are critics so often disappointed by Scott's endings? Stein sums up the issues: "What is objectionable is the stereotyping, yet this too has an obvious function: clarity of moral perspective. . . . At the same time, the character of these conclusions suggests something about the nature of the novels they belong to: the texts *can* be closed; there is a final, total perspective from which everything can be understood . . . there is a last word, and it belongs to the author" (224). Critics, I suggest, subject themselves to Scott's strong "sense of an ending." But in Scott, the ending generally is not.

Scott deliberately constructs unsatisfying endings. He certainly knew they were problematic. Writing to Lady Louisa Stuart about *The Black Dwarf*, he admitted, "I found I had circumscribed my bounds too much & . . . that my imagination not being well in hand could not lounge easily within so small a circle. So I quarrelled with my story, & bungled up a conclusion."[19] Yet he did nothing to change his practice. Lady Louisa commented on *The Heart of Mid-Lothian*, two years later: "The latter part of the fourth volume unavoidably flags to a certain degree; after Jeanie is happily settled at Roseneath, we have no more to wish for. But the chief fault I have to find relates to the reappearance and shocking fate of the boy. . . . I cannot say what I would have had instead; but I do not like it either; it is a lame, huddled conclusion. I know you so well in it by the by!" (Lockhart, 4:177–78).

Although the reviewers affirmed Lady Louisa's critique over a sequence of novels, Scott embraced and replicated the inadequacy of his endings. Was it simply because, as Lady Louisa interpreted, "you grow tired of yourself, want to get rid of the story, and hardly care how" (178)? The author upset reviewers, readers, and critics because he actively refuses an end. Consider the final move of *Old Mortality*. If the novel's opening gestures implied it belonged to none of its many narrators, the story proper anticipated the modes of classic realism. For three volumes, the reader has experienced no serious concerns about the construction of the text, only worries about that of Henry Morton. With Morton now recuperated as hero, the tale suddenly fractures itself—by insisting upon an ending. On top of a truncated and inherently dissatisfying romantic resolution—in two pages Evandale is shot, Burley drowned, the returning Morton barely recognized by his heroine—Pattieson offers a conclusion in which Scott weaves together reader and tale. The reader is characterized: Martha Buskbody. As mantua-maker, one who caps identities, Miss Buskbody seeks the conventional end to the tale. Pattieson supplies it: "The marriage of Morton and Miss Bellenden was delayed for several months, as both went into deep mourning on account of Lord Evandale's death. They were then wedded" (351). Yet the effect, as Kenneth Sroka points out, "seems improper for it jolts the reader back into the linear progress of events" (193). Jane Millgate helpfully interprets: "[the conversation] about endings . . . is unashamedly deconstructive" (128). It deconstructs both text and our readerly expectations.

Scott goes out of his way to prevent closure. He actually reviewed *Tales of My Landlord*, First Series, himself. Denying his authorship even to his London publisher (through John Ballantyne he dealt with Blackwood in Edinburgh, and kept Murray at a distance), he cavilled: "I have a mode of convincing you that I am perfectly serious in my denial . . . and that is, by reviewing the work, which I take to be an operation similar to the extent of quartering the child."[20] Where a lesser author might have seized the opportunity to ratify his novel's greatness, Scott looks on this as a means to pull his book apart. In the review, he criticizes its form, pointing out its problems: "[The author's] stories are so slightly constructed as to remind us of the showman's thread with which he draws up his pictures and presents them successively to the eye of the spectator. He seems seriously to have proceeded on [the] . . . maxim—'What the deuce is a plot good for, but to bring in fine things?'" (Scott & Erskine, 431). Scott undoes his novel's coherence, and points to its constructedness: "the author errs chiefly from carelessness," he says (431). "There may be something of a system in it however." That is, he invokes his usual self-deprecating cover for structures that call attention to themselves—carelessness—but he takes care to seed another idea: "with an attention which amounts even to affectation, [the author] has . . . thrown his story, as much as possible, into a dramatic shape. In many cases this has added greatly to the effect, by keeping both the actors and action constantly before the reader, and placing him, in some measure, in the situation of the audience at a theatre" (431). Meaning is constantly making, not in the text, but through us.

Nor does Scott close down history in *Old Mortality*—whatever his critics' concerns. He stimulates lively debate about it. Ina Ferris documents the argument that erupted across denominations, classes, and politics as a result of Scott's novel (chapters 5 and 6). She explains that the nineteenth-century representatives of Calvinism—Reverend Thomas McCrie and Josiah Conder—attacked Scott's novel because it substituted for history.[21] To them, it falsely told the story of the past, which had its own religious logic, ethics, and coherence. As I have argued elsewhere, "McCrie sensed an encroachment on his inheritance" ("Thinking," 304). But where Ferris sees Scott avoiding confrontation with history as it is lived by hiding behind a screen of narrators (166), I consider that Pattieson's plea to "rake not up the ashes of our fathers!" only disingenuously serves to avert dissension; in truth, Pattieson invites it (14).

McCrie actually invoked Pattieson's words as the site of contention: "your fathers! If you mean the Presbyterians, they acknowledge you not" (*Vindication*, 44). Not only was Scott pilloried by Conder and McCrie, his novel stimulated two self-consciously and assertively dissident tales. John Galt produced *Ringan Gilhaize* "explicitly . . . as a counterstatement to Scott's novel," while James Hogg, who claimed his novel predated Scott's, nonetheless brought it to oppositional publication on the appearance of *Old Mortality* (Ferris, 162 and chapter 6). As McCrie went on to criticize: "*you* [Scott] only are to blame for the stirring of those ashes with which time was slowly covering the memory of . . . infamous deeds" (*Vindication*, 44–45).

And Scott was enjoying the rumpus. For someone who sought to avoid disagreement, he stirred it up. Although he told Lady Louisa that "I have not read [McCrie's *Vindication*], and certainly never shall," he goes on to name "my suspicions of that very susceptible devotion which so readily takes offence."[22] One line later, he reveals his fighting stance: "such men should not read books of amusement" converts into: "do they suppose, because they are thought virtuous, and choose to be thought outrageously so, 'there shall be no cakes and ale?'—'Ay, by our lady, and ginger shall be hot in the mouth too.'" Scott gloried in making it "hot." His review, written jointly with William Erskine, ridicules *Old Mortality* for its historical anachronisms, thereby attacking the text along with those who invoke history against it, but making their claim trivial: Dalzell "was *not* at [Bothwell Bridge]"; the author exhibits him "as wearing *boots*, which . . . the old general never wore" (463). The review sympathizes with "these unfortunate men," the Cameronians (extreme Covenanters), yet does not vindicate them, and so maintains a perspective other than simply doctrinal (464). It refuses to translate "deceased heroes into deities," and implicitly throws a challenge to religious readers for this "pagan" practice (470). It defends a contested portrait of Claverhouse precisely on the grounds that it is contested (470–71). And, exacerbating the novel's offence, the review celebrates its "unprecedented popularity," which means that "we cannot suggest a consideration which a perusal of the work has not anticipated in the minds of all our readers" (466). The novel already has exceeded critical control. The battle is joined.

Scott kept it going. Early in 1817, he colluded with Charles Kirkpatrick Sharpe to publish an edition of James Kirkton's *The Secret and True His-*

tory of the Church of Scotland—a text he well understood the Presbyterians might view with a proprietary eye. He repeats his fighting words, now to Sharpe: "it would be most scandalous to let the godly carry it off there—If they are virtuous shall there be no cakes and ale—Aye by our lady & ginger shall be hot i' the mouth, too."[23] Scott even enters with verve into a physical tussle over the original text. "It is very odd," he continues, "the Vol. of Wodrow containing the Memoir of Russell concerning the Murder [of Archbishop Sharp] is positively vanished from the library. . . . Surely they have stolen it in the fear of the Lord." In early February, he crows to the editor: "My dear Sharpe,—It was not without exertion & trouble that I this day detected Russells MS. also Kirkton & two or three others which Mr. Macrie had removed from their place in the library and deposited them in a snug & secret corner. . . . I have given an infernal row on the subject of hiding books in this manner."[24] Yet when the book actually appeared, Scott gave it a mixed review. He interestingly casts Sharpe as an "antiquary," who "finds the solitary enjoyment of gazing upon and counting over his treasures deficient in interest" (could this be a slap at the cupboard-loving Presbyterians?) "and willingly displays them to the eyes of congenial admirers" (Scott, Review, 503). Kirkton's text he considers "highly valuable and important. It has been quoted by every Scottish historian of the period as the work of an honest and well-informed man" (530). Nevertheless, he is not afraid to characterize Sharpe as "an episcopalian and a tory" who has "contempt of the covenanters, and dislike of democratical principles" (531). He actually asserts his lack of sympathy with the man he encouraged to edit the work—"we are far from uniting our own views of the subject with those of Mr. Sharpe"—and goes on to castigate both the Covenanters and the cavaliers of the past (532–33). Scott stirs the pot from both sides—and with Aiken Drum's lang ladle!

He argues on through *The Heart of Mid-Lothian*. Scott had been recalling the Quaker part of his family history during 1816.[25] Now, he invokes it to evade but also reanimate the contention over *Old Mortality*. Jedidiah takes to himself the religious and historical criticism levied against the novel: "these cavillers . . . have impeached my veracity and the authenticity of my historical narratives!" ("To the best of patrons," 4). "It has been demanded of me, Jedidiah Cleishbotham, by what right I am entitled to constitute myself an impartial judge . . . seeing . . . that I must necessarily have descended from one or other of the contending parties" (5). With Jedidiah, Scott slips the noose: "O ye powers of logic! when the prelatists and presbyterians . . . went together by the ears . . . my ancestor . . . was one of the people called Quakers" (5). Scott moves in the gap constructed between supposedly all-inclusive religious definitions of Scottish subjects—and he draws attention to that movement once again, inviting others to register it and participate in its celebratory play.

Tales of the Author

Richard L. Stein considers that "the gaps [Wolfgang] Iser finds inherent in the reading process are for Scott traps to be guarded against" (223). I argue that the active response required by the twisted tellings, many tellers, various tales, and problematic endings of Scott's first two series of *Tales* implies the reverse. So does Scott's life at this time. In 1815, Francis Jeffrey had slyly doubled Scott and the Author of Waverley: "if [the novel] be indeed the work of an author hitherto unknown, Mr Scott would do well to look to his laurels."[26] As debate raged but opinion predominated for Scott, the author, rather than confirming his claim to the novels, complicated it wildly. He circulated against "the Author of Waverley" the author of *Tales of My Landlord*; he adopted a (recuperated) Matthew Bramblesque persona to produce *Paul's Letters to His Kinsfolk* (1816), supposed traveler's letters from post-Napoleonic Europe. When the reviewers wondered about the identity of the Author, he raised other possibilities—even with relatively close acquaintances. In a rash of speculations from 29 November to 28 December 1816, he declared to Lady Abercorn that "I cannot think it at all likely that Young Harry Mackenzie wrote these books," and offered: "His brother James might be more likely to amuse himself in that way." But Scott took away that option too: "I think this is also unlikely."[27] To Joseph Train, Scott offered: "Why the author should conceal himself, and in this case even change his publishers as if to insure his remaining concealed is a curious problem. I get the credit of them and wish I deserved it but I dare say the real author will one day appear."[28] And with the unfortunate Lady Abercorn, he debated but did not debunk a further rumor, that they were written by his brother: "if Tom wrote these volumes he has not put me in his secret."[29] As in his novels, Scott persistently opened up gaps within which he encouraged creative speculation—even about himself.

Scott's careers equally were multiple during these years. Millgate notes that "To read his letters from the early spring of 1815 to the spring of 1816 is to be overwhelmed by a sense of constant public activity, unremitting energy, and sheer comprehensive appetite" (*Scott*, 85). Scott was involved in everything: "Whether he was playing the anonymity game with the Prince Regent, trading compliments with Byron, hob-nobbing with Wellington . . . engaging in detailed legal arrangements about a young friend's marriage settlement, or putting in bids for more land around Abbotsford, no effort was spared and all possibilities seemed open." Scott, I suggest, was impelled to multiply, to throw voices into opposition, to move between the clashes. He circulated himself, and made the meaning that was Walter Scott, as insistent (though inaccessible) presence in the gap. Scott, like his stories, was pitched toward the future; anonymity plus multiplicity meant possibility in the minds of future readers.

Is it a coincidence that, as John Buchan and then Edgar Johnson point out, through this period Scott gathered into his care all the lands once walked by "True" Thomas the Rhymer?[30] Thomas's truth resided in his ability, circulated through multiple prophetic fragments, ever to participate in future meaning making. Perhaps in Abbotsford, and with a certain humor, Scott's antiquarian impulse assembled a space that suggests the persistence of the past and invites, by the absent presence of the Author of Waverley, a future ever to be met and to make anew.

3

Chancing Scotland

Playing for De/Valuation in *The Fortunes of Nigel* and at the King's Visit (1822)

"luck in a bag"

By 1822, Scott had constructed a Scotland ever new by its circulations through tomorrow's readers. The degree to which success depended on the antiquary/miner—tossing up hidden fragments to require and challenge present valuation—and the occulted author—spinning value in a place and time constantly arriving—is evident by Scott's persistent use of these figures. Edie Ochiltree/Thomas the Rhymer/Walter Scott are alive and well in the epigraph to *The Bride of Lammermoor* (1819):

By cauk and keel to win your bread,	[fortune telling]
Wi' whigmaleeries for them wha need,	[fancies; toys]
Whilk is a gentle trade indeed	
To carry the gaberlunzie on. (3)	[wandering beggar]

In his "Dedicatory Epistle" to *Ivanhoe* (1820), "Laurence Templeton" comments on the Author of Waverley's achievement: "It was no wonder . . . that, having begun to work a mine [of antiquities] so plentiful, he should have derived from his works fully more credit and profit than the facility of his labours merited" (6).

Such activities seemed as yet playful and creative. When Scott was elected president of The Royal Society of Edinburgh, he humorously melded his two metaphors, writing to William Laidlaw in November/December 1820: "I would have you in future respect my opinion in the matter of *chuckie-stanes* [jacks], caterpillars, fulminating powder, and all such wonderful works of nature. I feel the spirit coming on me, and never pass an old quarry without the desire to rake it like a cinder-sifter" (*Letters*, 6:304).The months before he began *The Fortunes of Nigel* saw Scott encouraging others to play along. With his friends Lady Louisa Stuart and J. B. S. Morritt, he contemplated a series of "Private Letters of the Seventeenth Century" (*Private Letters*, "Introduction"). He wrote to Morritt on 16 June 1821: "I hold you account-able for two or three academical epistles of the period, full of thumping quo-tations of Greek and Latin in order to explain what needs no explanation and fortify sentiments which are indisputable" (*Letters*, 6:479–80). The "Adver-tisement" for this unabashed fraud commended the work as "worthy the attention of all who are desirous of knowing, from the most accurate sources, the manners and habits of their forefathers" (56). Apparently, Scott enjoyed churning together past and present, tales and tellers, truth and lies, and wait-ing to see what meaning erupted where certainty could never ensue.

Yet play was anything but free. Yoon Sun Lee comments that "the prin-ciples through which [antiquarianism] established the value of its objects . . . bore a disquieting resemblance to those of . . . the marketplace" (540). Scott's circulation of Scottish artifacts, texts, and tellers stands subject to valuation within a system outside itself. Of course, Scott played this market. Trading through pasts and texts in money and reputation, Scott's stock was rising: "Within a single year [1819, Scott] had written and published one short novel, *A Legend of Montrose*, and two full-length novels, *The Bride of Lammermoor* and *Ivanhoe*, all three selling better than any of their seven pre-decessors" (Johnson, 1:691). He was able to sell his early copyrights—which he laughingly termed his "eild kye" (old cows)—for £12,000 (1:640). The novels coined value elsewhere, too. In February 1819 there was "a spectacular opening night at the Edinburgh Theatre Royal—a dramatized version of *Rob Roy*. [The anonymous author's appearance] . . . was the signal for a burst of enthusiasm in the crowded theater" (1:640). They also produced reputa-tion. Critics north and south applauded *Ivanhoe*: "The *Quarterly* called it a 'splendid masque.' . . . Sydney Smith . . . said roundly, 'There is *no doubt* of its success'" (1:686). In 1820, Oxford and Cambridge both offered Scott honorary degrees (1:708).

The author's stock was high enough, he used it to float other Scots. He wrote of his nephew, "I will do all that is in my power to stand in the place of a father to him," and offered to bear "the expense of his equipment and pas-sage-money" for "a cadetship in the East-India Company's service" (John-son, 1:710). John Wilson (*Blackwood's* Christopher North and a dubiously qualified candidate) he supported for Edinburgh's Chair of Moral Philoso-phy (1:710). They were among many who begged and received his help.

All seemed to prosper. But it is one thing for Scott's tellers and tales to circulate within the closed economy of the Waverley novels, quite another to enter the larger marketplace, with its different structures and unpredictable play, and Scott found that he was perhaps circulating too much and as too many. *Nigel* derived in part from the drafted *Private Letters* when, Lockhart says, Scott's friends informed him he was "throwing away in these letters the materials of as good a romance as he had ever penned" (Lockhart, 5:138; *Private Letters*, 38–41). Value may depend on scarcity, on moving the right item through the best market. Further, Scott's texts produced his day's "designer imposters." Upstart authors tried to substitute their own works for those of "the Author," circulating so smoothly and valued so high. In October 1819, an advertisement for a fourth series of *Tales of My Landlord*, purveyed by "Jedediah Cleishbotham," appeared in the *Morning Chronicle* (Johnson, 1:685–86). As a result, Scott decided not to adopt yet another persona for *Ivanhoe* but to work the market more precisely in a text where Laurence Templeton references the Antiquary and all folds back to "The Author of Waverley" (once more on the title page). Scott registered the risk that, as a term seeking valuation by circulation, even the space that was "the Author of Waverley" could be usurped and revalued—thus devalued.

Indeed, Scott did become implicated in the utterances of others. Scott was a silent, non-circulating sponsor for the Tory *Beacon* (1821).[1] It pilloried James Stuart of Dunearn and James Gibson. Gibson subsequently traced fiscal responsibility for the journal to a few eminent Tories—including Walter Scott. Serving as an equivalent for the *Beacon*, and brought into circulation against Gibson, who thought he had penned the offending articles, Scott found himself subject to comment that located the ineffable "Author" within the limiting discourse of petty politics. He risked the ultimate devaluation when Gibson contemplated challenging him to a duel. His worth was in no way enhanced when Stuart challenged and did kill an author for the *Glasgow Sentinel*, who also had ridiculed him, and then postured in a tawdry trial.[2] A Scott inscribed in tragedy played out as low comedy stood liable to trivialization.

Worse, the body that was Scott suffered outside the Author's control. From 1816 through 1819, Scott was often ill. In late March 1819, he suffered "a fourth very severe spasmodic affection which held me from half past six last night to half past three this morning in a state little short of the extreme agony . . . / I sighd and howld / And groaned and growld / A wild and wonderous sound."[3] J. H. Alexander suggests Lockhart exaggerates Scott's pain while composing *The Bride of Lammermoor* (*Bride*, 271). Still Scott felt enough at risk that on 23 March 1819, he informed Constable: "If the worst come to the worst I am putting my things into such order that you my good friend may not have inconvenient loss" (*Letters*, 5:324–25).

Given the unpredictability of gaining worth in any circumstances, and the difficulty of maintaining a circulable self, what were the chances of achieving value in the British market of finance and reputation? By 1822, Scott had spent some years exchanging Scottish narration for, he hoped, English valuation. Across successive poems and novels, he had aimed to earn money and respect, but also recognition for a Scotland sorely in need of affirmation within the technically "united" kingdom. In 1820, his Scottish performance seemed to have met and shifted British presumptions. His was the first baronetcy of George IV's reign, and the honor came at the King's behest.[4] Scott's prolific authorship had earned a high accolade within the perverse hierarchies of British economics and class. Moreover, it had earned respect for Scotland. Thoroughly inscribed within the discourse the author had supplied, the King anticipated a northern visit enhanced by all the pseudo-panoply of Scott's literary State. He did travel to Scotland in August 1822, a few months after *The Fortunes of Nigel* was published.[5]

In 1821, however, Scott realized that even as he achieved success, the terms of his texts placed all Scots and Scotland itself on the brink of failure. At George's enthronement, Scott witnessed the troubles of Glengarry. Wearing the highland costume Scott had defined for Scotland and romanticized to the English, this claimant to chieftainship functioned as a walking manifestation of Scott's national construction. Menaced with ejection because his highland pistols coded him in London as an assassin, Glengarry demonstrated the contingency of Scotland's valuation through Scott's narration.[6] As a literary construct, Scotland achieved worth; as a physical presence at the scene of English (supposedly British) self-affirmation, things Scottish suffer devaluation. The performance stands subject to the whims of the dominant audience. This reality haunted the author. Glengarry's embarrassment found its way into *Nigel*, and the novel became a worried consideration of how authorial, literary, and national value rises and falls within the dynamic of southern exchange (306).[7]

Scott's awareness was already growing through *The Bride of Lammermoor*. Here, "Pattieson," who considers it improbable his narratives "will ever become public during the life of their author," still imagines their sale would locate him "'as a lion' for a winter in the great metropolis" (3). While asserting he "cannot rise, turn round, and shew all my honours, from the shaggy mane to the tufted tail, roar ye . . . and so lie down again like a well-behaved beast of show" (4), Pattieson nonetheless assumes that his circulation would mean valuation—or perhaps devaluation. Dick Tinto, source for the story that follows, makes the problem clear. Dick exhausts his Gandercleugh market and degrades his art by painting a sign for the Wallace Inn, so he goes to Edinburgh. There, "he received dinners and hints from several distinguished judges of the fine arts," but no money (9). Dick next seeks "London, the universal mart of talent," where he "threw himself headlong into the crowd which jostled and struggled for notice and preferment" (9). But "Poor Dick was doomed. . . . In the fine arts, there is scarce an alternative betwixt distinguished success and absolute failure" (10). London, site of specie, is the arbiter of a value that overrides intrinsic worth and polices Scott's type of playful, differential performance. Terms in circulation tend to devaluation. So how could one play the British markets of money and reputation—and win?

The Mis/Fortunes of Nigel

"I never heard ye were a great gamester . . . my lord"

The "Introductory Epistle" to *The Fortunes of Nigel* (1822) shows the problem resides in the very telling of the tale. Can the ineffable author tell a story that will not get devalued when it is exchanged as cultural coin within the British market? Is all telling a telling *down*? After editorial persona "Captain Clutterbuck" meets his Author, he gushes: "[I] beheld . . . the person, or . . . the Eidolon, or Representation, of the Author of Waverley !" (4–5). Overcome with filial respect, Clutterbuck exclaims "*Salve, magne parens!*" But if the child recognizes the father, he nonetheless has trouble describing him—turning him into a site of valuation or even usable currency. The "person" who quickly slips to "Eidolon" and even "Representation " evades inscription:

> I . . . endeavoured to note the features. . . . But . . . I can give . . . no satisfaction. . . . the verses of Spenser might well have been applied—
> Yet, certes, by her face and physnomy,
> Whether she man or woman inly were,
> That could not any creature well descry.

Authority may be immanent, but it is also indeterminate. Indeed, it is evanescent.

Clutterbuck recognizes that in the literary marketplace, authority is produced through exchange between novelist and community and depends on limited circulation of worthy texts. The source of Scott's authority is thus also a liability: "Ah, sir," the Captain laments "would ye but . . . try to deserve at least one-half of the public favour you have met with, we might all drink Tokay!" (8). He continues: "Are you aware that an unworthy motive may be assigned for this succession of publications? You will be supposed to work merely for the lucre of gain" (13). Even as Scott produces saleable novels, their currency undermines their value and his authority. Because his work is a commercial triumph, the Author of Waverley flickers ever at the instant where transcendence dissipates into ephemeral popularity and reputation is lost. The success of Scott's texts may constitute him not as a site of hidden origins, but as a term in circulation and subject to devaluation.

Scott's response can be understood through Goux. Valuation depends on the exchange of equivalent terms, and is therefore unstable. However, one term can be constructed as the general equivalent—the father, phallus, or logos that transcends the system by repressing its own origins and appears to hoard and determine value. Yet because the general equivalent itself is merely a sign, its role established by exchange and convention, it also signals a lack. Every instance of valuation is thus inevitably a gesture toward deferral, devaluation, and back to limitless play. It is the tension between general and contingent equivalency, excess and lack, value and loss, and loss and play, that Scott explores in *Nigel* as a result of his unpleasant encounter with the complex realities of personal and national exchange through the circulations of narrative.

Young Nigel maps the relationship between novel and author and nation and narration. Lacking a father—as a novel by the "Author of Waverley" lacks a figure of authorship and the post-Union nation a tale of origins—he leaves Scotland for London in search of that supposed governing term, the King. Surely the King can revalue Nigel's inheritance and Nigel himself as Scot. According to the Scottish proverb, after all, "A King's face / Should give grace."[8] But James immediately brings into question his determinative power: "The scene of confusion . . . was no bad picture of the state and quality of James's own mind. There was much that was rich and costly in cabinet pictures and valuable ornaments, but they were slovenly arranged, covered with dust. . . . inconsistencies in dress and appointments were mere outward types of those which existed in the royal character; rendering it a subject of doubt amongst his contemporaries, and bequeathing it as a problem to future historians" (66; Wormald). James lacks the mental fortitude, the physical presence, and thus, unsurprisingly, the mounds of specie to serve as marker for national value. While he aspires to be a British Solomon, deciding between the claims of the English Buckingham and the Scottish Nigel, this Scotsman who has headed south in the capacity of value has lost it in the process.[9] Not only is he incapable of fixing Nigel's worth, he himself constantly is in search of capital. His attempt to re-establish Nigel's inheritance requires the King to pawn his jewels to underwrite money loaned through the most debased of markets: Alsatia, with its highwaymen and usurers. Nigel's loan guarantee from the King is purloined by old Trapbois, but in being stolen, it circulates where the King's jewels already have gone in its support. There is no value, merely a system of circulations. Lacking value in himself, James seems the site only of devaluation.

In fact the King reveals the dominant term's foundation in lack. As James VI of Scotland reinscribed as "I of England," he foregrounds not monarchical transcendence but rather the absence that requires substitution (for Scotland) and (in England) the substitution that implies loss. Nigel's servant, Richie Moniplies, remarks that "The King's leaving Scotland has taken all custom frae Edinburgh" (35). But since he "came fleeing down the back-stairs of auld Holyrood-House, in grit fear, having [his] breeks in [his] hand," the monarch himself is in circulation (47). Scottish courtiers who pursue him in hope of valuation stand degraded, like Nigel, and further degrade the King. English courtiers, who should look to the King for their status, claim both that they could have sent his warlike ancestors "back to the north again," and that such Scots would have been more manly than the poor substitute, James (110).

The King, too, is subject to exchange. Claiming the role of "second Solomon," for an English innkeeper the King becomes "a sort of [Jew]" (298). Employed in "constructing a palace, from the window of which his only son was to pass to die upon a scaffold before it" (65), his dynasty already is undone; in 1822 James VI and I is precipitated in the direction of devaluative exchange through his achieved deferral in the place and time of history. More, subject to personal rumor through what Isaac D'Israeli considered "His idle correspondence with Buckingham . . . often misunderstood. . . . an infamous Vice" (possibly homosexuality), the King stood always and already devalued in British social discourse (Scott, *Private Letters*, 35). Even the monarch—especially the Scottish monarch circulated south—signals not valuation, but its deconstructive other, equivalence.

Having demonstrated that equivalency, whether in national or literary authors, can never be fixed, Scott considers the reality that is circulation. At first, as representative Scot and putative text, Nigel refuses to define or name himself outside the court, insisting on his inherent worth that requires only recognition from the King. Yet all the time, the young man's value rises and falls depending on his social and economic alignment. To his English landlady, he is a Scot on the make. But because she herself married a Scot, and because Nigel is more attractive and more noble than her usual clientele, she recommends: "go back [to Scotland] again if you like it . . . unless you think rather of taking a pretty, well-dowered English lady. . . . [The] great Turkey merchant's widow . . . married Sir Awley Macauley . . . old Serjeant Doublefee's daughter . . . jumped out of window, and was married at May-fair to a Scotsman with a hard name" (41–42). Dame Nelly's mode of valuation inevitably undermines the self-consciously noble Nigel.

Even in the context of George Heriot, an undisputed figure of worth in England and Scotland, past and present, fiction and history, Nigel's value, and thus his identity as Scot and as subject, remains uncertain. Within the text, Heriot owes his success as the King's goldsmith to his origins in Edinburgh and his valuation by Nigel's father. Deferred through history, Heriot's name resonates across nineteenth-century Scotland as that of the son who went south but remitted value back home. George Heriot's high school has encouraged the successful circulation of generations of Scotsmen. Heriot's character rings sterling in all respects. Yet neither Heriot's recognition of

Nigel as worthy because of the young man's descent, nor his gift of funds, nor his intervention with the King based in his own worth as faithful subject and underwriter of the monarch's debts, can stabilize the young man's value. Heriot cannot remove Nigel from the system of exchange where he is seen at once as noble yet degraded, kind yet spoiling for a fight, brutal yet cowardly, truthful yet criminal. In fact, depending on how Nigel and other Scots are related at a given moment through the vagaries of circulation, Heriot too values incorrectly. Assuming all orphan Scots worthy, Heriot invests in the dishonest Andrew Skurliewhitter (120; 372–73). Nigel he reads through "the fatal case of Lord Sanquhar," who caused "[English] men [to] exclaim they will not have their wives whored, and their property stolen, by the nobility of Scotland" (327). When Nigel appears to have gambled away the King's guarantee and stolen David Ramsay's daughter, he falls outside the carefully governed class speculations of the rising merchant capitalist that enable George Heriot to see him as valuable. And Heriot reads the nation's worth through the exchanges of its subject. "[Our] national character," he concludes, "suffers on all hands"—Nigel's included (327).

In Nigel, we see the terror of ongoing devaluation for self and Scotland. This is most obvious through Dalgarno, Nigel's Scottish likeness who similarly hopes for recognition in an English market. Nigel and Dalgarno should provide mutual valuation, but to circulate even in context of one's reflection can only undermine worth. As Goux points out, "every commodity must, to express its value, enter into relation with some other commodity," but this relationship evokes other comparisons (15). This "extended value form" is "a situation of rivalry, of crisis, of conflict." Through his equivalence with Dalgarno, Nigel is repositioned and his value declines. Thus, Nigel's innocent relationship with Dame Nelly brands him as womanizer, sexual braggart, and physical and moral coward (126, 130–31, 168–72). When Dalgarno gambles and induces the reluctant Nigel to play, he gains respectability while his friend becomes known as a reckless gambler and a miserly exploiter of others. Nigel's actions and intentions matter little; circulation is all.

Further, through Dalgarno Scott clarifies that the circulation inevitable for the post-Union Scot and the northern author produces *self*-devaluation. Dalgarno hopes to lower his friend's value to the point that Nigel's property transfers to him and buys influence at the English court. Finally ejected by the court as it recognizes Nigel's value and his friend's duplicity, Dalgarno enacts all the sins of which Nigel has stood accused and suffers the ultimate devaluation of meaningless death. He reveals that such devaluation is almost a national project. Behind Dalgarno stands Alexander Skurliewhitter, who abjures honest work for George Heriot and embraces Dalgarno's assault on Nigel's character and property and his attempt on English valuation. Or there is Sir Malachi Malagrowther, the King's erstwhile whipping boy, who replicates Dalgarno's twisted logic in his twisted body and vindictive enjoyment of his countrymen's misfortunes. There is honest John Christie, Nigel's hapless, half-Scottish landlord, who by his marriage to an Englishwoman and kindness to Nigel has produced his own cuckoldry at Dalgarno's hands. There is Nigel himself, whose naïve notions of self-worth lead to a carelessness about the realities of valuation that hastens his decline. Scots who try to "pass" in English society and on English markets—right through to George Heriot, who Nigel's servant first considers "an Englisher"—appear complicit in the necessity of circulation (34). They construct the terms of their own degradation, undermine the Scottish community, and sell Scottishness short.

Scott leaves no doubt that personal and national identity stand at risk. When Nigel realizes the negative effects of his relationship to Dalgarno, he challenges his one-time friend to a duel, and thus risks sacrificing his right hand—the site of meaningful self-inscription—to the law. Worse, he sacrifices his name. There may be no self to signify. Fled beyond the terms of English governance into the inverted society of Alsatia, Nigel is constructed as criminal, but he is deconstructed, too. Nigel Olifaunt, Lord Glenvarloch, attempts to save his skin by offering an alias to his new associates. That alias maintains an oblique reference to his origins through his mother, yet even this weak connection to identity cannot be maintained. Olifaunt becomes Grahame. This is instantly rendered as "Grime." "I said Grahame, sir, not Grime," Nigel testily replies. "'I beg pardon, my lord,' answered the undisconcerted punster;' but *Graam* will suit the circumstance too—it signifies tribulation in the High Dutch, and your lordship must be considered as a man under trouble'" (192). Then, when written into the books of Alsatia, Nigel unfortunately transmutes into "Niggle" (195). Even this status he must maintain through "a con-si-de-ra-tión," constantly paid and repaid to a landlord who recognizes nothing but money (243). More seriously, Nigel can attain value in this doubly foreign circulation only when serving as a friend to England and thus no Scot. His admission to Alsatia challenged on the grounds that he is "a beggarly Scot, and we have enough of these locusts in London already," Nigel gains access "for giving the bastinadoe not to an Englishman, but to one of his own countrymen" (195; 196). Once in circulation, the Scot must lose national identity and debase the identity of Scotland.

Yet while Scott traces the devaluative necessity of circulation, he implies it is a game that can be played to the appearance and so with the transient effect of valuation. Everything depends on the spirit with which you cast the dice and embrace your luck. Lured to the gambling table, Nigel models his behavior as a player in the game of life. Sir Mungo Malagrowther taunts:

I never heard ye were a great gamester . . . my lord. . . . I call *him* a gamester, that . . . stands by the fortune of the game, good or bad— and I call *him* a ruffling gamester . . . who ventures frankly and deeply upon such a wager. But he, my lord, who has the patience and prudence never to venture beyond small game, such as, at most, might crack the Christmas-box of a grocer's 'prentice, who vies with those that have little to hazard, and who therefore, having the larger stock, can always rook them by waiting for his good fortune, and rising from the game when luck leaves him—such a one as he, my lord, I do not call a *great* gamester, to whatever other name he may be entitled. (170)

Perhaps like an author with his eye too resolutely fixed on the market, Nigel plays neither recklessly nor even with enjoyment, nor earnestly and sincerely. His one English friend, Lowestoffe, significantly "was Treasurer to the Lord of Misrule last year"; Heriot circulates money and compliments to make his market with the King, and acts with "sagacity and good-humour"; but Nigel plays cautiously and to win, never suffering the game to run beyond his luck (185; 29; 154). He thus fleeces the good-hearted apprentice Jin Vin, and is rumored to have caused a shopkeeper's suicide (162; 169). Consequently, he earns dislike even as he makes money. Nigel holds himself distant from life, too. He brings Sir Mungo's attack on himself when he objects: "You take me for a noted gamester . . . I am none such" (170). Equally, he invites disaster when his nobility discourages him from seeing to his own business. George Heriot comments: "it behoves every man to become acquainted with his own affairs, so soon as he hath any that are worth attending to" (124). When Nigel would fold his cards, declaring "Fortune has taken the field against me at every point. Even let her win the battle," "Zouns!" Heriot exclaims, "you would make a saint swear" (330). Nigel suffers the vagaries of circulation to an extreme degree because he is not honest with himself or with others, and does not play with his whole heart.

Who can play successfully, and how? Nigel is not saved by Lowestoffe, Heriot, or old and noble friends (such as Dalgarno's father). These are committed to established orders. Although they understand circulation, they are subject to it, so cannot project themselves into its vacancy to serve another— even Lowestoffe, nominated next year's Lord of Misrule, languishes in jail for helping Nigel (185; 248). Neither can young Lord Glenvarloch be saved by a new Jeanie Deans, moving as absence between clashing Scottish and English equivalents, for the book goes out of its way to show the limitations of female possibility. Yet Dalgarno does not manage to destroy Nigel. Obsessed with Nigel and with vengeance, exiled from the court and pushed north to the home he despises, Dalgarno becomes entirely a thing of relationships and the epitome of devaluation. Moreover, despite Dalgarno's efforts and example, the novel suggests it is possible to manipulate the market of British equivalence. Powerful players are those who stand outside circulation. Oddly, in a context that privileges youth, money, beauty, and class, the most powerful operator is the unpromising Richie Moniplies. It is through Richie that Scott demonstrates a strategy for personal, national, and literary valuation.

We first encounter Nigel's servant through the mockery of English apprentices:

> "See how he gapes at every shop, as if he would swallow the wares. . . . his grey eyes, his yellow hair, his sword with a ton of iron in the handle—his grey thread-bare cloak—his step like a French-man—his look like a Spaniard—a book at his girdle, and a broad dudgeon-dagger on the other side, to shew him half-pedant, half-bully. . . ."
>
> "A raw Scotsman . . . just come up . . . to help the rest of his countrymen to gnaw old England's bones." (27)

Richie is so degraded as a Scot, he might as well be a Spaniard or a Frenchman. He has no worthwhile country, no class, no clothes and, we soon discover, no money, no food, and no couth. Yet he has a strong sense of identity: "I am no more Jockey than you, sir, are John," he objects to Heriot, who as yet appears English (33). Richie strives to talk up Scotland as worth: "I hope there was naething wrang in standing up for ane's ain country's credit in a strange land, where all men cry her down?" he tells the dubious goldsmith (34). In fact, because Richie runs so counter to the English system of valuation, he serves to expose it. As Nigel's servant, he presents Lord Glenvarloch's supplication to the King. But as another of the King's debtors for "Twelve nowte's feet for jellis—ane lamb, being Christmas—ane roasted capin in grease for the privy chalmer, when my Lord of Bothwell suppit with hir Grace" (sundry butchers' fare delivered to the King's unfortunate mother Mary Queen of Scots for her liaisons with her paramour), Richie makes ludicrous Nigel's appeal, and reveals the tawdry reality of seeking value through the monarch (54). Small wonder that when he flourishes his "sifflication" along with Nigel's he almost unseats his transcendent majesty from his horse, and does precipitate James into an act whereby the King rejects all petitions from the north and thus degrades himself and his fellow Scots.

However, Richie demonstrates that although one cannot step outside circulation, one can move oppositely and thus successfully. When Nigel thoughtlessly adopts Dalgarno's practices and insists they are the legitimate pastimes of honorable men—and moreover "I never play but for small sums"—Richie withdraws his services (160–61). He contravenes his class position to assert: "you are misled, and are forsaking the paths which your honourable father trode in; and, what is more, you are going . . . to the devil with a dish-clout, for ye are laughed at by them that lead you into these disordered byepaths" (163). Subsequently, Richie circulates but enjoys no point of evaluative contact with those around him. The cuckolded Christie ejects him on the grounds that his master has stolen away with Christie's wife. And neither Nigel's servant nor Christie's companion any longer, Richie notes the inappropriate, damaging, and complicit exchanges of each: "It's an ill bird that fouls it's own nest" [sic], he says, "and a pity it is that a kindly Scot should ever have married in foreign parts, and given life to a purse-proud, pudding-headed, fat-gutted, lean-brained Southron, e'en such as you, Maister Christie" (289).

By thus swimming against the southern tide, and despite his many faults, Richie merits valuation. Moreover, ejected from society, Richie finds himself in a position to help one equally beyond the dynamic of social valuation. With her usurer father murdered, the ungainly and unfeminine Martha Trapbois seems adrift in London. Richie's kindness earns her gratitude, her hand, and her money. That is, Richie gains the mounds of specie that trump all other evaluative terms—even those of transcendent monarchism. When he buys up Nigel's mortgage and presents him with his inheritance, returns the King's missing jewels and earns a knighthood, Richie demonstrates that while circulation is inevitable and its play unending, the Scottish subject can gamble successfully *because* against the odds.

But if the issue for *The Fortunes of Nigel* is whether subject and nation can retain value within the circulations of narrative, in the end the novel offers a solution that is possible only in, and not true of, fiction. Circulation is inevitable, and wayward circulation may even prove rewarding—yet at the end of *Nigel* the hero has recovered his estate and seems likely to withdraw there with his wife. By the intervention of the King, romance overcomes money and delimits play. Circulation has ceased because value is achieved.

This is why Scott's "Introductory Epistle" is so important. It forces the reader to be skeptical, stressing ahead of the game that Richie's is the model for the writer caught between nation and narration. Nigel sought a father and appears to have been recreated as such himself. The end of the novel establishes him as patriarch, projected to a fantasy space of permanent value, his paternal estates in Scotland. However, the Author of Waverley refuses to serve as governing term either in himself or for his texts. Although Clutterbuck begs his literary parent to abjure circulation and thus raise value for his characters, his text and himself, the Eidolon cultivates indeterminacy and embraces play. He preens himself as the critics' "humble jackall, too busy in providing food for them, to have time for considering whether they swallow or reject it" (9). "To the public," he claims, "I stand pretty near in the relation of the postman who leaves a packet at the door. . . . the bearer . . . as little thought on as the snow of last Christmas." If Clutterbuck cannot register the Author it is because the Author insists on movement. Through the Author's feints the Captain cannot describe "what it is probable the Personage before me might most desire to have concealed" (5). The Author even insists: "to say who I am not, would be one step towards saying who I am," and when Clutterbuck catches on to a hint that he has served in the military he responds: "I have—or I have not, which signifies the same thing" (9; 11). He is in circulation—and he likes it so.

Knowing that all valuation of nation through narration and author through text means participating in the necessity of circulation and trembling ever on the brink of loss, Scott asserts in the guise of the Author: "I am not displeased to find the game [of authorship] a winning one; yet while I pleased the public, I should probably continue it merely for the pleasure of playing" (15). There is only the game. Every gain could as easily be a loss, and gains are the matter of a moment. "*Tempora mutantur*," Clutterbuck learns (13). But the game must be played or there is only loss. It must be played with open eyes and a whole heart. The Scottish author seeking to establish worth must embrace circulation while yet moving oppositely. Like James VI, that "wisest fool in Christendom," he must reside playfully yet precariously in the gaps of circulation—he must constantly resituate nation, text and narration at the site of valuation (67).

George IV in Scottish Circulation, 1822

"I call *him* a gamester, that plays with equal stakes and
equal skill—and stands by the fortune of the game"

Within months, Scott played the game for national stakes. From the battlements of Edinburgh Castle the King flourished his hat. Below, a sea of tartan swelled and roared, while above, royalty responded with enthusiastic gratitude (Mudie, 201). Moved to less cynical words than usual, *Blackwood's Magazine* welcomed the Scots' "hereditary Prince" to the national fireside (12, no. 68: 260–63). Had the King "come into his own, again," as the *Edinburgh Weekly Journal* proclaimed when it declared "it seems we had 'The auld STUARTS back again'" (21 August 1822: 267)? The year was 1822; the figure was the portly George IV. Surely, at this moment, Scotland lay neither outside of nor becalmed within history, as Cairns Craig has come to fear. Perhaps, from the mutual recognition of King and people at the heart of Scottish signification, streamed a future rooted in the past but constantly renewable through negotiation between powers and across the sign—a future Homi Bhabha would recognize.

Commentators generally interpret George IV's visit, performed through Walter Scott's pageantry, as an imaginative completion of the Scottish past that left Scotland looking backwards. Constructed as a mere space of story, the nation stood fixed in misrecognition and vulnerable to English appropriation. For John Prebble: "Scotland could not be the same again once it was over. A bogus tartan caricature of itself had been drawn and accepted. . . .

With the ardent encouragement of an Anglo-Scottish establishment . . . Walter Scott's Celtification continued to seduce his countrymen, and thereby prepared them for political and industrial exploitation" (364). Even scholars who assert the ongoing political energy of Jacobitism argue that the author did not recognize his images' vitality and deployed them with a deadening hand. To Murray Pittock, the game was one of loss. With Sir Walter's "transference of Jacobite symbols from the Stuart to the Hanoverian cause," Scott "helped dull the radical edge of the Jacobite critique" (*Invention*, 90). "[Truly] the Wizard of the North," he "buried the Stuart myth of regenerative power" (90). And it is Scott's persistent articulation in his novels of a narrative lacking connection to present and therefore future that Cairns Craig blames for pushing Scotland into the past and out of history in the first place. Craig argues that "narrative became part of the world that was framed by art, while the order of progress could only be narrated from somewhere else"—presumably England (*Out of History*, 39). For these critics, England held—and perhaps continues to hold—an unbeatable hand.

Such readings echo those of Scott's skeptical acquaintances. Stuart of Dunearn, still holding his recent grudge, sniped that "Sir Walter Scott has ridiculously made us appear to be a nation of Highlanders, and the bagpipe and the tartan are the order of the day."[10] Lockhart saw the visit as an anachronistic performance that deluded even its author and lead actor. With a nod to Scott's friend and perhaps theatrical consultant for the visit, the actor-manager Daniel Terry, he termed it "a sort of grand *terryfication* of the Holyrood chapters in *Waverley*; George IV, *anno aetatis* 60, being well contented to enact 'Prince Charlie,' with the Great Unknown himself for his Baron Bradwardine" (Lockhart, 5:192). For critics early and modern, the King's visit ratifies Scott's inscription as one who "loved his country, but denied its contemporaneity," and thus lost the national gamble for his time and ours (Pittock, *Invention*, 87).

Yet these assertions may reveal more about Scott's critics than about his tales or himself. Given recent arguments for the power of the very terms Scott deploys, to insist that through him they have operated only on England's behalf is to reveal that we ourselves are limited by a primary assumption of Scotland's subjection. It may be we who resist the play of the sign, denying it to Scott and, to a degree, forcing the narrative of Scottish appropriation, malformation, and the exile from time.

Past and present, Scott's significations precipitate a complex, often subversive, and sometimes developmental interplay that asserts the nation as narrative and economic value. Lacking no moral courage with regard to the factors that construct a nation, Scott manipulates signs that must invoke the question of Scottish value and across which it may be renegotiated. He stands forth as a relatively conscious and hard headed practitioner of creative play in a national context. The example of the King's visit suggests that his success at least matches his failure. He gives the idea of Scotland a lasting forward momentum through a phenomenon scholars have long considered evidence of his backwardness.

Over numerous adventures in national signification, Scott had come to appreciate narrative as a space for economic and political exchange. Indeed, Scott was establishing his own value in terms of ready money exchanged for his texts, and that of his nation as a purchasable space inscribed in narrative. Most importantly, he was pursuing the possibility of telling as a site for the constant renegotiation of national worth. So by the time of the King's visit Scott was a practiced literary and economic entrepreneur well versed in the operations of signification as valuation.

But how to lessen the odds in the play of national equivalences? For Pierre Bourdieu, economics underpins all relationships, but economies are enacted through symbolic exchange that obscures their self-interest. All economies depend on *"institutionally organized and guaranteed misrecognition"*; social value is established and maintained at the level of the significant gesture—the sign (171–72). Consequently, symbolic capital may be accumulated through literacy, or control of the sign. Literacy "enables a society to move beyond immediate human limits—in particular those of individual memory" and "enables particular groups to practise *primitive accumulation of cultural capital*" (187). This theory opens a space for those who manipulate the signs available in the form of culture. For Goux, also, although value may be an illusion, that illusion appears through the sign: "commodities are universally evaluated only through . . . signs, masks, representations" (38). Across these two theories, we can see that the author stands at a privileged site: she or he deals in the signs by which alone value may be established.

The author who happens to be located between two systems of signification is surely especially interested to negotiate value through what Bourdieu calls the "symbolic violence" of the sign (191). Certainly, when George IV came into conjunction with Scotland through his visit of 1822, Scott responded as one with hoarded literary capital and the market experience of his own and his texts' circulation. The author's attendance at George's coronation had intensified Scott's understanding of the role of exchange to maintain the monarchical Sign and the signified People. In a letter published by the *Edinburgh Weekly Journal*, Scott remarked upon the mutual valuation that established George as King: "it was impossible, without the deepest veneration, to behold the voluntary and solemn interchange of vows betwixt the King and his assembled People" (*Letters*, 6:494–502). So informed, Scott recognized in George IV's progress north an opportunity for Scotland's revaluation. By entering circulation the King revealed the constructedness of his role; he became vulnerable to revaluation through exchange, and could allow the renegotiation of Scotland itself. Now, Scott deployed Scottish signs to shift the value of the King and, consequently, Scotland. He fulfilled the dream of McCrone et al. that Scotland deploy its images in the present without constantly bemoaning their past; he showed that "heritage icons are malleable," as McCrone and his colleagues both lament and desire (*Scotland*, 5). In fact, he fully participated in Scotland's "glamour," that condition they seek to appreciate once more and that still carries connotations of "magical powers . . . enchantment and witchcraft, even the power to bamboozle or deceive" (7). The author cast a glamour that does not delimit Scotland or commit her to the past, but creates a space of play through the past and with an ever present purpose. He opened up the future.

Scott gained assistance from the most unlikely of sources—the King. By 1822, George IV should have stood as transcendent signifier for all things British. It should have been the people who circulated around him to establish their value by his ineffable meaning. Thus, the Scottish visit should have produced what the critics assume—the delimitation of Scotland through the evaluative power of an English king. But George served as a particularly contingent Sign. He had suffered a distressingly long career in the circulation that reveals all value as a matter of exchange before blazing forth in the role of monarch who fixes meaning. He who had been an appealing young man had grown into an unattractive old one; he had been a Whig and a Tory; he had figured as an illegitimately married man through his morganatic alliance with Mrs. Fitzherbert, and as a bigamist by his legitimate marriage to Caroline of Brunswick (Smith, xi–xii). Through this last relationship he had appeared ridiculous even beyond the moment of his monarchical inheritance. At a time when he should have been translated into the always and already national Sign, the notorious adulterer sought to divorce his wife and deny her the title of queen. In so doing he kept himself visible as a figure whose value depended on the positioning of another—and one whom he publicly abjured. He provided the opportunity for the maligned Caroline to declare to all and sundry that she was no adulteress—or at least had offended only once, with the husband of Mrs. Fitzherbert (Smith, 120)! George's wide and varied circulation undermined any idea of his monarchical function.

Of course, after his father's death, George had taken steps toward confirming his position. Goux suggests that transcendent terms gain their authority through a series of substitutions that constitute them within convention. Immediately after his Coronation (an event from which Caroline was barred), the King set out to circulate through systems that should admit his role and thus make it so. Crowned on 19 July, he disembarked in Ireland 12 August—having just received the happy news of his wife's demise (7 August). The Irish acknowledged George as their King. William Maginn described their welcome in *Blackwood's*: "he was received with an enthusiastic burst of joy . . . swelling from the inmost recesses of the heart."[11] But in the absence of a dominant term, or during its formation as at the

King's visit, value depends on an exchange between two equal commodities capable of mutual recognition. It is surely telling, then, that when the King landed at the wrong place he went unrecognized by the Dublin luminaries and unwelcomed except by "the casual crowd which the dense population of Ireland exhibits in all its sea-ports" (224). The King's worth was not enough to inspire acknowledgement at the requisite level. Rather, it precipitated a response that further undermined him from an Ireland ever the poor relation of the United Kingdom: "The procession to the Phoenix-Park was more like the march of a popular demagogue, at the zenith of mob-favour, than of a King on a visit to an ancient kingdom" (224). Even more embarrassing, aligned with the King, the Irish themselves lost value. A year after the visit, the *Scotsman* invoked it as a monitory example for the Scots: "The conduct of the Irish . . . ought to be a lesson to us. The delirium into which they were thrown . . . and their absurd and extravagant conduct, did more to prejudice the Irish character . . . than any thing that ever occurred in the history of that country" ("The King's Visit," 3 August 1822: 244). Neither King nor people maintained worth adequate to fix the value of the other in this, the first of George's progresses in search of the recognition that implies transcendence.

Consequently, the King set out for Hanover. Four generations earlier, Hanover had given Britain her monarchy when the Elector, George Louis, succeeded to the throne in his deceased wife's place. Surely this place of familial and monarchical origins would recognize the King and ratify his role? The Hanoverians, like the Irish, welcomed the King with glee—and also much pomp. Christopher Hibbert, comments: "a hundred and one guns roared their salute and the people cheered him as though he were a hero returning triumphant from the wars" (230). But where and what was Hanover? The British hardly knew. Declared an "Electorate" in 1692, governed by absentee monarchs (Georges I–IV), constantly tracked across by European armies on their way somewhere else, seized by Prussia in 1801 and 1805, by the French in 1803 and 1806, divided and incorporated into the French Empire and Westphalia and only reconstituted as a kingdom in 1819, like Ireland it hardly enjoyed the value necessary to acclaim a King.

George remained in circulation. But if his early wanderings through political parties, notorious boudoirs, and the like had destabilized his value, his excursions had begun to expose him as a Sign in search of a ratifying system. Lord Dudley blightingly remarked that in Ireland the King "behaved not like a sovereign coming in state and pomp. . . . But like a popular candidate come down upon an electioneering trip" (Hibbert, 213). Then, in July 1822, just a month before his visit to Scotland—when rumor still went this way and that about his impending arrival—*Blackwood's* opened with an ode "To the King" that at once celebrated the monarch and critiqued his

construction (12, no. 66: iii–iv). The poem exhorts: "HONOUR TO THEE, O
KING, AND PRIDE IN THE GLORY OF BRITAIN!" George is "Mirror of brilliant
Kings!—the PRINCE and GENTLEMAN blended!"—a dominant term if ever
there was one (iii). Yet the poem concludes: "What dost thou think, my liege,
of the metre in which I address thee? / Doth it not sound very big, very
bouncing, bubble-and-squeaky . . . ? / (It into use was brought of late by thy
Laureate Doctor— / But, in my humble opinion, I write it better than he
does)" (v). Then it adds a "Peroration," in turn undercut by a "Postscript to
the Public," and "Postscript the Second," each of which diminishes the initial compliment by its twaddling literary content and its very presence (v, vi).
The poem constructs the King, then thrusts him into circulation through the
literary forms and even the literary hacks supporting him. Evidently, having
got around too much, the King still needed to move appropriately—through
a strong and relevant system, not an Ireland or a Hanover, and not in the
public press. He needed a system whose recognition could stabilize him as
monarch so forcefully it would obscure its own operations, rendering "natural" the relation between acknowledged King and willing people. George IV
needed Scotland.

Scott was ready for him. The author had long echoed Brummell to term
the King "our Fat Friend."[12] But having actively participated in the monarch's devaluation, Scott was the more prepared to renegotiate the roles
of monarch and man through the exchange of signs. Scott claimed that he
had been roped into service for the King's visit at the last moment. He told
Joanna Baillie: "The whole business of this Reception was hastily and suddenly thrown on my hands" (18 August, *Letters*, 7:220–24). In reality, he had
expected the visit since the eve of the Coronation, when he wrote to George
Craig "It seems almost certain that the King comes to Scotland" (11 July
[1821], *Letters*, 6:493). Three months later, he recognized that the King's
earlier trips could operate to Scotland's advantage. Although Scotland's
"colder and more reservd manners" might have suffered beside Ireland's
enthusiasm, "the German sour-crout and some of the not unwholesome bit-
ters of London will sharpen [the King's] appetite for such fare as we can
afford him," he joked to Maria Edgeworth (October 1821, *Letters*, 7:24–26).
From 24 May 1822, at the latest, Scott plotted a particular arrangement of
signs around the monarch on the occasion of his visit—he started to debate
with Lord Montagu the appropriate badges for the various clans (*Letters*,
7:172–73). And according to so authoritative a source as Robert Peel, "Sir
Walter took an active lead in [the] ceremonies."[13] To Sir Walter's house guest
during the visit, George Crabbe, the author seemed "more engaged than any
Man in England at this Time" (Crabbe, 287). He was engaged in all the symbolic violence available to an author. Byron, a Scot on his mother's side, educated in Aberdeen, and latterly the author's friend, knew well what was going
on. He asked in *Don Juan:*

And where is 'Fum' the Fourth, our 'royal bird?'
Gone down it seems to Scotland, to be fiddled
Unto by Sawney's violin, we have heard:
'Caw me, caw thee'—for six months hath been hatching
This scene of royal itch and loyal scratching.[14]

Scott carefully deployed Scottish signs to raise the King's value, but in so doing quietly subjected the monarch to a Scotland constructed as transcendent Sign. He turned the King to Scottish use.

How could Scott determine George IV as the nation's dominant term, but Scotland as his site of meaning? The author locked King and people in a dynamic of mutual valuation through the narrative of "return." Neither George nor any other Hanoverian king had ever set foot north of the border, and the stream of Stuart blood ran thin in the King's German veins, yet in the texts that set the tone for the visit, particularly in his manual for the Scottish reception, Scott insisted that "this remote part of the empire" received him home (*Hints*, 7). "Carle, now the King's Come!" Scott's execrable doggerel to welcome the King, echoed a Jacobite rant of the same name and thus located George IV within the Stuart myth.[15] The King had "been a weary time away" (verse 3), and by implication, he had come into his own again. Through this trope, Scott connected the King to his lowliest countryman by the body and the blood. In *Hints Addressed to the Inhabitants of Edinburgh, and Others, in Prospect of His Majesty's Visit*, Scott stressed: "King George IV. comes hither as the descendant of a long line of Scottish Kings. The blood of the heroic Robert Bruce—the blood of the noble, the enlightened, the generous James I. is in his veins. . . . he is our kinsman" (6–7).

Scott fulfilled, in the most literary and yet most physical of ways, the need that terms serving as equivalents be mutually recognizable. Further, Scott's deployment of "return" initiated the dynamic of recognition and substitution: the trope's familial intensity founded in body and blood achieved the effect of repetition and authorization. Thus, in one exchange, Scott established the King as already the nation's transcendent Sign: "we are THE CLAN, and our King is THE CHIEF. Let us, on this happy occasion, remember that it is so; and not only behave towards him as a father, but to each other, as if we were, in the words of the old song, 'ae man's bairns'" (*Hints*, 7). And through the idea of return the people stand translated too. The same exchange of signs that constitutes George as "son" and thus "father" manifests Scotland as end and therefore origin—it is "home," in the first place and the last. Edinburgh is "the ancient capital of the most ancient of [George's] kingdoms" (3). Scotland is the King's prior term without which there is no value at all. For a moment, then, Scott fixes King and people in the impossibility of mutual transcendence—their shared afflatus registered by their eruption into upper-case letters!

Of course, Scott did not rely merely on virtuoso placement of a single term. As numerous critics have noted, Scott energetically communicated the notion of Scotland as highland home. Moreover, he did so despite his own knowledge to the contrary. A letter repeated in many versions to hail the Chiefs to Edinburgh weaves together the pretense of Edinburgh's Celtic Society and the regional ethos of the north into the appearance of a highland nation. The July 22 letter to Macleod of Macleod of Skye reads: "The King is coming after all. Arms and men are the best thing we have to show him. Do come and bring half-a-dozen or half-a-score of Clansmen, so as to look like an Island Chief as you are. Highlanders are what he will like best to see, and the masquerade of the Celtic Society will not do without some of the real stuff, to bear it out" (*Letters*, 7:213–14). Meantime, the Minstrel of the Border, than whom there was no man better versed in lowland history, himself assumed the tartan for at least part of the visit. "A Goth" could not resist exclaiming in *Blackwood's*: "When I read for the first time in the papers, that Sir Walter Scott had gone up to the Castle of Edinburgh in a coach full of Highland chiefs, they and HE all alike plaided and kilted, I swear to you, I thought some of your own merry class had been playing pranks upon the poor Editor. A Scott in tartan! Good gracious!"[16] And through these false substitutions, Scott constructed his nation as a place perhaps marked as past, but thereby exoticized as origin and consequently ever operative in the present. With the King constituted in a state of return to a highland home, Scott had actually energized the Jacobite myths that critics such as Craig Beveridge and Ronald Turnbull consider he buried. Beveridge and Turnbull see a lively Scotland encoded in highland/Jacobite signs: "A complex set of mythic undercurrents shape the way in which Jacobitism was and is perceived by Scots. Its legendary associations, which originate within Gaelic culture, are not of ultimate defeat, but of the restoration of Scotland as a Celtic civilization" (*Scotland*, 69). Scott exploited this phenomenon to the full, encoding a King within the myth of Scottish origins.

He went further. The King had to be located as dominant term through the operations of Scottish exchange, but if Scotland was thereby to find value, then he needed to recognize it in turn—he needed to feel "at home." Scott worked hard to establish Scotland not merely as "home," but as "homely." He recommended: "Let our King see us as nature and education have made us—an orderly people, whose feelings, however warm, are rarely suffered to outspring the restraint of judgment" (*Hints*, 6). He orchestrated the smallest detail to ensure that Scotland appeared a place of order and thus of reason. Scott likely participated in the Magistrates' determination for uniform dress among those not garbed in tartan, and certainly publicized this sartorial signification of a nation as Enlightened through its dress. In *Hints* he stressed, "the Magistrates expect all gentlemen to appear in an uniform costume, viz. Blue Coat, White Waist-coat, and White or Nankeen Pantaloons. The ancient national cognisance of St Andrew's Cross, white upon a blue ground, is also to be universally worn by way of cockade" (12). He strove to maintain order even in the ladies' deportment, advising them: "A considerable difficulty is presented to the inexperienced by the necessity of retiring (without assistance) backwards. . . . those who have never worn such dresses should lose no time in beginning to practise this" (25). According to Sir Arthur Mackenzie, Scott oversaw the seating plan for the stands on the day of the King's progress to Edinburgh castle that ranged participants according to class, region, occupation, and gender.[17] The author actually congratulated himself on his general success, writing to William Stuart Rose, "we contrived that the whole demeanour of the population should be the most regular and imposing which you ever saw. . . . All stood perfectly firm and untill the King had passed quite silent while his progress was marked by a rolling cheer which accompanied him from the palace to the castle each body taking it up when he came in front of them for they were all separated into their own different classes and crafts an excellent receipt for insuring good order among the most riotously disposed" (4 September 1822, *Letters*, 7:229–32).

Long years past Hugh Miller remarked of Scott's Jacobitism that it "formed merely a sort of laughing-gas that agreeably excited the feelings" (85). N. T. Phillipson has argued that Scott "taught Scotsmen to see themselves as men whose reason is on the side of the Union and whose emotions are not, and in whose confusion lies their national character" ("Nationalism," 186). But here we see something different. Through highland and lowland images both, through signs exotic and orderly, Scott confirmed Scotland as "home" in the present moment. He accomplished the repeated substitutions across the range of Scottish signs that could locate King and country together as the equivalents upon which valuation depends.

Scott's substitutions proved so compelling that he received assistance from those who promulgate a national culture. Hordes of Edinburgh's literati adopted and developed the signs and systems of his exchange. Many characterized Scotland as "home," the place of origins and ends. Their discourse echoes with assumptions of the King's return, his role as scion and sire, as chief in the blood. *The Royal Scottish Minstrelsy* [anon] contains many of the songs published during the King's visit. "Auld Guidwife, Holyrood" welcomes George "to your ain house!" (61–64: verse 1). "Stanzas for the King's Landing" manifests the King as Scotland's child, and thus her father (84–89). He is "Son of her Lords" (verse 1), consequently "The King—the Sire of All!" (verse 8). For *Blackwood's*, "Scottish loyalty partakes of the nature of the domestic ties . . . it is something akin to filial reverence, and . . . to fraternal affection," thus the King is "a kinsman . . . imperishably connected with the very being and substance of the kingdom—an honour in his blood." Significantly, "Independent, therefore, altogether of his matchless personal claims, the King [is] the heir and descendant of 'Scotland's royal race'" (12, no. 68: 264). Indeed, without a qualm, *Blackwood's* published among its numerous songs "The Chief and his Tail," with its rousing if perplexed declaration: "Long life to the Brunswick, the head of the Clan!" (351–52, verse 2).

Equally, Scottish authors spread the notion of Scotland's homeliness—its rationality and order. In the face of recent radical disruptions and two risings in just over one hundred years (see Ellis and Mac A'Ghobhainn), *Blackwood's* described "the . . . circumstances in which we, as a people, have for some centuries been placed":

> Scotland has long been a calm, quiet, happy, and improving country. We are strong in our deep and placid domestic affections . . . in our sound, plain, hearty, honest, good, common, or, if you chuse, commonplace sense—in an intelligence of perhaps a higher order than was ever before general among all ranks. . . . We do not fear to say, that such is our National Character. A loftier and a wiser people are not to be found now upon the earth, nor do the records of any such survive. (12, no. 68: 255)

Scott seems to have accumulated enough cultural capital, and brought it enough into circulation, that his compatriot authors do not recognize its constructedness, self-interest, or economic operations. They simply deploy its terms.

At the same time, the peculiar emphases in these authors' comments show that while we may not be aware of the operations of symbolic capital, we are nonetheless invested in it. Edinburgh's authors exchange Scott's terms in ways that render their value more certain. If Edinburgh is orderly and thus a home, it is the more so by contrast with Ireland and even England. *Blackwood's* obsessive rendition of Scotland as the land of order stretching back through recorded time stands in direct opposition to Ireland. When the King visited Ireland, "Erin clasped to her green bosom the Monarch of the Isles," yet "[t]here was something disturbed in the physiognomy of the people, as there was, and long had been, and long will be, something disturbed in their souls" (12, no. 68: 253). As for England, according to the *Edinburgh Advertiser* when the King visited Scotland the only disruptive elements expected in the north were English criminals ("The King's Visit," 2 August 1822: 77–78). Indeed, the papers frequently stress that the King's inheritance of the English throne derives from his Scottish blood (however thin). The *Advertiser* continued:

> it is through the Royal Scottish line that our Sovereign is descended from the Saxon Kings of England. Malcolm Canmore who was crowned at Scone, 25th April 1057, married Margaret, Grand Niece of Edward the Confessor, and their posterity have reigned over Scotland for more than seven centuries. We need scarcely remind our readers,

that in the Sacred Person of his Majesty King GEORGE the Fourth, they hail a descendant of the first of Scotia's Heroes, King Robert Bruce, and of which descent His Majesty we have heard is greatly and justly proud. (78)

Although other lands may claim the King, only Scotland is truly home.

And only this King can "come again." Marking the Stuarts as maybe kin but less than kind, the author of *A Narrative of the Visit of George IV* declared that although George's was "a visit made from no state necessity, and for no political purpose, but dictated by kindness on the part of the King. . . . Never before had this been the case since Scotland and England came under the sway of the same sovereign" (93). This writer sets aside James VI and Charles I. These "came from the south to carry into effect schemes to which a large proportion of the nation were known to be decidedly averse; so that their visits were regarded with vigilant and jealous distrust." The author others the Stuarts as English in their hearts and thus with no right of return. Accepting Scott's currency, Scottish authors advance his methods; they clear away possibilities for exchange in different directions—they deny rival places and persons any substitution through the discourse's privileged signs.

They push Scott's exchange as far as it can go. Time and again, the terms "King" and "People" meet in mutual recognition. *Blackwood's* "The King" emphasized the visit's purpose: "King and people would see and be satisfied with each another" (12, no. 68: 253), while James Simpson avers within two months of George's departure that "Our King *has* seen his people, and they have seen their King" (11). But this recognition, which values King and people together, depends on Scotland's prior worth and requires George IV explicitly to value Scotland. In *Blackwood's*, the people test the King: "when our King . . . came among us, we tried him, unconsciously, and without arrogant intention, by a very lofty standard" (12, no. 68: 262). Consequently, the king attains value. The magazine asserts the "delighted pride which we, in common with all our countrymen, felt in the whole conduct of our King" (261). This puts George in the position to value Scotland. In *A Narrative*, the King comes, is recognized, and recognizes as son and father: "George IV. came among his people of Scotland as the descendant of their ancient race of kings, as the common father of all classes of his subjects, and as the protector of all the rights and privileges enjoyed by them under the sanction of the laws,—to exchange with them the sentiments of mutual confidence and affection" (93).

The *Edinburgh Weekly Journal* for 28 August makes explicit this cycle of exchange, linking King and people through a national love overtly inscribed as origin and end: "It is a homely saying [note the term], but it is a very true one, that love begets love; and if we were to point at any one feature of the Royal visit, as more distinct and conspicuous than another, it would be THE

LOVE which the KING has upon all occasions shown for his Northern people" ("Tuesday August 27": 274). King and people stand as equivalents—with Scotland just that little bit, impossibly, prior.

Through this exchange of signs and balance of equivalences, Scott's followers developed their land into a charmed space of new possibilities. To the anonymous author of *A Full Account of King George the Fourth's Visit*, looking back after sixteen years, the visit seemed a moment of creative paradox where monarchy and democracy coexisted. He imagined the people's cheers as an acclamation: "This is a great Sovereign, and he is our Sovereign [note the possessive],—the Sovereign of the freest people in the world" (37). Similarly, for the *Edinburgh Weekly Journal*, the King's visit allowed an afflux of "independence" ("Tuesday, August 20," 21 August 1822: 267). This free Scotland became a place where the King could achieve and multiply his value. An article in the *Edinburgh Observer* with an Inverary by-line stressed in lyric form:

> Here *Wallace* found in brave *Sir Neil*
> A patriot firm and true. . . .
>
> Here *Bruce* found Highland hearts and blades
> T'assert his regal rights. . . .
>
> Here *William*, too, found hearty friends,
> In crushing all his foes. . . .
>
> *Great George* we hail'd; with joy sincere
> We say the Monarch crown'd.
> God save the race we all revere,
> Its enemies confound. (22 August 1822: [3])

A song called "The News" even hinted to the King that his value depended on staying within Scotland. The song declared: "Lang reign in peace our lawfu' King, / We'll aye his rights maintain, man," but it indicated the precariousness of the monarch's position, continuing: "And while he stays 'mang Scotia's hills, / He'll aye be wi' his ane, man" (*Royal Scottish Minstrelsy*, 71–74 verse 6). Courtesy of Scott's emulators, the author's circulation of monarch and men through Scottish signs reveals its ultimate exchange. For George, going to England now should be to leave home and abandon value. The King deploys his power from a Scottish base; he belongs to Scotland.

Not everyone bought into this system. Evidence of Edinburgh's construction as symbolic capital—in all senses of the word—was not hard to spot. Witness the physical reconstruction of the city: "Repairs were instantly commenced at Holyrood. . . . A new entrance was opened . . . a number of mean buildings . . . were removed; an elegant porch was erected . . . and thence a carriage road was formed through the park. . . . The Weighhouse . . . was sold and taken down to the foundation" (*A Narrative*, 6–7). There was also the daily spectacle of the city's social climbers squeezing into the ill-fitting rental clothes supplied from London and everywhere advertised in the papers. The following, from the *Edinburgh Advertiser*, is typical: "COURT DRESS / Messrs. Batey & Finley, Tailors, &c to their Royal Highness [*sic*] . . . beg leave to acquaint the Nobility and Gentry, that . . . they have just arrived with a Splendid Assortment of every Equipment necessary for COURT DRESSES" (26 July 1822: [1]). Jane Grant registered the silliness of: "Old Mr. Hamilton . . . quite vain of his appearance, enduring with the most complacent countenance the operation of the curling tongs, which my Uncle wielded with great gravity . . . Gertrude equally busy about William's stock, and Fanny with a long red shawl, pinned on by way of train, practising courtseys before Papa, who played King, and was trying to use the royal privilege" (Skinner, "Contemporary," 115).

Running his practiced northern eye over "the sedate and sober citizens of the Scottish Metropolis," her father, John Grant of Rothiemurchus, remarked upon "[their] whimsical affectation of a sort of highland costume" (88). And Lockhart, closely bound to the author who hoarded and deployed symbolic capital, resisted Scott as "stage-manager" working from his Castle Street "greenroom" (Lockhart, 5:192).

Those outside the system, too, could grasp its pretense. The English architect C. R. Cockrell described the King's progress into town as "a scene in a play," and perhaps slyly observed: "much pleasure in the people who called it *awful*" (Watkin, 152). The invisible authors of the London parody *Kilts and Philibegs!!* understood perfectly well how the visit was put together and what was at stake. "Sir Wattie" presents a song to "Geordie, Emperor of Gotham," that reveals the visit's lying constructedness: "all allow'd Munchausen done over, / By Geordie, the great modern Gulliver" (8). Scott exposes his own role:

> All *Paternoster-Row* shall shortly flame
> With the "*Imperial Geordie's Northern Tour*,"
> Which shall the *Ursa Major's* so eclipse,
> As is my fame superior to *Sam. Johnson's*. (7)

The parody goes on to identify the end of Scottish exchange. A discussion between three comic Scotsmen locates the King as the object of Scottish valuation:

> *Second Man*. . . . he is an emperor of our ain, lineally descended from our royal race of Jamies. . . .

Second Man. . . . He shows some signs of being [wiser than James II/VII], by coming amangst us, the maist ancient, the maist noble, the maist learned, and maist polished of a' his three kingdoms, for ye mun ken, mon, that a' the Southrons are but a mongrel race, and that we are the only pure descendants of Adam.

Third Man. Troth, then, we do the emperor no less honour than he does us. (30–31)

Further, the King's welcome avers:

> Blessings with unsparing hand
> Kindly scatter through the land!
> Commerce thriving,
> Arts reviving,
> Grandeur growing,
> Plenty flowing,
> Peace and pleasure
> Without measure!
> Be these the glories of the day!
> Be these the marks of Geordie's sway! (31–32)

Both Scott's methods and their economic imperative stand clearly visible.

Nevertheless, King and people eagerly asserted themselves within Scott's system of exchange. George IV accepted his valuation and replicated its terms. Before the King set down foot at the Port of Leith, Scott had translated his "Fat Friend" into "THE FIRST PRINCE and THE FIRST GENTLEMAN in the world," who would necessarily recognize and create order (*Hints*, 5). "Let our King see us as nature and education have made us—an orderly people," he exhorted, and added that "the presence of our King may be the signal for burying in oblivion that which is past, and the pledge of better things in the time to come" (6; 8). The King stepped right into his role as dominant term constructed by the people's recognition and operating to fix their value. Describing the King's entrance into Edinburgh, Robert Mudie writes: "There was not one whose behaviour would have been offensive in a private drawing-room. . . . We may trust, however, that to a prince distinguished for his good taste and discernment, our loyalty will not be the less acceptable, because it is engrafted upon sober reflection" (109–10). The people hail the King through their good behavior, and Mudie expects a response from a monarch established as the arbiter of taste and discernment, those markers of reason and enlightenment. Happily, he is able to report "[t]hat the manner of his reception was as grateful to our King, as it was solemn and impressive. . . . His Majesty observed, that 'he had often heard the Scots were a proud nation; and they had reason to be so, for they appeared to be a nation of gentlemen. He himself was proud of them'" (110). George IV accepted his transcendent role on the basis of his supposed reasonable qualities and, in a comment much bruited around Edinburgh, promptly recognized and revalued the Scots.[18]

Equally, the King accepted his coding within the myth of origins. George had already circulated a fascinating selection of signs in pursuit of self-valuation. Notoriously precise in his dress, in recent years he had become entranced by military uniform. His contemporary biographer Robert Huish acidly comments that "the King of England, the most powerful monarch of the world . . . braved the perils of the ocean, and the almost impassable sands of Hanover, to bring away with him the pattern of a German uniform" (334). He had also worked to bring himself into a position of exchange and valuation with the exiled and now defunct Stuarts. According to J. H. Plumb, "when the last Stuart . . . died, George IV had a vast memorial erected at his own expense in St. Peter's, Rome. . . . [he] bought up all the Stuart papers, along with what remained of their jewels. . . . His sense of identity with the Stuarts and with Scotland was very close" (232). Thus, the King's predilections were served by Scott's maneuvers to inscribe him within a Scotland imagined as the site of British origins. At his levée, the King assumed Scottish dress under the direction of Scott's partner in pageantry, David Stewart of Garth.[19] Maclean and Skinner list George's £1354.18.0 accoutrements (11–12). Then, after a week of assurances that the people were the clan and the King their Chief, George rose at the Provost's banquet to toast: "All the chieftains and all the clans of Scotland, and may God bless the Land of Cakes!" (Mudie, 238). Lockhart remarks: "So completely had this hallucination taken possession, that nobody seems to have been startled at the time by . . . his Majesty's impression that the marking and crowning glory of Scotland consisted in the Highland clans and their chieftains" (Lockhart, 7:67–68). Nor did the King register any inconsistency. Fully inscribed by Scott's circulation of Scottish signs as the Chief of chiefs, he valued himself and consequently all things Scottish within the dynamic of highland yet homely exchange.

As for the Scots, they too participated in the symbolic violence of Scott's revaluation through signs. They showered the King with gifts that created and recognized his power—just hours after his arrival in Leith Roads, George received Walter Scott who presented him with a worked St. Andrew's Cross and "from a lady. . . . a spoon, knife, and fork, all of pure silver, formerly the property of the unfortunate Prince Charles" (Narrative, 16). Yet more notably, the Scots struggled to present themselves within the system to which they contributed. The mania affected Whigs as well as Tories. Despite their humorous recognition of the pretense behind both highland Edinburgh and their own self-presentation, the Whiggish Grants at times completely lacked self- and situational criticism. Father John directed his absent wife to signify the King's centrality by the exchange of Rothiemurchus's distinctively northern fowl: "As possessing the highest mountains in his dominions, I think I ought to send [the King] Ptarmigan. . . . I shall expect not less than 25 brace" (Skinner, "Contemporary," 88). A few days later, after discovering that "[the King] drinks nothing but *whiskey*, and he is an admirable judge of glen livat," Grant requested "Pray send a dozen of our best" (134). As they worked to figure the King and also themselves as Scots through culinary signs, the family charted its proximity to monarchy. John Grant proudly remarked that "[Jane's] approach to the King, and her reverance after he saluted her were *perfect*" (122). The whole family agonized over tickets for the Peers' Ball—with Grant's "Joy! joy! a *second* ticket for the Peers' Ball!" sadly turning out to be incorrect (133; 135–36). Even quiet Mary Frances succumbed, taking satisfaction in the King's comment: "he had never seen so few diamonds or so little dirt. 'In London,' he went on to say, 'they put on their diamonds to hide their dirt, but it don't do'" (144). By the exchange of signs, the Grants constructed the King as Scot, themselves as prior Scots, and imagined they had situated themselves closer than the English to the not very obscure object of their desire.

Sir Evan Murray McGregor, expecting that the King would visit his father-in-law the Duke of Atholl, wrote to his Lordship that he planned "to prepare some of my Highlanders quietly in case of need in the proper garb" (21 July, ACR 68/12: 215). When the King determined to stay in Edinburgh, he offered again: "if . . . You shall be of opinion that all our Tartan ought not to be thrown away—and intend to distinguish yourself from Lowland Lord Lieutenants by going to Holyrood House—with some of Your Highland followers in your train—I have no doubt it will be in my power to add to your Suite—from 40 to 60—picked Men of my Clan properly equipped & who will feel, with myself, proud and happy to be near Your Graces person—when You wait on Your Sovereign in the palace of his Ancestors" (29 July 1822, ACR 68/12: 237). He evinced delight at the Duke's invitation to serve: "I have now to thank Your Grace for thinking of including me so promptly in the list of Deputy Lieutenants—and also for adding me to the number appointed to assemble in Edinburgh on the occasion of the King's Visit to his Scottish Capital" (ibid.). Similarly, Mary Stewart Mackenzie stressed her Highland credentials and willingness to present them to "*George the Fourth in Scotland*": "there is not a Chief among them all *so* [anxious] to pay their duty to their Sovereign and in *proper stile too* as I poor shadow . . . am. . . . I would have paid my duty to my King with '*a tail*' that would have reached from here to Johnny Groats house."[20] Bound to her home by sickness, she struggled to assert her position in absentia by an appeal to Scott. She asked: "Will you be the organ there of My most humble apologies to His Majesty for not presenting myself with the homage of my obeisance." And to the last moment, she begged "a sofa . . . at a friend's house" so that her four-year-old son might serve as her proxy.

It was not simply individuals who jockeyed for placement. According to Maclean and Skinner, the Royal Company of Archers was founded "in the late 17th century as a sporting club," "received a Royal Charter from Queen Anne in 1704," and spent the eighteenth century as "a hunting-shooting fraternity with the social overtones of a dining club of restricted member-ship" (6). They enjoyed a mild reputation as "a Jacobite body" from 1715 to 1745. However, at the King's visit this assemblage of great and middling, lords and merchants, lawyers, accountants, military men, customs officials, students, and sons of important people skillfully placed themselves within Scott's signs. "With a proper uniform, according to the pattern settled by the Council of the Royal Company on 26th July [1822]," they mustered within traditions of Scottish and even English romance (Anon, *Report*, 6). Mudie says they "astonished those who were strangers to their appearance, by the elegance of their uniform,—a Robin Hood tartan jacket, tartan trews, the Highland hose, the flat blue bonnet, the ruff, Robin Hood belt, and white satin bow-case, worn as a scarf" (29). Showing substantial market acumen, on 1 August they appointed general officers, including the Earl of Hopetoun, Duke of Atholl, and Walter Scott, and "[claimed] their ancient privilege of forming his Majesty's Body Guard during his stay in Scotland" (*Report*, 7 and 8; 5). Such virtuoso deployment of signs could only succeed. They did serve as the King's bodyguard and were among the first to greet him and last to see him. On the day of his arrival, they performed "the service of deliver-ing a pair of Barbed Arrows to his Majesty, as the tenure by which the Royal Company hold their privileges under the charter from Queen Anne," and on the day he left they attended Hopetoun House where they paraded as honor guard and played at archery on the wet lawn (*Report*, 13; Maclean & Skinner, 23 and 28).

Even Scotland's towns competed within Scott's signs. An address from "The Magistrates and Town-Council, and Inhabitants of the Town Council [*sic*] of Musselburgh" typifies municipal efforts. Musselburgh had hoped to entertain the King as he returned from the Cavalry Review on Portobello sands, but he took a different route (Mudie, 212–13). So the town then strove to indicate its Scottish priority through a suggestion of return—though obvi-ously not to Musselburgh. The *Edinburgh Advertiser* remarks how local dig-nitaries rejoiced "to behold the descendant and representative of an ancient race of Kings in the country of his forefathers, and in the Palace of his ances-tors" ("Address of the Town of Musselburgh," 3 September 1822: 154). Leith and Newhaven squabbled over their authenticity as a site for the King's landing given previous Scottish royal progresses. A disgruntled "Subject" snarled: "It may be true that King James the Fifth of Scotland, and James

the First of England . . . landed at Leith, when, like them, they had no better place to which they could resort; but . . . there is well-grounded hope
for believing that his present MAJESTY will make use of those advantages . . .
which the spirit of improvement has laid open to him, by landing at the elegant and convenient structure at Trinity" ("To the Editor of the Advertiser,"
Edinburgh Advertiser 6 August 1822: 86). Lord Melville actually had to mediate the dispute.[21] Leith also found its privilege contested by a family that
claimed prior right. The *Caledonian Mercury* reports:

> it was in contemplation to have had a meeting of gentlemen of the name
> of LOGAN, with their retainers, mounted on horseback, and habited in
> their ancient costume, for the purpose of doing homage to their Sov-
> ereign, and accompanying him from Leith to Edinburgh, according to
> ancient custom, when the Scots Monarchs passed through the barony
> of Restalrig.
>   . . . Leith is built on the ancient possession of the chiefs of this
> name . . . so that when the first King who has visited Scotland since
> the Union sets foot on the '*Yird*' [earth] of Caledonia, it will be on that
> which for centuries belonged to this family. ("The King's Visit," 10
> August 1822: [4])

People from every condition and class proved eager (McCracken-Flesher,
"The Great Disturber"). John Galt burlesqued the evacuation of Glasgow,
tracking for *Blackwood's* the exchange eastward of "Greenock Folk," "Pais-
ley Bodies," and "Glasgow People" in the persons of Mrs. Goroghan the
ship-owner's wife, Mrs. M'Auslan the Captain's wife, and Miss Nannie
Eydent the Irvine seamstress (12, no. 68: 306–32). When William Murray
determined "not to alter the prices . . . for the one night the King [attended
the Theatre-Royal]," Edinburgh crammed the box office (Skinner, "Contemporary," 82). Mudie notes: "This was an event which all classes of the
community had looked forward to with the most anxious anticipations. His
Majesty was now to be brought into closer contact than he had yet been with
his Scottish subjects," and he recalls the disorderly rush for admission by
"the indiscriminately collected multitude" (Mudie, 272):

> The situation altogether was so eminently *revolutionary*, that persons
> at the extremity of the crowd had no reason to despair, while those
> upon the very threshold of the door could scarcely venture to hope. . . .
> we observed . . . a lady who had just recovered from a swoon; and such
> was the enthusiasm of her loyalty, that she persisted, though pale and
> almost lifeless, in her attempts to gain admission.
>   . . . . A stout, athletic Gael,—whose little finger would have been a
> grievous burden to some *petit-maitres* who stood beside him,—deter-

mined to let them feel the weight of his loins; and, mounting upon their shoulders, regardless of their groans, he scrambled over the heads of those in advance of him, till he came to the door, through the upper section of which he bolted with the agility of a harlequin. (Mudie, 275–76)

His Majesty had commanded *Rob Roy*, and all Edinburgh struggled to stand instantaneously within the signs of Scotland as established in literature by the national bard, and close to the King.

Scotland seemed flung into activity. The *Caledonian Mercury* remarked: "Such is the influx of passengers to Edinburgh, that not less than 450 passengers were landed from the Stirling steam boat, at the chain pier, on Saturday evening" (12 August 1822: [3]). It quoted the *Glasgow Courier*: "The number of persons leaving this city (Glasgow) for Edinburgh is scarcely credible. Every vehicle is engaged for days to come. . . . The canal boats and the extra boats . . . are insufficient to convey the passengers pressing to the metropolis, and we are told that coal punts have been put in requisition."

But at the same time as the Scots rushed to locate themselves figuratively and literally within Scotland, they worked to take the King out of circulation. On his departure, the *Edinburgh Advertiser* assured its readers that though the monarch may be gone, his image would remain: "Our KING has not only been affectionately received by us, but he will also long be remembered with partiality and kindness" ("Departure of His Majesty," 30 August 1822: 144). Moreover the King would remain unchanged with regard to Scotland: "The feelings of the people have found a warm response in the bosom of the SOVEREIGN. . . . It is made known to us on the best authority—communicated by the command of the SOVEREIGN himself." Indeed, the King should remain unchangeable within Scotland. The Institution for the Encouragement of the Fine Arts in Scotland began a subscription in order "that a memorial should be erected in the City of Edinburgh, to commemorate, in the most lasting manner, his Majesty's auspicious visit to Scotland" ("Equestrian Statue of the King," *Edinburgh Advertiser* 23 August 1822: 131). Hence Edinburgh's Equestrian Statue of the King, despite the fact that George IV never bestrode a horse within the city. The Marquis of Lothian not only "caused a new approach and gateway to be formed" for the King's visit to his home at Newbattle, he also marked the imprint of his Majesty's first footstep onto his land with a brass rim.[22]

Why did Scots throw themselves into circulation yet try to interrupt the movement of the King, which had precipitated their action? Two examples reveal a population largely subject to Scott's dynamic of valuation through the exchange of signs. The various assemblies of George's visit enjoy lengthy and colorful description in the many journals of the day and books on the subject. Equally important are the lists of participants, as is evident when someone is inadvertently dropped. A Mrs. Campbell, mentioned by the *Edinburgh Observer* but without information as to who presented her, considered the omission a challenge to her veracity and attendance. The paper had to publish an exculpatory paragraph: "We stated that we had not seen Mrs. Campbell of Dalserf's card . . . [but] we had no conception that Mrs Campbell would have so far misunderstood us as to have supposed that we meant to question the truth of her having been at Court" (26 August 1822: [3]). Meantime, the *Caledonian Mercury* published two columns of omissions from the gentlemen present at his Majesty's levée (22 August 1822: [4]). Scots proved anxious not just to operate within Scotland's signs or in proximity to the monarch, but to be seen to do so.

The case of the Countess of Sutherland and Marchioness of Stafford, Scotland's "premier Earl," makes matters clear. Although a great lady in Scotland, the Marchioness had seen her value slip by her English marriage and titles, but even more through her social policies. She had presided over the clearance of her estates. Now, James Loch, her man of business, lobbied to make the Marchioness visible according to Scott's signs and within the monarchical presence. He wrote to Scott arguing "Lady Stafford's claim to carry the Sceptre as [Countess] of Sutherland": "I trust her Ladyship will come up and pay her Court to His Majesty. . . . I would undertake that she should in one week stand at the cross; at the head of the finest set of men in Scotland & the most numerous except Macallumore of any Scottish Chieftain—It would more effectually disprove the tales that have been told than anything she could do."[23] At the head of a body of highlanders, in possession of the Sceptre, and close to the King, the Marchioness should find her value reestablished. That is, having once created George IV as their governing term by substitution through Scottish signs, the Scots constituted themselves according to those signs, and by circulation around the King established their value where it mattered—in the public eye.

With their valuation thus affirmed, however, the Scots found themselves locked within a cycle of exchange. George, after all, was only a sign. Thus, they simultaneously circulated around the King, and struggled to signify him as that impossibility, the transcendent Sign and permanent arbiter of value. In a 3 September letter, the Marchioness declared to Scott: "I rejoice to think that this visit of the King's to Scotland . . . will do a great deal to excite the energies of the Country in every way, & to bring the Highlanders forward" (NLS MS 3895: 75). Circulation has been achieved for her highlanders, and value initiated. Yet at the same time she wistfully remarked that her people "deposed their colours and their targets here [at Dunrobin Castle] . . . till a second Visit from H. M. may call the men & their arms again" (ibid). The great lady dreamed of a repeat visit, the consequent stabilization of the transcendent Sign within Scotland, and the permanent determination of Scottish value. Scott's system had become self-perpetuating in its many players—a triumph of its kind.

Scott, the Site of King and Country

"I call *him* a ruffling gamester, or ane of the first head, who ventures frankly and deeply upon such a wager"

Here we encounter the visit's major fascination. The people measured themselves against the King; the King achieved meaning in relation to the signs of Scotland; those signs drew their value from Walter Scott. George IV's visit foregrounds an author's ability to hoard capital in the form of literature and, importantly, to use it to determine national worth. But more, it reveals that the postcolonial author speaking from the margins himself may serve as the system's defining term. Consider how Scott operates during the visit. He seems to do everything. He goes so far as to design crosses and buttons— "the motto on the St. Andrew's Cross, to be presented to the King, is '*Righ Albainn gu brath*,' that is, 'Long Life to the King of Scotland,'" he writes to Daniel Terry (31 July 1822, *Letters*, 7:214–15). "'*Righ gu brath*' would make a good motto for a button." He composes addresses, writing even on behalf of the undoubtedly competent Faculty of Advocates: "we beseech your Majesty's favourable acceptance of the unreserved tender of our devoted submission and inviolable attachment to your Majesty; in whom we have the proud satisfaction of beholding the descendant of a Race of Kings, whose rightful possession of the Sceptre of this Realm has been coeval with the first foundation of the monarchy" (NLS MS 3134.f175). With David Stewart of Garth, whose highland and military credentials were impeccable, the author delivers their colors to the Celtic Society ("Celtic Society," *Inverness Courier*, 22 August 1822: [4]). Moreover Scott seems to be everywhere. He is in the parade to the Castle to receive the Regalia, and at the progress to return it; he is on the King's yacht when it arrives, and at the landing (Mudie, 46, 193, 88, 100). The author of *A Narrative* situates him at small gatherings with the King on at least three occasions (*Narrative*, 97–99). Yet he is in Castle Street entertaining George Crabbe and assembled noisy highlanders: "there met at the sumptuous dinner, in all the costume of the Highlanders, the great chief himself and officers of his company.... Then we had Sir Walter Scott's national songs and ballads.... and Sir Walter was the life and soul of the whole" (Crabbe, 294–95). Which is to say he seems prior, originary, omnipresent—the site of meaning and worth.

Scott's role to determine value supports this reading. In "Eben Anderson's Account," The *Edinburgh Magazine* naïvely assumed the authenticity of Scotland's bogus pageant on the grounds of Scott's involvement: "The procession at last moved on, in a long line of chivalrous and heraldic order, such as . . . her own Scott alone could have mustered up into keeping, and bearing, and historic truth" (August 1822: 237–40). Others turned to Scott for recognition on a less extensive but no less personally important scale. "An obscure individual" requested that he deliver a bramble bead (improbably the property of Mary, Queen of Scots) "from the idea that the value of the gift, if at all acceptable, would be highly enhanced from being presented to his Majesty by the hand of Sir Walter Scott."[24] A perfumer, having tried Mr. Mash (Lord Chamberlain's office) and the Lord Provost, turned to Scott as the one capable of conferring value on his request of "being appointed perfumer to his Majesty."[25] George Tough, Minster of Ayton, intercepted the King on his private visit to Holyrood and begged his acceptance of "an Orrery, upon an improved plan, constructed by Mr. Tough himself,—and also a Sermon," but finding his gift neglected, asked Scott to establish its proper worth and therefore his own (Mudie, 252–53). Concerned that his sermon had proved offensive, he begged Scott: "If you have had leisure to look into it, might I request that you would favour me with your opinion whether there be any thing objectionable in it?"[26] Resisting comment, the author duly commended the orrery through Sir William Knighton and, as A. Aspinall observes, "It is now in the Royal Library, Windsor Castle."[27] David Wilkie, too, found that Scott's name translated into opportunity when "Sir Walter Scott recommended me to go | to the levée] and to make use of his name on my presentation card" (Cunningham, 2:85–86). This gained him "the privilege of entrée" and a point of observation within the Presence Chamber.

The great seem equally aware of Scott's power to establish value. James Loch and the Marchioness of Stafford together agreed that only through Walter Scott could they fix the right to bear the Sceptre. Loch reveals he knows where the real power of valuation resides when he informs the Marchioness that he has "written to Capt. Ferguson the keeper of the Regalia, stating your claim to carry the Sceptre—and enclosed it to Sir Walter Scott."[28] The Marchioness herself told Scott in her letter of 3 September: "I should have been grieved to have lost [the privilege of bearing the Sceptre], such good Friends have helped me to retain it, which doubles its value" (NLS MS 3895: 75). Even those to whom Scott officially bowed, or who did not number among his uncritical admirers, turned to him. Having averred that "Scott . . . was equally Ignorant of certainty of The Kings motions," the Duke of Atholl grudgingly asked him for help: "I was anxious to procure for the Lieutenancy . . . of Scotland a safe place to See the Procession and a Platform on the Castle Hill where Sir W: Scott could command the Ground appear'd the best."[29] And even Glengarry, who bowed to no one, remained within a Celtic Society he despised because he found his own value raised by proximity to Scott. When he abandoned the Society because of its supposedly fraudulent behavior during the King's visit, he carefully renegotiated his own position. The Society might be bogus, he wrote to the *Edinburgh Observer*, but the company was grand. Of his first attendance, he remarks: "I never saw so much tartan *before* . . . with *so little Highland material.* The day went off pleasantly, to be sure, but how could it do otherwise to any man seated on one hand of Sir Walter Scott?" ("To the Editor," 5 September 1822: [3]). Scott is the agreed upon Sign around which all circulate in search of valuation.

For the King, as well, Scott served to set worth. George had long admired Scott for his poems and novels. In 1815, when they first met, the then Regent exchanged and capped stories with the author, all the time calling him "Walter" and indicating an established value that exceeded the bounds of normal princely intercourse (Lockhart, 3:341–43). In 1821, when the King charged Sir Thomas Lawrence to paint the most distinguished men of the age for Windsor, "His Majesty desired [the portrait] of Sir Walter Scott [his first baronet] to be the first" (Johnson, 1:728). So when the visit north wavered in possibility, Lord Melville invoked Scott to firm up the monarch's intentions: "there is one [invitation] which [I] humbly [submit] for [Your Majesty's] perusal, though evidently not intended to be so honored.—It is from the pen of Sir Walter Scott."[30] Now, when Scott embarked to welcome his King, George exclaimed: "What! . . . Sir Walter Scott? the man in Scotland I most wish to see!" (Mudie, 88). The King found his meaning in a northern author.

Scott already stood credited as the hub of circulation and thus valuation to a remarkable degree. The *Edinburgh Observer* marveled that passengers heading to London could travel by "the Sir W. Scott light post-coach, from this to Carlisle" (29 August 1822: [3]). For the visit, those coming from Glasgow could take either of the first two passenger boats on the three-month-old Union Canal—the *Flora McIvor* or the *Jeannie* [sic] *Deans* (Maclean & Skinner, 2). But during August of 1822, the urgency of movement around Walter Scott transfigured the author's role. "Eben Anderson" in the *Edinburgh Magazine* considered him "our Master Magician" (August 1822: 240). Sir A. M. Mackenzie wrote to the Duke of Atholl that "Sir W. Scott . . . is FacTotum."[31] On 10 August, Mary Stewart Mackenzie effused to the author: "I congratulate Scotland upon our King's visit happening in [your] day, as every thing, and almost every person, will appear quite in a different light to His Majesty from your wisdom and judgment pervading the arrangements" (NLS MS 3895: 43). Even Lockhart saw his father-in-law as a power—if behind the throne. He remarked later: "Scott could . . . have played in other days either the Cecil or the Gondomar; and I believe no man, after long and intimate knowledge of any other great poet, has ever ventured to say, that he could have conceived the possibility of any such parts being adequately filled on the active stage of the world, by a person in whom the powers of fancy and imagination had such predominant sway, as to make him in fact live three or four lives habitually in place of one" (Lockhart, 5:207). Scott had become a site of excessive meaning that the perfumer, the minister, the King—and a mass of people including even J. G. Lockhart— recognized, set apart, and deployed for the purposes of their own valuation. Moreover, as Bourdieu would expect, they considered it natural and took it for granted (Bourdieu, 171–72).

Obviously, however, there was nothing natural about any of this. Scott worked to present a deferential front. He wrote to Melville in terms that suggested his Lordship's authority, but his letter reveals he is the one running the show. Scott writes as if under direction: "I am now to inclose the petition for the Regalia." Nevertheless, he tells Melville what to do: "If you approve & ratify it by your signature I will obtain the signature of two other officers of state" (August 1822, *Letters*, 7: 218). Further, he wrote himself into the terms of exchange during the King's visit. His *Hints* characterize him as "An Old Citizen," already with the priority and authority of age (*Hints*, title page). They anticipate his presence with the King at the moment of his arrival: "Before quitting the yacht," Scott informs us, "a beautiful St Andrew's Cross, wrought in pearls, is to be presented to his Majesty by Sir Walter Scott, in the name of 'the Ladies of Edinburgh'" (*Hints*, 9). A contemporary commentary on said cross indicates that Scott planned even this, noting: "it was suggested by Sir Walter Scott, that the ladies should embroider and offer [a St. Andrew's Cross] to his Majesty on his arrival."[32] It is not then surprising—and Scott may justly have expected—that the cross "was presented in the name of the ladies by their chosen knight, the Bard of Chivalry" (ibid.).

The incident that best manifests Scott's construction of his own and thus others' roles is Howison Craufurd of Braehead's service to His Majesty at the Provost's banquet. Accompanied by "[Masters] Charles and Walter Scott . . . as pages," Craufurd knelt to the King and proffered him a basin and napkin to wash his hands (Mudie, 234–35). But Scott's intrusion was more pronounced and otherwise located than through his son and nephew. The ceremony purported to arise from a service unwittingly offered James II or III by Craufurd's ancestor, and in reward for which the family held Braehead (Mudie, 234–35 n.). While the story fits medieval theories of the dynamic of recognition between a King in disguise and a worthy subject as defined by Louise Fradenburg, this particular version received its authority from Walter Scott (Fradenburg, 69–70). According to Mudie, he "told the . . . story to the King, who was very highly amused with it" (Mudie, 235 n.). Yet Scott's involvement is prior to the King's visit. Craufurd's body service echoes that offered the Chevalier by Baron Bradwardine in *Waverley*: "Cosmo Comyne Bradwardine . . . claimed permission to perform, to the person of his Royal

Highness . . . the service used and wont for which under a charter of Robert Bruce . . . the claimant held the barony of Bradwardine, and lands of Tully-Veolan. His claim being admitted and registered, his Royal Highness having placed his foot upon a cushion, the Baron of Bradwardine, kneeling upon his right knee, proceeded to undo the latchet of the brogue, or low-heeled Highland shoe" (*Waverley*, chapter 50). Scott understood the resonance of a cultural narrative. By redeploying the tale of service between king and subject, he confirms both in a dynamic of mutual exchange. Moreover, by using a tale already recognized as his, and constructed by him elsewhere as comedy, Scott strategically foregrounds himself as the source of both authority and critique.

Thus, it is small wonder that when "The Author of *Waverley*, whoever he is" was toasted at the Provost's banquet, Scott responded with more humor and less obliquity than usual. *Blackwood's* tells us: "this was drunk with great hilarity, Sir Walter Scott leading the way in acclamation" (12, no. 69: 492–97, see 496). It is fitting that "Stanzas on the Evening Before the King's Landing" should exhort:

> Now bumper your glasses, brave boys, brave boys,
>   I'm sure that you'll empty them too;
> Oh, well in such Son may old Scotland rejoice,
>   For his equal go search the earth thro':
> 'Tis his in her honour to shine and surpass;
>   To enoble the name of the Scot;
> Oh, ne'er when in friendship we send round the glass,
>   Be the name of Sir Walter forgot,
> (*Royal Scottish Minstrelsy*, 97–98, verse 1)

Scott had deliberately circulated signs such that, by their acceptance, he stood constituted as the site of valuation. The author controlled the moment.

No doubt we can trace to Scott's self-inscription as the arbiter of meaning behind and through the King's visit the fact that he carries the blame for the occasion's failures. Looking back from 1834 John Galt mocked: "The Edinburgh citizens cuckoo about George the Fourth calling them gentlemen, and their town a city of palaces, as if he had not read enough of other places to know the truth, and thought but of outdoing them in cajolery" (241). Certainly, even the moment of the visit carries within it the fact of Scotland's devaluation through Scott's use of literary signs. Think of George's construction. This was a matter of signification, and the King himself merely a sign. George's value would continue to rise and fall—not three weeks after his death, the *Times* sourly remarked: "The truth is . . . that there never was an individual less regretted by his fellow-creatures than this deceased King. What eye has wept for him? What heart has heaved one throb of unmercenary sorrow" (16 July 1830: [2])? Still, the role had real effects. First, a dominant term depends for its power on its distinction from other signs. We must forget that we made it (Goux, 33). In Edinburgh, neither King nor subject easily registered the monarch's constructedness. This reduced the opportunity for self-conscious critique of the kingly role. Second, the dominant term serves to apportion relative value between commodities, but its own inflated valuation levels whatever it encounters (Goux, 39). As Goux writes: "The monarch can settle disputes, according to his rule, only if he eliminates all differences and *distinctions*." Taking himself for granted, the King will subject all others. This is the case for 1822 Scotland.

Wilkie wanted to depict the King at church, humble among his people, but "dazzled by the splendour of the Highland tartan, captivated by the nodding of the plumes, and nursed as he had been in etiquette and ceremony . . . the King . . . fixed upon his admission to the palace of his ancestors" (Cunningham, 2:89). Further, he instructed Wilkie that he "'Stood! . . . not as I stand there [in a preliminary sketch], but thus;'—and he set his foot forward, threw his body back, put on 'a martial and swashing outside,' and said, 'There!'" (Cunningham, 2:90). The King could only see himself as transcendent within Scott's signs. In fact, he could only recognize the Scots within those signs, too. At the Caledonian Hunt Ball, the King requested "Scots reels and strathspeys in abundance, but none of your foreign dances." He declared: "I dislike seeing any thing in Scotland that is not purely national and characteristic" (*Edinburgh Advertiser*, 6 September: 163; Mudie, 257). By the role Scott had established for him, King and people stood locked in a relationship of dominance and subjection.

Worse, George invited others into the cycle of valuation. With the monarch elevated through Scottish signs, people who looked to George would seek to locate themselves within those signs. Goux suggests that "the social organism" is shaped by the conjunction not just of terms but of systems, each with their own centers and dynamics (45). Although Scott or Scotland might seem to dominate, there are equivalencies located elsewhere—in England, for example. These negotiate value differently. For one thing, the English could deploy "an absolute commodity (gold)" (Goux, 17). They could lay out wealth to purchase proximity to His Majesty. Sir William Curtis provides the best example of such intervention in Scott's exchange. On 5 August, well before the King arrived, the *Caledonian Mercury* sensed English money in the offing. It quoted the *London Star*: "a worthy City Baronet, of great *weight* wherever he goes, is determined to afford his Majesty, in his visit to Edinburgh this year, the benefit of that *preponderating* loyalty which he last year threw into the *scale* of the Dublin Corporation. Sir William has just purchased from a Highland tailor in the Haymarket; a complete suit of tartan, *philibeg*, and 'all those sort of things,' with which he means to invest himself, as the appropriate costume, to meet his Royal Master in Edinburgh"

(5 August 1822: [3]). Curtis's weight—personal, physical, and financial—will turn the scale in Scotland, directing value through Scottish signs but south of the border. Scott's very success revealed what Bourdieu might term the repressed of symbolic capital: all is interested; all is economic; money trumps every exchange.

Worse still, Scotland potentially stood devalued through Scott's exchange of signs. If meaning depends on the King, yet the King is but a sign, then all value is contingent and unstable. George IV may have fixed Scottish worth, but he simultaneously brought it into question through Scott's central terms. In Scott's narrative, heart speaks to heart. Scotland as origin welcomes the King through return as the heart of the nation such that the *Edinburgh Weekly Journal* declared: "[The King] is the centre [to] which every feeling gravitates, the life-spring from which at this moment are sent out the [str]eams that animate and invigorate every mem[b]er of the body politic" (21 August 1822: 267). However, the heart was a fickle sign that already had circulated too much. In Ireland, George exclaimed, "my heart has always been Irish." "From the day it first beat," he assured his eager listeners, "I have loved Ireland" (Huish, 2:320). In Hanover, George asserted "that he felt a joy which he could not express in finding himself on the native soil of his illustrious predecessors" (Huish, 2:333). This trade in hearts had become such a feature of the King's visits that it was openly mocked. "William Heath depicted [the King] in a red coat of foreign cut and a round Teutonic cap, smoking a meerschaum pipe and carelessly tossing coins to excited Hanoverian subjects one of whom says, 'He is indeed a Hanoverian at heart,' to which another replies, 'No, he is an Irishman, he says'" (Hibbert, 238). Nor could anyone forget the King's heartfelt devotion to the ladies. Madame de Lieven remarked upon the "indescribable oglings" at the opening of Parliament in February: "he caught sight of me—a smile. A row higher, his eyes fell on Lady Cowper—another smile. Higher still, Lady Morley—he beamed. . . . The signalling never stopped for a second" (Hibbert, 246). Even in Edinburgh the King proved easily distracted from his love for Scotland by his attraction to the ladies: "When he looked towards the balcony on the Exchange, filled with an attractive assemblage of fair ladies, he placed his hand upon his heart, and bowed" (*Narrative*, 49). The King was a big, aching heart looking for love in all the wrong places. His devotion was worthless—except that it undermined its object, bringing it to a level with all the other places and people he adored.

The wits who produced *Kilts and Philibegs!!* chortled:

lest jealousy should cause heart-aches,
Geordie resolved to view the *Land of Cakes;*
And mighty were the preparations made
By sea and land for the advent'rous blade;

Whose setting off by *steam* (a pretty joke)
May, like the Irish jaunt, end all in smoke. (6)

But this was the best scenario. Craig argues that "any significant work con-
sumed within the core culture is then assimilated to its tradition and is
denied any role within the culture from which its creator derived" (*Out of
History*, 19). As we have seen, generations of Scottish critics have suggested
that through the King's visit Scott caused even more damage: he delimited
his nation as a space subject to English purchase, his people as subject to
English construction, and his land as a devalued vacancy. Beveridge and
Turnbull sum up this perspective: "Scots have connived at the manufacture
and peddling of clownish, contorted versions of their history and culture,
for reasons of economic gain and British-imperial participation, and as a
way of evading the harsh realities of the Scottish condition. This prolonged
and shameful undertaking . . . has led Scots actually to accept a kind of
dream history of their nation" (*Scotland*, 58). All this courtesy of Scott's
"pickling of a dead culture and cause" (74). Scott's literary intervention
in national valuation seems to have caused its own failure and the nation's
effective demise.

Ironically, however, this critical vision credits England with a power to
stabilize signs and determine values that is theoretically impossible. If we
pay attention to the implications of Scott's strategy, and not simply its inter-
mediate stages (such as centering the King), different possibilities emerge.
Remember that the dominant term is established through repeated signification, and it is therefore under pressure to reveal that exchange. Thus, it
is always forced toward collapse in the direction of the sign—which is all it
is. And signs can circulate freely and be exchanged creatively, as *The Antiquary* and *Nigel* suggest. To accept the valuation of a moment, therefore,
is to subject ourselves unnecessarily and dangerously to the Sign—which
the example of Gow the musician makes clear. After dinner with the young
Duke of Buccleuch, George IV thanked the players: "'I am happy to see the
representative of Neil Gow in this place; and long may he live to delight his
friends!' . . . When the King had withdrawn, Gow . . . was heard to utter,
'I'm perfectly contented to die now'" (Mudie, 187). Whether we submit
to the Sign as positive (like Gow) or negative (like the critics), the effect is
equally deathly. We abjure an opportunity that Scott has provided and that
his contemporaries developed even as they tried to fix their value through the
King. The practical experience of Scotland's people during George IV's visit
reveals that courtesy of Scott the margin is a Bhabhaesque space of disruptive play where value can and must constantly be renegotiated by exchange
across the sign and between all parties.

Scott opened the opportunity for such play as much through his failures
as his successes. At the moment of George IV's visit, the Scots struggled for

proximity. In so doing, they revealed their effective subjection to the idea of the King. But they further revealed that all positions stand equally constructed by the interplay of signs. All are contingent; each is a space of possibility. The Whigs and the Tories offer an example. Scott noted "Party feeling . . . has of late years risen much higher [here] than any sensible person . . . could possibly imagine"; "[it] is really too much to have people divided in this manner"—and he folded both groups into the homely myth of unity and order (*Hints*, 7–8). However, throughout the visit order stood at once established and demolished. Each party attempted to determine itself against the other and met vicious resistance. Although the Whigs began by sourly questioning the King's visit and stressing his role as the "first Magistrate of a free state," they situated themselves against the Tories and thus as unique in the context of the King: "we hope [our countrymen] will not forget that they are freemen, and that a constitutional King can have no esteem for those who try to recommend themselves to his notice by an ultra display of zeal, or by fawning and servility" ("The King's Visit," *Scotsman*, 3 August 1822: 244). The Tories rose against this assertion of Whiggish value. In "The Sorrows of the Stot"—the Stot being a gelded bull, and representing the *Scotsman* and Whiggery in general—*Blackwood's* mocked the Whigs' binary response to the news of the King's impending visit: "The disloyal dunce began to bite his thumb even on a holiday. . . . [he] endeavoured to bring up a smile on his countenance from the dark, deep, dank drawwell of his unfangled heart, and with that most grievous grin to fall into the ranks of leal and joyous citizens, and with restless and uncertain feet to keep time with the tread of loyalty that shook our streets like an earthquake" (12, no. 68: 333–43, see 334). Predictably, too, the Tories decried their own depiction: "This is very unintelligible stuttering of the Stot's. Who are the desperadoes and the devils he complains of? . . . is this the language of a man, or the growling of a beast" (334)? And the cycle continued. Aspiring to value through the King, each group tried to situate itself beside the monarch by a process of differentiation. Each group defines the other and locates themselves against it. However, every gesture in this direction produces a countermove, for as we know, signification precipitates uniqueness only through uncontainable play. In that play comes opportunity: the contest for signification and its resultant instability allows mobility—the condition of possibility.

The sartorially defined Scots manifest the same phenomenon. Again, Scott tried to fold two bodies into one Scottish narrative. To the Celts, he presented their colors; for the assembled multitude from the far north, he served as adjutant-general (*Inverness Courier*, 22 August 1822: [4]; *Narrative*, 109). But like any such managed equivalence, this also fell apart. Alastair Macdonell of Glengarry and the Celtic Society immediately embroiled themselves in a squabble over the right to wear tartan. In a two-installment letter to the editor of the *Edinburgh Observer*, Glengarry, who claimed chief-

tainship of the Macdonalds and had founded the Society of True Highlanders, attacked:[33]

> I never saw so much tartan *before*, in my life, with *so little Highland
> material* [as in the Celtic Society]. . . . I take this opportunity of with-
> drawing my name publicly from this mixed society. . . . their general
> appearance is assumed and fictitious, and they have *no right to burlesque
> the national character or dress of Highlanders*. . . . I have seen a mulattoe,
> a Jew . . . and some other foreigners equally preposterous, appear in
> the George's Street Assembly Rooms, with scarfs almost down to their
> heels, in the same night, winter was a year.[34]

With unabashed racism Glengarry asserts the fictionality and belatedness
of the Celtic Society, and thus his legitimate claim to the signs in circulation
around the King's visit. Not surprisingly, he erupted at the moment of the
monarch's arrival—accoutered in all the supposed splendor of a highland
chief, he broke ranks, "[forcing] his way through every obstacle, and, advanc-
ing close to the royal carriage, exclaimed 'Your Majesty is welcome to Scotland'" (Mudie, 101). He reckoned his value thus established. When Scott
forwarded Peel's letter of thanks to the various chiefs, Glengarry responded:
"I considered it my Duty to lay your agreable communication with its *favourable testimonial* before the Public [in the papers], as the surest, & far the most
expeditious means of getting at all the Gentlemen concerned; who will *not
fail* to notify their Followers, that most gracious acknowledgement, transmitted *through you* by the Secretary of State, of the Esteem and approba-
tion of their Sovereign."[35] Having set himself before and against the Celts,
Glengarry situated himself close to the King and appropriated all valuation
therefrom.

Furious, the Celts questioned Glengarry's position within the discourse
of home. The mild-mannered David Stewart of Garth fulminated: "Glengarry is a conspicuous man, and is held up as a model of the Highland character. . . . [but] he does infinite injury to his poor countrymen in the false and
erroneous views he offers to the public of what he is pleased to call a true
Highlander."[36] Glengarry is neither Highland nor a gentleman, and the Society moved to obviate his resignation by expelling him (*Edinburgh Observer*, 7
September 1822: [3]). Further, the Society trumped Glengarry by petitioning the King:

> The object of the [Celtic Society] is to preserve unimpaired amidst
> the refinements of the times in which we live the habits & manners of
> the Highlanders; habits and manners with which is associated a tone of
> feeling not less commendable for its delicate sensibility than for its gal-

lantry and generosity; blending harmoniously the wild freedom of the Mountaineer with the ardent loyalty of Subjects to their Prince. . . .

[The Society] humbly entreat that Your Majesty may be pleased to confer on the Celtic Society the highly distinguished honour of receiving it under the Royal protection and enabling it proudly to boast that the Sovereign is its Patron.[37]

With their suggested "delicate sensibility [and] . . . gallantry and generosity," the Celts set their faces against Glengarry. Evidently, with the same signs playing in opposed systems, Glengarry can be directly addressed by the King's thanks, yet the Celts appropriate their monarch's patronage.

But by raising their competition to the level of public notice, Celts and highlanders unwittingly invited others to compete for placement within those signs that both groups considered their own. "Christopher North" declared in *Blackwood's*:

We never . . . sported the kilt, even at a masquerade. Our fidelity to breeches had been unquestioned. . . .

Why, then, we ask, should a Society be instituted for the suppression of breeches in the Highlands of Scotland? . . .

When . . . A. R. Macdonell, Esq. of Glengarry . . . comes forward on his high horse, as if he would ride over all the old women and children of the metropolis. . . . we have just as good a right as he has to sport a Tail [of attendant highlanders]; and confound us, if we do not, next time the King comes. . . . We will switch away with it, like a lion as we are, and it shall be as stiff and bristly as that of Mac-Mhic-Alastair himself.[38]

Overly energetic competition within the sign has revealed the playfulness of signification and opened a space for the Edinburgh wits, who were unrelated to the original debate.

The maneuvers of those with established value reveal some consciousness that the terms of Scott's exchange opened a space of danger, where value might be negatively renegotiated, but also offered opportunity. The fourth Duke of Atholl, chief of the Murrays and Privy Councillor, had expected the King to circulate to him (Prebble, 147; Mudie, 149). No doubt the visit would prove a bore. His son-in-law, Evan Murray MacGregor, on 21 July assured him he had understood that His Majesty's sudden decision to visit Scotland "from the difficulty of finding Tartan &c at such very short warning,—would hurry and inconvenience Your Grace" (ACR 68/12: 215). When the King decided not to visit Dunkeld and Blair, McGregor registered his disbelief: "This is quite inexplicable—and I can scarcely credit the intelligence" (ibid.). Immediately, those who took their value from the Duke, but recognized the function of the King, scurried to push Atholl into circulation. McGregor offered him highlanders, and John Findlater began to amass a force from the Atholl estates:

> I have already a List of upwards of 50 Young Fellows, Servants & Sons of Tenants of His Grace all Upwards of 5f-9in. . . . The Blue Coats are in every one's possession, or can be had in Lone from their Neighbours we have considered it proper for Mr. Stewart to Set off to Perth . . . to procure the Waist Belts & Dirks, Purses &c. . . .
>
> We shall do every thing possible to appear Respectable & I will engage for the Clans being among the first & surpassed by none. If I had, but had, 8 days Drilling of them, But even on the Road we will bring them wonderfully forward. (ACR 68/12: 254)

Yet the Duke refused to circulate except on behalf of the Lieutenancy of Perth, for whom he presented an address.[39] His "Memoranda" for 15 August make clear he did not appear in the Royal Progress into Edinburgh: "not being in the Procession I was at a Window in the Waterloo Hotel," he writes (Mudie, 102; ACR 1026/35:2). Moreover, he refused to let others move on his behalf. Having agreed with Scott that quite enough highlanders now swarmed Edinburgh's streets, he remarked on 10 August, "I trust this foolish fancy wont be insisted on by others and that I wont be obliged [to be] equally foolish" (ACR 1026/34: 35–36). He even lobbied to prevent further incursions by the Gael: "wrote to Mr. Peel & Ld Melville who quite coincide with me in all Counts" (36). John Findlater never set out for Edinburgh. The Duke, then, saw no need of circulation. In fact, he recognized its risks. "The Mania is the Highland garb," he noted in his journal of 15 August, after the King's progress, and he watched "a considerable Procession of Troops, Highlanders and the different Persons dressed up by [Sir] W: Scott in fantastic attire."

Nonetheless, though he termed the visit *"one and twenty daft days,"* and though he determined not to participate himself or let others operate for him, the Duke manipulated events so as to appear that he had duly circulated and maintained his supposedly unquestionable value (1 September 1822, ACR 68/12: 289). While he strove to interrupt the flow of highlanders, he also ensured that authoritative voices supported his position and even claimed responsibility for it. He elicited from Peel the helpful comment: "Considering the Time that necessarily must elapse before your Highlanders could make their appearance, and considering too the number already in Edinburgh subject probably to no very severe discipline . . . I am inclined to think that it might be as well not to summon the Men of Athol" (11 August 1822, ACR 68/12: 252). Peel actually assured him: "Should Your Grace concur with me I will not fail to explain to His Majesty the only reason which will have induced Your Grace to abandon your Intention, and to take upon myself my share of Responsibility." On 19 August, he duly reported: "I took the earliest opportunity of Explaining to the King the Sole cause of the absence of the Athol Men. . . . Lord Melville & I had entreated Your Grace to stop them" (ACR 68/12: 267). If the Duke saw no need of circulation either by himself or his representatives, he nonetheless acknowledges its power when he works to get credit for a movement he never performed.

At the other end of the scale stands Alexander Rodger. Under the names Alisander the Seer, Andrew Whaup, and Humphrey Henkeckle, Rodger the weaver produced political satire. In honor of the King's visit, he parodied the same Jacobite rant Scott favored. His version, published in the *London Examiner*, ran in part:

Sawney now the king's come,
Sawney now the king's come,
Down and kiss his gracious———,
       Sawney now the king's come.

Tell him he is great and gude,
And come o' Scottish royal blood,
Down, like Paddy,—lick his fud,
       Sawney now, &c.

Tell him he can do nae wrang;
That he's mighty, high, and strang;
That you and yours to him belang,
       Sawney now, &c.

And when he rides Auld Reekie through,
To bless you wi' a kingly view,
Let him smell your garde-loo,
       Sawney now, &c.[40]

This poem articulates the devaluation Scots risk by revolving around the King. Yet the piece itself circulated in such a way as to claim priority and therefore value. In the 1842 "Brief Sketch of the Author's Life," which precedes Rodger's selected poetry (edited by himself) and a sanitized version of "Sawney," we are assured that "[a] copy of this having been sent by some of [Rodger's] friends to the London Examiner, it was published in that paper with some laudatory remarks. The publication reached Edinburgh on or about the day of the king's arrival. Sir Walter Scott, having written a piece to welcome his majesty, beginning 'Carle now the King's come,' the coincidence of their appearance and measure gave the greatest annoyance to the

'Great Unknown'" (Rodger, ix; 15–18). In reality, Scott's poem appeared in the *Examiner* on 11 August, but Rodger's was not published even there until 1 September, and I have yet to locate it in the Edinburgh papers. Thomas Carlyle, who grew "disgusted with the fulsome 'loyalty' of all classes in Edinburgh towards [the visit]" and "resolved . . . to quit the city altogether and be absent and silent," seems the exception to the general rule (*Reminiscences*, 222–23). Cases as disparate and unlikely as those of the Duke of Atholl and Alexander Rodger confirm the necessity for all Scots to circulate in the contest for placement. They demonstrate the consequent possibility for identification, differentiation, and the access of power.

Indications are that Scott sensed his carefully balanced equivalences would devolve into destabilizing yet creative and potentially powerful exchange, and that he found it something to encourage. Of course, the King's response pleased him. On 7 October, he wrote to his son, Lieutenant Walter Scott: "The King has expressd himself most graciously to me both at leaving Edinr. and since he returnd. I know from sure authority he hás scarce ever ceased to speak about the Scotch and the fine taste and spirit of their reception" (*Letters*, 7:262–64). However, he took little action to fix King and people in place after the visit. James Simpson understood that he impinged upon Scott's literary/political opportunity when he presented his *Letters to Sir Walter Scott, Bart. on the Moral and Political Character and Effects of the Visit to Scotland in August 1822, of His Majesty King George IV*. He opened: "the writer, who now uses the freedom to address you, is unwilling to abandon the hope that the task of telling the tale and pointing the moral of that auspicious event,— with all the poetry, the painting, the high excitement of which it is susceptible,—will yet be performed by you" (Simpson, 1–2). Scott remained silent. In fact, he called the events "this most royal row," and remembered them as "the awakening of Abou Hassan to a dream of Sovereignty."[41] Despite all his pageantry, and his efforts to determine the details, he wrote to William Stuart Rose: "We were obliged to go to town and when there I found every [thing] in such confusion that the coronation . . . was calm water compared to it. The *purblind* is a king you know among the blind and the very little I know of courts and court like matters with some other considerations occasioned my being constituted a sort of adviser general in the matter of ceremonial and so forth" (4 September 1822, *Letters*, 7:229–32). Throughout, he considered his efforts of the slightest, and strikingly, he was happy to let everything go. "I cannot say that I have thought my own thoughts or wrought my own works for at least a month passd," he complained to his son on 28 August (*Letters*, 7:228). By mid-September, he was embroiled in his own financial, literary, and architectural affairs once again.[42]

Most impressively, Scott gleefully watched the relationships he had constructed fall into dissension. Of a spat between Glengarry and Lieutenant William MacKenzie, a Celt, he chuckled to Peel: "[MacKenzie] has behaved

I think with great temper and spirit in a late *row* betwixt Glengarry and the Celtic Society which began about a *piper*. I was in hopes that they would have fought it out with sword and target and stop'd at the first blood drawn. . . . It puts me in mind of the behaviour of our colly-dogs at church" (13 September 1822, *Letters*, 7:237–38). Scott participated in the dissension. He relished the Whig Duke of Hamilton's discomfiture during his speech at the Provost's banquet, writing to Morritt on 7 September:

> The Duke's speech was delivered like a school-boy, and lest we should not be aware of his folly, he spoke it twice over in great trepidation, and yet with an air of his usual asumption. . . .
> He spoke as if he were b——t   [beltit: drunk]
> And looked as if he smelt it.
> (*Letters*, 7:233–36)

Indeed, with the King gone, it was open season. On 14 September, the *Scotsman* griped, "It is somewhat ludicrous to observe the pains with which the Edinburgh Government scribes endeavour to press Sir Walter Scott into the front rank of the personages who occupied the *proscenium* during the arrangements for his Majesty's reception in Scotland. . . . It is a pity that the author of *Waverley* should deem it important to figure in every part of a corporation pageant" (289). And Scott replied with a will. Creatively deploying the system of exchange already established, he othered the Whigs and renegotiated his own value and that of Edinburgh's Tories by a correspondence with Sir William Knighton, the King's de facto Private Secretary. He detailed Edinburgh's Whig community, noted their associations with "the lowest shop-keepers and mechanics," and mocked their "great belief in the influence of fine writing and . . . that a nation can be governed by pamphlets and reviews," while noting its danger: "[they] conceive it adequate to set the revolutionary stone a rolling and then to stop it with their quills when it is in mid descent down the hill."[43] All the time, of course, he scribbled enthusiastically and disruptively himself.

Paying Forward: Scott's Tomorrow—Today

> "ye ken weel how to use that jilting quean, Dame Fortune,
> like a canny douce lad"

I have argued that although Scott may have seemed to transfer Scotland to the past and dehistoricize the present, by the mere entry into narrative he located the nation ever at the point of construction through the lively play of the sign. Let me go further. He thereby subjected England, even today, to a past both fictional and foreign. Scott's strategy may have established George IV as dominant term, but the symbolic violence of exchange through Scottish signs at the same time deformed the King and powerfully recoded English history.

Beginning with Jane Grant, Scots have found the Author of Waverley naïve in his deployment of Scottish signs. She embraced the Baron de Stael's opinion that "Sir Walter Scott. . . . is quite childish about the pageant he is preparing for the King" (Skinner, "Contemporary," 70). Further, Scots have assumed that the King remained unchanged by Sir Walter's efforts. It is not promising, then, that the *Scotsman* joined with the *Morning Chronicle* to dub His Majesty "the Royal Tourist" (3 August 1822: 246). Unfortunately, George IV had all the marks of the roving consumer as defined by James Buzard. Whereas "the traveller exhibits boldness and gritty endurance under all conditions" (and is subject to those conditions), "the tourist is the cautious, pampered unit of a leisure industry. Where tourists go, they . . . [remake] whole regions in their homogeneous image" (Buzard, 2).

But as James Hogg registered, behind Scott's pageantry Scotland was a place of lively faction liable to implicate its monarch. In *The Royal Jubilee*, the Grey Highland Spirit seeking to take up residence in Edinburgh exclaims:

Oh! master, master, whatever betide,
Here our heads we cannot hide;
There are spirits in fern, in flower-cup, and lin;
Spirits without and spirits within;
There are fairies, and brownies, and shades Amazonian,
Of harper, and sharper, and old Cameronian. (131)

The King only seems above this dissension. When Archy Campbell, the King's Officer and Guardian Genius of the High-street, intervenes "in the King's name," all and sundry immediately question "Who are you, Sir? Who are you? Who are you?" (140). The First Sea-Nymph remarks, moreover:

I judged there were greater crimes
Than giving my Prince a touch of the times;
So I whispered to him, in haughty tone,
What element he journeyed on. (111)

Although Simpson imagined the monarch "sweeping 'through the deep' with a giant's power; careering, engine-armed, against winds and tides and currents," as he rowed between ship and shore, George IV "was saluted by Mr Kent, who was walking upon the water" (Simpson, 39; Mudie, 98). Kent's eruption in the space of kingship implied what the rest of the visit proved: the King's value, too, rose and sank through the tides of significa-tion. In Walter Scott's Scotland, George IV was all at sea.

Because of Scott, in fact, the King's shape shifted and his system changed. We have only to consider the kilted King. Conventional wisdom reads George IV as usurping Scots dress and thus Scottish culture, forcing Scotland into the past (Prebble, 364). Yet the King's dress equally manifests his appropria-tion by Scott's myths. Bourdieu and Goux suggest that exchange depends on misrecognition. George carried the marks from his misrecognition of Scott's occluded economics on his body. Mrs. Scott of Harden described his glori-ous attire: "[At the levée] His Majesty wore the *Royal Tartan Highland Dress* with Buff colourd Trowsers like *flesh* to *imitate* His *Royal Knees*, and little Tartan bits of Stockings like other Highlanders half up his Legs."[44] Cos-tumed in this manner, the King stood outside his usual system of exchange. Even in Scotland, Atholl remarked to his journal: "many not expecting to see His Majesty in a Highland Dress got too close to the King before they recognized Him" (17 August 1822, ACR 1026/35: 5–8). Worse, the King stood in a different system, for which he did not know the rules. The jaun-diced Macaulay pondered the incongruity of the King "[disguised] . . . in what, before the Union, was considered by nine Scotchmen out of ten as the dress of a thief" (Macaulay, 283). Like Waverley, who fondly imagines that "the romance of his life [is] ended" after he leaves the Chevalier's army and "its real history . . . commenced," the King is in fact permanently dis-placed into Scottish history through his attire (60). If Waverley is confined within Scottishness through his sentimental depiction sporting the tartan, how much more drastic were the effects on the King? The be-plaided Waver-ley appears pathetic; George IV appeared bizarre. Henry Cockburn recalled that the Scots treated him as "a spectacle, at which they gazed exactly as they would have done at a Chinese Emperor with his gongs, elephants, and Mandarins" (Cockburn, 104). The emperor had too many clothes; George IV stood deformed and reformed by Scott's signs.

Further, when Scott constituted his nation as origin and George IV as son and father, he not only took the King out of English history, he rewrote Englishness under the sign of the monarch as Scot. Consider the case of Sir William Curtis. In compliment to George IV, he assumed the tartan. But if his financial and personal weight made him seem a threat, his clothing sub-jected him both to Scotland and to ridicule. The *Inverness Courier* quoted the *Morning Paper*: "The Highland dress made for Sir William Curtis is of the finest silk. His costume will be complete, as he is to have his dirk, and above all a knife and a spoon, with plenty of snuff in his pouch, and no doubt the Baronet will have the martial air also of a well fed Highlander" (15 August 1822 [4]). Sir William had taken a devaluing detour out of English history and into Scotland's constructed present, where he stood not as a city magnate but as a figure of fun. Even the earnest J. L. Adolphus wrote: "If it were possible to wish oneself a native of any country but one's own, I should certainly at [the time of the visit] have wished to be a Scotchman. The meanest Scottish subject . . . must have felt a triumph that could not be participated by the most distinguished visitor."[45] Englishmen who took their value from the King found themselves redirected through Scotland.

This proved a lasting effect for England's monarchy. Queen Victoria embraced her imagined Scottish heritage with enthusiasm. On her first visit, entranced by what she considered highland Scotland, she wrote to her mother: "We have heard nothing but Bagpipes since we have been in the *beautiful* Highlands,—& I am become so fond of it,—that *I* mean to have a *Piper*, who can . . . *pipe every night* at Frogmore" (Miller, 20). Before long, Scotland actually was home. A comment on Victoria's 1870s visit to Glencoe shows how far the signs Scott had set in operation now were taken for granted in Britain's Royal house. The Queen expressed "a sort of reverence in going over these scenes, in this most beautiful country, which I am proud to call my own, where there was such devoted loyalty to the family of my ancestors. For Stuart blood is in my veins & I am now, their representative & the people are as devoted & loyal to me, as they were to that unhappy Race" (19). Victoria's Windsor descendants seem no less enamoured of Scott's myths. As daughter to a Scottish aristocrat on her mother's side, Elizabeth II enjoys a more distinct claim to northern inheritance than her predecessors. Still, her decision to dub Philip of Greece (otherwise known as Philip Mountbatten, Baron of Greenwich, and Earl of Merioneth) "Duke of Edinburgh" seems perhaps evenhanded, yet also delusional. And millennium-era suggestions that Princess Anne make Edinburgh her official home, "effectively [becoming] a princess regent north of the Border," or Prince Charles serve as Lord High Commissioner for the 2000 General Assembly of the Church of Scotland, reveal that although the embattled House of Windsor may look to Scotland for the comforting glow of popular approval, the relationship has long since served its Scottish purpose.[46] Met with bemusement by Scots, the "Princess of Scotland" option resulted in embarrassing denials from the royal family, and the silence from the Church on the possibility that Charles would preside made a ludicrous idea a nonstarter. Thus, today's vision of Prince Charles in a kilt alongside his sartorially conservative sons only points up the deep disconnect in the monarchy's devotion to things Scottish. And it indicates Scott's ongoing success.

What of the English themselves? The oddity of a be-kilted monarchy has become visible to an England no longer addicted to romantic vistas and Landseer prints. Should we doubt, Donald Spoto reminds us: "Charles likes to take [Princes William and Harry] to the misty Scottish hills. Diana [preferred] to whisk them off with a few friends to Disney World in Florida" (471). Closer to the Stuart line than her husband, the Princess implied England's recent dissociation from Scottishness. Moreover, the drift of British tourism seems to have turned to more exotic spaces. However, the new Scottish Parliament suggests that while Scott's signs may finally be unattractive south of the border, they have taken political effect.

Obviously, Scotland as now constituted is a thing of laws produced by politics over generations. As Lindsay Paterson puts it, "Scots have recurrently asserted their separateness and have reminded the English that the Union is supposed to be a union and not an absorption of Scotland into England. Each wave of nationalist assertion managed to maintain a sufficient autonomy and a sufficiently distinctive ideology not only to satisfy that particular nationalist phase temporarily but also to provide the grounds on which the next wave of nationalism would thrive" (Paterson, 7). This assertion has taken the form of a Constitutional Convention, court cases like the one to produce the Cooper Judgement, land agitation, and devolution debates and votes.

At the same time, however, the Parliament depends on the notion of a distinct Scotland—one substantially different from a Sussex or a London; one whose borders are not permeable in Northumberland or imprecise in the islands, but clearly defined. Jonathan Hearn notes "the numerous ways in which 'Scotland' is reinforced as the given universe of discourse, in both explicitly political and relatively apolitical contexts," the "wide variety of media through which ideas about nationalism are created and disseminated," and "the density of multiplex social networks, so that key activists participate through various roles and contexts" (Hearn, 78). As Brown et al. point out, "[t]here can be little doubt of the ideological power of Scotland as a nation. . . . Scotland is not simply a piece of geography but a transcendent idea which runs through history, reinterpreting that history to fit the concerns of each present. To say that Scotland . . . [is a 'figment] of the imagination' is not at all to imply that [it] is false, but that [it has] to be interpreted as [an idea], made and remade. Above all [it is a place] of the mind" (Brown, 38). Even modern Scotland depends to some degree on its creative construction within a discourse at once political, but running through and energized by a literature not bound by the practices of law or government. James Mitchell has acknowledged: "For a self-government movement to be successful there must exist a 'self' which is worth preserving. In this, MacDiarmid and the Scottish renaissance played a considerable, if unquantifiable part"—a part that I would trace through a tradition powerfully revived by Walter Scott in 1822 (Mitchell, 27).

How does that tradition operate in modern politics? Brown et al. continue: "The key point about all social identities, including national ones, is that they are not given once and for all, but are negotiated. People's claims to an identity have to be recognized to be valid and operative. We have to be able to read the signs" (Brown, 218). Scott activated a set of signs in such a way that their mere movement signifies Scottishness at home and abroad for un/willing Scots and un/informed others. When Tony Blair claimed *Ivanhoe* and appropriated the portrait of Sir Walter; when the Queen dressed as a thistle and praised "above all the strong sense of identity of the Scottish people" at the opening of the Scottish Parliament; when Donald Dewar proclaimed: "This is about more than our politics and our laws. This is about who we are, how we carry ourselves"; when early drafts of the White Paper on Scotland's Parliament had to be redrafted to seem less "Braveheartish," all concerned manifested the rush of a cultural stream running under the tide of political progress.[47] Insofar as Scotland is an idea negotiated through signs, as well as a praxis enacted through laws, however much Scots may resent their depiction as homely or highland, however much they may cringe at the naming of Sir Walter or the swing of the kilt, they owe their Parliament in some small part to Scott's signs and the delusions they have practiced on both the southern population and themselves.

Anticipating the King's visit, Scott wrote: "Highlanders are what he will like best to see," thus implying that Scotland served an English market (*Letters*, 7:213). It is not strange, therefore, that speaking about Scott's use of Jacobite signs, Murray Pittock should comment: "Scott . . . [made] this pageant of the past Scotland's gift to the Empire: a way of showing Scottish distinctiveness while minimizing political threat" (86). But Scott's was a dangerous gift that continues to pervert the receiver and open opportunity for the donor—it is a gift that has revealed its interest. In *Kilts and Philibegs!!* Sir Willie Curt-his asks the King's mistress "An't I quite the thing now, my lady?" "Quite *a thing*, 'pon my honour," she replies. "Yet *things* are certainly pretty much exposed, too," laments Sir Willie. "I must take devilish good care, and keep a sharp look out, or I shall lose all the little I have— '*speedy and soon*'" (20). When Scott established his land as culturally prior and constituted the King within its signs, he set England apart from her own history and exposed her to a distinctly northern blast. For England, Scotland has become a cultural unit that, as other yet originary, cannot quite be approached yet must often be accommodated. Thus, in the early months of the Scottish Parliament the British government found itself shifting cautiously around disliked Scottish policies on student tuition, political asylum, and mad cow disease—to the degree that New Labour's Matthew Taylor lamented: "Devolution gave the people of Scotland the right to elect their own Parliament, not to redesign the political platform of their own party," and that there is occasional talk of a parliament for England—even of liberating the monarch (see McCracken-Flesher "Tartan Politics"; Crawford "The Crown"). To a degree, England bends to Scotland. Indeed for some Scots, England has lost its lure: "in a remarkable role reversal," a *Guardian* pundit noted, "England has become inferior."[48] Occulted within the sign, Scott's land north of the border may be learning to enjoy the luxury of noisy opposition and lively difference—a creative play that England, as dominant yet detoured, finds harder to accomplish.

So Prebble's misty-eyed romantic, who "clearly wished to believe that the spiritual nature of a Stuart . . . had been made manifest in the fat form of the landlord of Brighton Pavilion," was also a hard-handed cultural entrepreneur and national opportunist (Prebble, 18). Homi Bhabha points out that 'Whisky' Sisodia in Salman Rushdie's *Satanic Verses* poses England's postcolonial problem: "The trouble with the Engenglish is that their hiss hiss history happened overseas, so they dodo don't know what it means" (6). For Bhabha in 1994, "The Western metropole must confront its postcolonial history . . . as an indigenous or native narrative *internal to its national identity*" (6). But through the King's visit, by hoarding and deploying cultural capital in the form of narrative, Scott had fixed England as a place whose history had *always* been elsewhere and some other time. Remarkably, he had freed Scottish history to play through the sign as a tool to manipulate the future. In 1822, Scott was a creative user of a lively past—constantly cutting a deal for the "possible Scotland," always pushing his land toward tomorrow through the imbalance of the sign.

4

Performing Other/Wise

The Talisman and *Woodstock*

"Art thou still so much surprised . . . as to wonder that men
are not always what they seem?—Thou thyself—art thou
what thou seemest?"

In *The Fortunes of Nigel*, the Author embraced his role as manufacturer of
monetary and cultural capital. "If the capital sum which these volumes have
put into circulation be a very large one," the Author of Waverley notes, it has
drawn in many compatriots: "from honest Duncan the paper manufacturer,
to the most snivelling of printer's devils" (13). When the class- and money-
conscious Clutterbuck objects, "[t]his would be called the language of a cal-
ico-manufacturer," the Eidolon brings him back to the market of literature
with a bump: "I do say it, in spite of Adam Smith and his followers, that a
successful author is a productive labourer, and that his works constitute as
effectual a part of the public wealth, as that which is created by any other
manufactor."

By the mid-1820s, Scott had become the manufacturer who controlled the
market. The "Introduction" to *The Betrothed* (1825) embraces this moment.
"MINUTES OF SEDERUNT OF A GENERAL MEETING OF THE SHARE-HOLDERS DESIGN-
ING TO FORM A JOINT-STOCK COMPANY, UNITED FOR THE PURPOSE OF WRITING
AND PUBLISHING THE CLASS OF WORKS CALLED THE WAVERLEY NOVELS" reports
"the Eidolon, or image of the author . . . unanimously called to the chair"
by a house composed not of Scott's publishers and printers, but of his many
personae. "[A] valuable property . . . has accumulated under our common
labours," he notes (xxv). Now the company is ready to step up production:
Dousterswivel, here "the ingenious inventor of the great patent machine

erected at Groningen, where they put in raw hemp at one end, and take out
ruffled shirts at the other" "is of opinion, that at the expense of a little mech-
anism, some part of the labour of composing these novels might be saved by
the use of steam" (xxvii–xxviii).[1]

In 1823, Scott's excessive productivity evoked Clutterbuck-type remark.
A review in the *New Monthly Magazine* led with an epigraph from *Macbeth:*
"What! will the line stretch out to the crack of doom? / Another yet! a sev-
enth!" The writer complained that "[n]otwithstanding the amusement which
the 'Novels by the author of *Waverley*' afford in the perusal, the astounding
rapidity with which they succeed to each other gives—the *reviewer* at least,
something more to do than is absolutely pleasant. . . . yet the necessity of
reading whatever bears the signature, or rather the enigma, of their author, is
absolute" (Hayden, 272). Still, the reviewer finds that the volume of Scott's
work bears down criticism: "the popularity of our author exempts us from
the necessity of analytical criticism. *Quentin Durward* every body has read, or
every body will read" (278). Scott continues to rule the market for the *Gentleman's Magazine* in its review of *The Talisman* (1825). This reviewer throws
up his hands: "Inexhaustible in his resources, we have here another annual
offering. . . . Who shall attempt the '*wasteful and ridiculous excess*' of lauding
him whom the King delighteth to honour? whose fame reacheth from one
end of the civilized world to the other!" (July 1825: 40). Through a productivity that exceeds the pace of criticism, serves by its romantic historicism at
the King's visit and in the novels as the source of "culture," and is recognized
by monarchy, Scott stands outside and perhaps in control of a discourse both
literary and national.

Sarah Greene thought so. If Scott had achieved that sincerest form of
flattery, imitation, from the authors of *Pontefract Castle* and *Walladmor*,
in *Scotch Novel Reading; or, Modern Quackery. A Novel* Really *Founded on
Facts* (1824), Greene anonymously gifted him with parody.[2] Fennel, father
of a daughter addicted to Scott's novels, abjures the Author's excessive productivity: "when [Fennel] found works pouring on us like a torrent from
one fertile pen . . . merely for *gain*, his indignation at this, what he called
quackery . . . knew no bounds" (1:35). Scott's role as "the unknown" and his
persistence in coining texts to produce money are both attacked. Yet Green
insists through her characters that "[i]t is his imitators that I find most fault
with" (1:9). James Hogg serves as Scott's surrogate for criticism. Fennel
rehearses his daughter's entanglement with that author: "never shall I forget poor Alice, when first she heard of the Ettrick Shepherd! . . . her dis-
appointment when she read through the, to her, rueful description given
of this hard-faced Scotchman [in Lockhart's *Peter's Letters to his Kinsfolk*
(1819)]. . . . but when she found that the Ettrick Shepherd was named Hogg,
her grief was beyond all bounds" (1:10–11). Green identifies Scott as the

model for "Scotch Quackery," but she is reluctant to challenge "the Great Unknown" directly, perhaps preferring not to risk the revaluation such an encounter might entail for her own work.

So Green focuses on how Scott's writing has revalued the English. Alice Fennel, nineteen years old and vulnerable to literary reconstructions, "has read [all Scott's novels], or rather skimmed them over, merely to say she *has* read them; without understanding one-half of what she has perused, and scarce comprehending one word of a dialect with which they abound, but which she affects to use on all occasions, generally misapplying every word . . . but she tells her companions, with an air of consequence, that she never reads any other novels than *Walter Scott's*" (1:4–5). A big girl, Alice likes to figure as an "*elfin female page*" (1:15). With double anachronism—"this prolific writer dresses his females as he pleases, and has no regard to the . . . ugly features of the costume of the times he transports us back to"—and national confusion, Alice affects the dress of Annot Lyle from *A Legend of Montrose* (1:92). Worse, her subjection to the signs of Scottishness deforms her. Young Mr. Butler, a prospective suitor, "knew not what to make of her, as to her manner: her queer pronunciation of Scotch words he thought proceeded from a want of articulation, from a disagreeable impediment in her speech; and he wondered she had not been born dumb, for there was surely some great defect in her organs of speaking" (1:51). Scott's discourse usurped English speech and degraded even southern beauties in the process.

The swap between Scottish signs and English money is so complete as to be obvious, yet not changeable. "[A]bsolutely picking the pockets of an infatuated public, to the prejudice of many a meritorious English writer," the novels display their agenda to resituate wealth north of the border (1:35–36). They succeed because the public is "infatuated," investing in a currency much inflated against an insider-trading monopoly. A "Cabal" of Scottish "quacks," literary doctors with the responsibility to heal the British nation, are "filling their Scotch pouches, and laughing to see how easily John Bull is gulled" (1:6). Alice, "her own apartment . . . littered with Blackwood's Magazine, and the Edinburgh Review, &c., wherein she found the *puff direct* . . . given in surfeiting abundance to her favourite novel writers of North Britain, and the poets also of the land of cakes," cannot see that, "Alas! they make cakes of many a silly English reader, who neglects his own bards to read what he does not understand" (1:43–44). The exchange is not purely literary and it is entirely national.

Green hints at one result of the King's visit. But she also projects a fall in Scott's stock based on its circulation through an English market temporarily duped, yet from its size and strength likely to realign values and terms over time. Alice encounters a real Scotswoman. The draggled Lady McBane, with a daughter who, as the inverse to Alice, is trying to pass as English, corrects the market. She tells Alice: "ken ye not weel that 'tis aw a fable . . . ? Gang down o' your knees, and be thankfu' that ye were born what ye are . . . I am often left wi'out siller or bawbee; and ye English ha' muckle o' that, and gude gear beside" (1:220). England commands the money. Then Alice meets a Scottish soldier. Having suffered in foreign wars on Britain's behalf, he lacks an eye, a hand, and a foot. Falling in love with the disguised Englishman who enacts this hero—and who enjoys the full complement of limbs and organs—Alice voices a comment crucial to the Scott who dominates the market of signs, but may suffer an adjustment within it. "Such a creature," she thinks, "is only fit to be kept for fighting" (3:76–77). Against the hero, Butler, with his inherited wealth, easy manners, and who "never read one novel through in his whole life," the Scot suffers limited circulation (here, military) within British systems (1:74). Perhaps he can function only through a reduced set of Scottish signs—and ones that deform in their turn. The prospects for Scots in British markets are attractive at first, but equivalent play is no romance, and those signs that at first seduce the English eventually are twisted by context toward the grotesque.

In *The Talisman*, before the financial collapse that would make Green's comments seem prescient, Scott himself ponders this logical extension of Scottish circulation. Trading widely, for a moment dominating the market, Scots still may suffer devaluation. They likely will be revealed, even where valued, as novel in their difference—from an outside point of view, for their deformity. Here, Scott hopes there is an operative power in the necessity of the Scot as Other to England and to himself. In *Woodstock*, however, written as Scott's financial gains and, he worried, his reputation, evaporated with a tumbling market, Scott considers the possibility that all is circulation, the mere performance—never the reality—of worth.

If all value is contingent, but can seem grounded by the construction of a dominant term that hoards cultural or literary worth and serves as the site of money and the law, then Scott, by circulating and amassing signs, by suggesting himself as the site of excess and lack, by making phenomenal amounts of money, commanded the market. On the national level, if a unifying discourse is constructed and complicated by its differing enactments, and if the nation narrates itself against what it is not, in so doing constantly folding in otherness from the national margin, then a Scot can gain control of British discourse, and *The Talisman*'s Sir Kenneth can work King Richard's crusade. But since value arises through the sign, it is subject to collapse by differential play. So Sir Walter might be at once dominant and different, centered and marginalized, delimiting perhaps—as Green argues—but playful, and playful nonetheless unable to achieve meaningful Scottish worth. This may explain why, in 1825–26, before his financial difficulties, Scott began *Woodstock* as an interrogation of whether there is anything *but* play, performance, and constant shifting for Scots and their significations.

"Other" Scots in The Talisman

"give me the dress of a slave"

After the success of the King's visit, but with a looming sense of that visit's limitations and the problems it might encourage, *The Talisman* and *Woodstock* consider the Britishness of Scottishness.[3] In *The Talisman* (1825), Sir Kenneth maps the career of the Scottish soldier mocked by Green. The problem displaced into an uncontroversial time and location, Sir Kenneth serves in King Richard's train within the Crusading army. Like many a real Scottish soldier, he fights (all anachronisms notwithstanding) for a British cause abroad.[4] Unlike Smollett's Lismahago in 1771, or Green's descendant of Rob Roy, however, Kenneth does not seem to have suffered devaluing differentiation—at least, not visibly.[5] Lismahago's skull is patched and his shanks exploded; MacGregor lacks an assortment of parts. Yet Sir Kenneth manifests the idyllic vision of military Scottishness: "The Frank seemed a powerful man, built after the ancient Gothic cast of form, with light brown hair, which . . . was seen to curl thick and profusely over his head" (chapter 2). He has a "full and well-opened blue eye." "His nose was Grecian." Notably, he insists that he is "One of [Richard's] followers . . . for this expedition . . . and honoured in the service; but not born his subject, although a native of the island in which he reigns" (chapter 3). A lot is at stake: "If the King of England had not set forth to the Crusade till he was sovereign of Scotland, the crescent might, for me, and all true-hearted Scots, glimmer for ever on the walls of Zion" (chapter 3). Sir Kenneth maintains a nineteenth-century notion of "separate but equal" within Britain.

There is no equality in separateness, however. If terms find relative value in circulation with others, then valuation is founded not just by recognition but through differentiation. Moreover, when the game is national, dominant terms retain their apparent worth by insisting upon the otherness at their margins. In a British market, extended into colonial space, and with Scotland playing a role both colonial and postcolonial, nations, persons, and signs may strive to circulate as "the same," but commonly will figure as "Other." England may be haunted by the deconstructive possibility residing in the differentiation that establishes her dominance—a King commanding overbearing numbers of men, and looming from English myth, may find his constitution, physical and governmental, undermined by his conjunction with the otherness of Palestine, just as George IV may have found himself refigured by his circulation through Scotland—but England still dominates. To Richard, not just the Muslims, but his Christian allies stand beyond the boundaries that make up Englishness. Although Leopold of Austria mocks Richard as "this King of half an island—this grandson of a Norman bastard" (a figure founded in differentiation and thus unstable like all others), the Marquis of Montserrat acknowledges: "the three lions passant of England . . . are become lions at all points, and must take precedence of beast, fish, or fowl, or woe worth the gainstander" (chapter 11). Every term in circulation is Other to another, and constructs its own Others, but Richard and England dominate the system, forcing all terms not entirely similar beyond the margins.

So Kenneth may differentiate himself from the Muslims as rabidly as the English cohort, telling Saladin, "I well thought . . . that your blinded race had their descent from the foul fiend, without whose aid you would never have been able to maintain this blessed land of Palestine against so many valiant soldiers of God" (chapter 3). He may aspire to align himself with Richard through a marriage with Edith Plantagenet. Yet despite and because of his role as similar Scot, and because he is almost "equal," he will always function as Other for England—and thus stand subject to English systems. Indeed, Kenneth's assertion of common cause yet national separateness has led his English allies to stress in him that primary marker of otherness, bodily difference. Richard's right hand man, Sir Thomas de Vaux, cannot immediately identify Sir Kenneth, but can categorize him as "a Spaniard or a Scot" (chapter 7). Like the Christian Spaniard, Sir Kenneth can serve in the English cause, but like the racially distinct Spaniard, he cannot be considered English. For Sir Thomas, Kenneth verges away from Occidental and towards Oriental. Once located as Other, the Scot stands voiceless, deprived of his function as speaking subject. De Vaux's first instinct as an Englishman, and consequently one of the crusade's elite, is to pass by Kenneth without speaking to him (chapter 7). Given that Sir Kenneth turns out to be a Prince of Scotland, David, Earl of Huntingdon, serving anonymously in the crusading forces, Scott offers no optimistic picture of his contemporaries' operations within the Union.

Their subjection is to some degree the Scots' own fault. England may inevitably dominate, but the Scots are complicit. If Scott sought to insert Scottishness at the heart of Britishness during the King's visit, Kenneth has sought to animate the crusade from within. In this space, his power has diminished: his cohort have died, or left, to the point that, given England's greater numbers in the first place, he now stands as a mere follower within King Richard's camp. A more skeptical Other, Saladin, notes that in this role he easily may be confused with "subject"—Kenneth can serve within the narratives of Britishness, but will become Other than he is in so doing (chapter 3). Like Green's MacGregor, his revealed otherness arises in proportion to his services. In the text, as a reward for bringing to Richard a Saracen doctor (Saladin) who cures him of fever, Kenneth receives the task of guarding the English standard. But tempted away by the bogus hope of seeing his English ladylove—significantly another moment when he would equate himself to Englishness—his punishment is death. Sir Kenneth seems caught in the systems he sought to negotiate. Worse, condemned to execution, he covers himself with remorse, and submits to Richard's summary judgment. As Alexander Welsh notes, when Kenneth declares, "I have deserted my charge—the banner intrusted to me is lost—When the headsman and block are prepared, the head and trunk are ready to part company," "not only is Richard prepared to execute the hero, but the hero is prepared to die" (chapter 15; Welsh, 217). If Sir Kenneth sought to be equal but separate, his supposed separateness from things English makes him a sufferer under her equal law. Sir Kenneth has lost the power of self-determination under a system that differentiates him to a terminal degree. Through Sir Kenneth, Scott casts a critical light on nineteenth-century compatriots who sought the gains of Union but thereby subjected themselves to English power. Their service may render them grotesque, and could deprive them of the voice that enables it. Sir Kenneth seems a critique upon a Scott who played the market of British signs and now wonders how he has reconstructed himself and Scottishness in the process.

Scott stresses, in fact, that negotiating Scottish value through a foreign code achieves little honor for the Scottish subject. When Sir Kenneth worships before a fragment of the true cross at Engaddi, he conjures up two oddly substantial visions. A parade of veiled women circles the shrine. As they pass Sir Kenneth, one drops rosebuds at the knight's feet. This, Sir Kenneth acknowledges, is Edith Plantagenet, his one true love, and he forgets the true cross in order to worship—as befits a Scottish Other—speechlessly at her English feet. After this vision retires, another takes its place:

> a long skinny arm, partly naked, partly clothed in a sleeve of red samite, arose out of the aperture, holding a lamp. . . . The form and face of the being who thus presented himself, were those of a frightful dwarf, with a large head, a cap fantastically adorned . . . and a white silk sash, in which he wore a gold-hilted dagger. This singular figure had in his left hand a kind of broom. . . . [As] if to show himself more distinctly, [he] moved the lamp which he held slowly over his face and person, successively illuminating his wild and fantastic features, and his misshapen but nervous limbs. (chapter 5)

With his tawdry accoutrements and deformed body, the dwarf parodies knightly nobility, but when he displays to Sir Kenneth his red samite rags, his peacock feather *fleur de lys*, his trusty broom, he stresses his role as the Scottish knight's similitude. The Scot, functioning in an English army, can only be a thing showing grotesquely through the signs to which he has subjected himself. Scott goes further. When Nectabanus is followed from the depths by "his lady and his love," an equally deformed apparition named "Guenevra," Scott mocks both courtly romance and Kenneth's aspirations to Edith Plantagenet; an alliance between Englishwoman and Scot can occur only in Sir

Kenneth's dark dreams or in the bodies of these perverse representatives. Then, when Nectabanus lures Sir Kenneth from his post guarding the English standard to fulfill a supposed assignation with Edith, Scott brings into question Sir Kenneth's very commitment to the crusade he espouses. The dwarf demonstrates that Sir Kenneth makes only a deformed, an ineffective, and perhaps even an insincere knight—a knight with a self-serving agenda. For Scott, then, the Scotsman in part subjects himself to Englishness, but without much visible gain and at considerable risk. He will not accomplish the alliances he desires; he will prove derelict in his duties to his adopted system; and he will lose, or severely deform, what he is.

Thus, in *The Talisman* Scott maps the conditions and trajectories of Scottish involvement within the colonial dynamic. The Scot seeking to renegotiate personal and national relationships with England suffers within that nation's necessary differentiation of itself from other Others. But Scott also works a way around the inevitable devaluation even of those hoarding British cultural capital, such as Scotland. If any nation requires otherness to specify itself, then the national self depends for its energy on that otherness. With Scotland constituted as yet another "Other" to England as "self," Scott recognizes an opportunity to explore Scottish otherness as agency—a differentiating play for Scotland, and deconstructive difference, perhaps, for uninterrogated notions of Englishness.

When we meet Sir Kenneth, he rides by the Dead Sea, an almost anonymous knight. Years of blows suffered in the crusade have blurred his heraldic device. Moreover, the design that looms uncertainly from his shield is that of a couchant leopard, underwritten by the words, "I sleep—wake me not" (chapter 1). As a Scot, Sir Kenneth sleeps, with the result that his identity has been practically obliterated. His value is obscured. Scott, however, begins to wake the Sleeping Leopard. He starts the long process of Sir Kenneth's re-education as a speaking Scot by confronting him with Saladin. This most alien of Others can teach the Scottish knight neither to hide his otherness, nor to accept its silencing through English systems, but to embrace it and to use it—to voice himself across it.

In the heart of the land, at a fountain of clarity and truth called "The Diamond of the Desert," Sir Kenneth meets Saladin (here Sheerkohf, the warrior; later El Hakim, the doctor). As a Scot in the matrix of England, and a soldier in the crusades, Sir Kenneth has studied to suppress difference in himself and in Palestine, so now, not surprisingly, he fails at first to recognize his kinship with this epitome of otherness: the two men do battle before becoming friends. But once Scott has established the friendship between Kenneth and Sheerkohf, he aligns his characters. Each fights well in battle, rides a horse perfect for him, eats appropriately to his needs, is sincere in his religion, respects women. For Bruce Beiderwell, they are "the two best representatives of their respective cultures' virtues" (85). Yet in every case,

Scot and Saracen also are distinguished from one another. Kenneth appears the perfect type of a soldier—from the North. "His form was tall, powerful, and athletic. . . . His hands . . . were long, fair, and well-proportioned . . . the arms remarkably well-shaped and brawny. A military hardihood, and careless frankness of expression, characterized his language and his motions" (chapter 2). Sheerkohf perfectly represents the warrior—from the Middle East. "His slender limbs, and long spare hands and arms, though well proportioned to his person, and suited to the style of his countenance, did not at first aspect promise the display of vigour and elasticity which the Emir had lately exhibited. But, on looking more closely, his limbs . . . seemed divested of all that was fleshy or cumbersome; so that nothing being left but bone, brawn, and sinew, it was a frame fitted for exertion and fatigue" (chapter 2). The men, although similar, are not the same; their every similitude comprises a difference. Kenneth and Saladin are the same only insofar as they are systematically different; they are brothers in their otherness.

As the more racially and geographically distinct of the two warriors, and consequently as the more unremitting and necessarily self-accepting Other, Saladin has a series of lessons to teach Sir Kenneth. First, he demonstrates that if one is delineated by dominant powers as inevitably and inalienably different, the best strategy may be not to resist or repine about one's designation, but to use it. Just as Sir Thomas de Vaux could not distinguish a Scot from a Spaniard, neither can the invaders individualize middle-eastern Muslims. Sir Kenneth himself takes Sheerkohf/Saladin for an Arab, and stands corrected: "I am no Arab. . . . I am Sheerkohf, the Lion of the Mountain . . . Kurdistan, from which I derive my descent, holds no family more noble than that of Seljook" (chapter 3). Yet far from being subjected by his erasure, Saladin turns it to his advantage. If his body renders him indistinguishable from the Arabs, and effectively invisible to the crusaders, then he can play different roles without drawing attention to himself. Thus, in the course of the novel, Saladin appears as the warrior Sheerkohf, then as the physician El Hakim, and only at last as himself. In these roles he negotiates a treaty, cures King Richard, and sets the Crusading camp to rights. Saladin transforms his bodily difference and its accompanying erasure into mutability and mobility; he uses his body like a cloak of invisibility under cover of which he can direct the course of events.

Second, Saladin shows that there are advantages in accepting one's otherness. Sir Kenneth asserts his distinctiveness, but does not live up to it, instead subjecting himself to English codes, and the more he insists on his similarity, the more he is exiled into difference; Saladin embraces the otherness in himself. Most obviously, he acts in the apparently exclusive capacities of warrior and doctor. As he explains to Sir Kenneth, the roles are necessary—if opposite—elements in the multiplicity that constitutes the complete man: "an accomplished cavalier should know how to dress his steed as well as how to ride him; how to forge his sword upon the stithy, as well as how to use it in battle; how to burnish his arms, as well as how to wear them; and, above all, how to cure wounds as well as how to inflict them" (chapter 23). As this complete man, Saladin manages both to kill crusaders and to cure their leader, in each case directing events toward a treaty in the Saracens' favor. One's own otherness, once embraced, places at a disadvantage those who, like Richard, focus on too narrow a personal and national self. It energizes a self never separate, but more playful and dangerous than merely "equal."

Third, Saladin reveals that one can use not just the otherness in oneself, but the principle of otherness. King Richard cannot moderate his Englishness even so far as to negotiate with his allies. When Scott first introduces the king, he notes that the crusade is already in decline because of "the jealousies of the Christian princes . . . and the offence taken by them at the uncurbed haughtiness of the English monarch, and Richard's unveiled contempt for his brother sovereigns" (chapter 6). By contrast, Saladin embraces even the otherness of death. As a doctor, he acknowledges death and gains the power of life; as a ruler, he accepts his own death, and thus uses his power more advisedly and effectively. In his tent, Saladin reclines under a spear, a shroud, and a banner that proclaims his power and its transience. It reads: "SALADIN, KING OF KINGS—SALADIN, VICTOR OF VICTORS—SALADIN MUST DIE" (chapter 28). Saladin brings this awareness to play in his closing scene with Richard. He hosts for Richard the tournament in which Sir Kenneth disciplines the real thief of the English standard, and afterwards he himself disciplines the Crusade's conspirators. In the celebrations that follow, not recognizing the possibility of death, Richard challenges Saladin to a duel for Jerusalem or, failing that, a friendly bout in the lists. He wishes a competition that would make otherness visible, easy—or that might simply end it. Saladin refuses: "The master places the shepherd over the flock, not for the shepherd's own sake, but for the sake of the sheep. Had I a son to hold the sceptre when I fell, I might have had the liberty, as I have the will, to brave this bold encounter; but your own Scripture sayeth, that when the herdsman is smitten, the sheep are scattered" (chapter 28). The ruler, in the knowledge of death, must preserve himself as the agent for his people. So Saladin lives in death's shadow, and works with it; he realizes that death comes even to kings, but on his awareness he builds careful action. He derives his power from accepting what others fear or—in Richard's case—lack the sense to fear.

Finally, if Saladin shows how to turn otherness into agency, he also demonstrates how to convert its forced silence into speech. Scott's novels strive to make Scottishness speak within a British discourse. At George IV's visit, it looked as if Scottishness, and Scott himself, might even control that discourse. But within a British context—or any context—such control can only be of the moment. What is more, its achievement typically produces a reaction—for instance, one where critic after English critic calls on Scott to stop producing novels at such a rate, and novels of Scottishness in particular. Ultimately, the voice of politics, money, and monarchy reasserts itself. So in this text Richard, as English monarch, fully enjoys the right and the power of speech; his loud voice echoes around the camp. In fact, Richard's speech risks fragmenting the crusading alliance—it unavoidably others even England's friends. Richard's words are too powerful; he constantly must call them back. He cajoles his offended royal brothers, "Richard is a soldier— his hand is ever readier than his tongue, and his tongue is but too much used to the rough language of his trade. But do not . . . throw away earthly renown and eternal salvation . . . because the act of a soldier may have been hasty, and his speech as hard as the iron which he has worn from childhood" (chapter 19). Apologizing for his dominance by self-deprecatingly allying his word with his sword, Richard hints at the terms of his power, and once more establishes it. The word of English governance, even when retracted, always asserts control.

Saladin acknowledges this when Richard declares, in response to pleas from his women and from Kenneth's confessor that the delinquent knight's life be spared: "Ladies and priest, withdraw, if ye would not hear orders which would displease you; for, by Saint George, I swear—." "Swear Not!" Saladin intervenes (chapter 17). A word of kingly power must not be lightly uttered, for it governs value and changes realities. Kenneth's word has no power; he serves as a vehicle for the crusading voice and cannot speak even his own name, David, Earl of Huntingdon. By contrast, Saladin enjoys the power of speech. If Saladin is overborne by crusading voices, he has not, nonetheless, given up his own culture's modes of speech. At different points in the story he speaks as warrior, doctor, and even muezzin. Furthermore, he has found ways to speak as ruler within his own system: he has but to imply a sign to accomplish real power. He tells Sir Kenneth: "When I send one [eagle-feathered arrow] to my tents, a thousand warriors mount on horse-back—when I send another, an equal force will arise—for the five, I can command five thousand men; and if I send my bow, ten thousand mounted riders will shake the desert" (chapter 3). Saladin's speech is so powerful, he does not have to open his mouth. But if Saladin has found alternate forms of speech, unlike the garrulous Richard, he understands the power of not speaking. When Richard challenges him to fight, Saladin withholds consent. First, he refuses the challenge because he already holds Jerusalem, and would stand only to lose in the encounter. Second, he refuses the contest because, Other though he may be, he can yet resist the lure of inclusion in the dominant culture that lies behind Richard's invitation to participate in the discourse of English chivalry. It is not, then, that Saladin cannot say yes, but that he will not say so. Saladin demonstrates how to assess a situation dispassionately, and how to take control of it; he shows how to exercise and assume power by remaining silent, remaining Other.

Sir Kenneth makes no promising pupil. Insisting on separateness, he oddly refuses to recognize his otherness, holding instead to an English culture that rejects him. On the one hand, he claims similarity to his fellow knights—against even their indications to the contrary. Despite being constantly othered by crusaders like Thomas de Vaux, Kenneth constitutes his body as English when he subordinates it to Richard's punishment. Then, saved from death by Saladin, he resists the knowledge that the Templars they meet will certainly slaughter him along with the Saracens; he mis/recognizes them as "my comrades in arms—the men in whose society I have vowed to fight or fall," and has to be forced to flee men who epitomize his adoptive code of honor, but do not adhere to it (chapter 22). On the other hand, Kenneth maintains that he cannot be compared with the Saracens. When he meets Saladin his instinct is to fight him. Later, though saved by Saladin, Kenneth churlishly rejects even hospitality as a dishonor. For him, as for the crusaders, the Saracen seems immutably and negatively Other. Saladin has suggested that: "Man is not . . . bound to one spot of earth. . . . Thine own Christian writings command thee, when persecuted in one city, to flee to another; and we Moslem also know that Mohammed . . . driven forth from the holy city of Mecca, found his refuge and his helpmates at Medina" (chapter 14). But Kenneth sneers: "I might indeed hide my dishonour . . . in a camp of infidel heathens where the very phrase is unknown. But had I not better partake more fully in their reproach? Does not thy advice stretch so far as to recommend me to take the turban?" Kenneth is so committed to finding his meaning within the Crusade, he cannot accept a brotherhood based on the Scot's and the Saracen's differentiating otherness. Small wonder that Saladin has to drag him first from the camp, and then from the Templars, to initiate his recuperation as Scottish Other and Saracen brother.

In the course of *The Talisman*, however, Saladin does help Sir Kenneth to embrace his otherness. The Saracen Other who is yet a brother teaches the Scottish knight not simply to succumb to or adopt the crusading culture's view of the world, but rather to act expediently, across his othered body; he shows him how to speak across silence. In the depths of his despair, Kenneth asserts that rather than become a Muslim, he would wish "that my writhen features should blacken, as they are like to do, in this evening's setting sun" (chapter 14). Saladin recognizes in this death wish an opportunity to separate Sir Kenneth from his false brothers, and to connect him with his otherness; thus he transforms the Scottish knight into a Nubian slave. Judith Wilt considers Kenneth's transformation "one final humiliation," but Scott makes clear that it is not loss, but gain of identity that is at stake (Wilt, 182). Saladin stresses that in this black body, "not thy brother in arms—not thy brother in blood—shall discover thee" (chapter 23). Kenneth will be separated by the barrier of his racially distinct body from his false brothers; what is more, in this othered body, he will finally attain agency, even equality—he will be able to explain the events surrounding the theft of the standard. All he has to do is accept himself as Other, and model his behavior on that of his brother. As Saladin tells him: "Thou hast seen me do matters more difficult—he that can call the dying from the darkness of the shadow of death, can easily cast a mist before the eyes of the living" (chapter 23).

But in this backened body, Kenneth will be voiceless. His blackness will render him thoroughly Other, and as such, he will become functionally invisible—for all intents and purposes, mute. Moreover, Saladin insists that as Nubian slave, Kenneth lacks not just the ability to make himself heard, but also the basic power to articulate. Sir Kenneth, of course, has been subsiding into voicelessness in the course of the text, but now Saladin offers him an opportunity to influence events and achieve identity once more. All he must do is voice himself out of the silence of subjection by means of that which renders him most visibly subject, his othered body. This he accomplishes. With a certain ingenuity, Kenneth communicates in writing, and with the help of man's best friend, his dog Roswal. However, it is his body that initiates the train of events leading to the discovery of the thief and to his own recuperation as a distinct, Scottish entity. A Marabout makes an attempt on Richard's life; Kenneth, in his role as slave, sees the fanatic approach mirrored in the shield he is cleaning, and aborts the attack, but in the scuffle, he sustains a possibly poisoned flesh wound. Predictably, Richard's courtiers refuse to suck the poison from such a visible Other—no matter that his actions have served their purpose, and what they may cost him. Long Allen protests, "methinks I would not die like a poisoned rat for the sake of a black chattel there, that is bought and sold in a market like a Martelmas ox" (chapter 21). But when Richard himself sucks the poison, he sucks away some of Kenneth's black dye, and realizes this is no Nubian, but some other Other— perhaps, learning Saladin's lesson, even to him a sort of brother. Of course Richard, as prime mover in the dominant culture, cannot yet quite grasp Sir Kenneth's situation. After the tournament wherein Sir Kenneth has begun the rout of evil, and re-established himself as Scot, Richard opines: "thou hast shown that the Ethiopian *may* change his skin, and the leopard his spots" (chapter 28). However, Kenneth has not so much changed his skin and his spots, as acknowledged them and learned to use them. Sleeping no longer, and speaking loudly through his (Scottish) knightly body, he is now, truly, the "Knight of the Leopard" (chapter 28).

According to *The Talisman*, then, the Scot in the matrix of England has two obvious options: like the early Sir Kenneth, he can accept his subjection, and effectively die as a distinct self, or, like the Marabout who is mirrored in Richard's shield as Kenneth's inverse, he can openly resist, and be completely othered. But Scott recommends Saladin's more creative strategy. Saladin teaches Kenneth to accept his otherness, and thus neither to reject the boundary between himself and the crusaders, nor to transgress it. Indeed,

Saladin insists on delineating boundaries clearly: he lives under the sign of death; he welcomes Richard to his camp with a shower of arrows that demarcates the English monarch's acceptable space—if the crusaders exceed the room Saladin allows them, they risk dying; and even to Kenneth, to whom he claims he is a brother, Saladin presents himself not as slavemaster, or physician, or friend, but "as your ancient foe . . . a fair and generous one" (chapters 22 and 23). Why all this emphasis on recognizing one's difference? First, as Saladin stresses to Sir Kenneth, "Knowledge is the parent of power" (chapter 14). To him, difference realized constitutes the subjected Other's only locus for agency; bodies and boundaries are to be recognized for what they are—and used. Second, if Others can honor one another for their difference, they can truly become br/others; they can multiply their agency across their varied bodies. And, as Scott demonstrates in his novel, the strategy works. Through his br/other Kenneth, Saladin manages to negotiate a treaty with Richard; through his br/other Saladin, Kenneth manages to operate within the crusading system without sacrificing his identity. The knight who first appeared with arms effaced now blazons forth on his shield a leopard with collar and broken chain; Scots can circulate with and as a *différance*.

The Performance of Woodstock

"thy nation so easily entertains suspicion, that it may well
render themselves suspected"

Woodstock suggests that it is hard for the Scottish author, or his tales, to circulate as different enough. Or rather, perhaps they merely circulate. Perhaps no national effects are possible in a circumstance where all signs are equivalent, but English signs are "more equal" than others. This may be the argument of *Woodstock*.

In 1825, as he began the novel, Scott maintained his high place in British letters. Constable had offered "£2000 for a six-volume edition of his miscellaneous prose writings" and contemplated a *Miscellany*, "a great national work" in which the Waverley novels would figure prominently (Johnson, 2:895; 942). When his London partner objected to undermining the sales of current Scott inventory, Constable fielded the idea of a sumptuously produced, "New Edition" (2:942; Scott, *Journal*, 57). "The book trade," Johnson sums up, "was thriving as never before" (2:948). That trade, however, depended on the circulation of specie, as well as books. And in January 1826, the bottom fell out of the money and thus the literary markets.

It is tempting to read *Woodstock* (1826) from the perspective of Scott's fall. The author's finances, already entangled with Constable's through his printing and publishing concerns, were drawn into an English circulation specifically devaluative through Constable's links to London publishing houses. Abbotsford stood at risk, much like Woodstock under the encroachments of Cromwell's Commissioners. Scott worried that his reputation was in ruins—and in *Woodstock*, the space that is the site of history and fiction is partially destroyed by its intersection with the present moment. It is easy to see Scott's antiquarian fancies and playful telling exploded in the collapse of money markets and one of the towers whereby fair Rosamund, secluded like the Author of Waverley, kept her illicit, nation-shifting trysts with an English monarch of long ago (Sroka, 190). But the novel was into production before Scott's lesson in how money underpins and makes a mockery of all other types of valuation. Through *Woodstock*, then, we see Scott anticipating in literature the problems of maintaining worth that he was about to encounter in life.

Scott's consideration and practice of the intertwined economics of literary and national construction here moves beyond early and perhaps idealized investments in occulted telling, conflicting tales, and differential tellers. Having achieved momentary control of markets both literary and national at the King's visit, having managed in *The Talisman* to deploy as energizing principle the inevitable othering of a Scottish subject within a British context, Scott here begins to recognize, and no longer in a positive way, the contingency of valuation. On 1 January 1826, when his imminent financial collapse still seemed "troublesome pecuniary difficulties which however I think this week should end," Scott pondered the difficulty of effecting change:

> the whole human frame in all its parts and divisions is gradually in the act of decaying and renewing. What a curious time-piece it would be that could indicate to us the moment this gradual and insensible change had so completely taken place that no atom was left of the original person who had existed at a certain period but there existed in his stead another person having the same limbs thewes and sinews, the same face and lineaments, the same consciousness—a new ship built on an old plank. . . . Singular—to be at once another and the same. (*Journal*, 63)

Singular—to change so much, and be so little different. In the context of the novels, distressing to perform difference so persistently, but maybe accomplish little.

Woodstock foregrounds the problem of difference as performance within the dynamic of national valuation. To stabilize value we insist upon a transcendent term that seems to govern the play of equivalents and to set worth, but such terms are still only signs. Value is transient and circulation is constant. Moreover, although the nation seems to determine meaning, it asserts itself against what it establishes as its margins. Those margins are implicitly acknowledged and effectively folded into the culture such that they open a margin in the middle. While the culture is thus shifted, the change is not permanent—for shifting is ongoing. There will always be new margins and thus new constructions of the nation. Therefore, Scott's opportunity to fold in otherness is necessarily and problematically recurrent. Scotland must keep performing itself. And since performance is ongoing, its effectiveness is questionable. On 18 December 1825, with disaster looming, yet perhaps still avoidable, Scott confided to his journal: "Once more, 'Patience cousin and shuffle the cards'" (49). What if a Scott in search of national and personal valuation could merely shuffle, then reshuffle, and only shuffle again the cards?

It is this possibility that disturbed *Woodstock*'s critics. *Woodstock*, an unusual number of Scott's critics agree, is a flawed text. Even Scott's supportive contemporaries found themselves at a loss when confronted by its lapses. So much so that many reviewers chose not to critique the novel, but merely to repeat it. Typical is the reviewer for the *Literary Chronicle*: "A long introduction to an account of a new work by the author of Waverley would be as tantalizing to novel readers, as a tedious grace to a gourmand as a prelude to a corporation feast. . . . We purposely abstain from criticism . . . confident that, to the public at large, every line not appropriated to an analysis of the work will be thought unnecessary."[6] Yet this was a different avoidance from that practiced by Sarah Green. The reviewer serving the *Westminster Review* begins: "It was in an evil hour that the author of Waverley left the ground on which he had moved with the ease of a person perfectly at home, and betook himself to English history" (5 [January–April 1826]: 399–457; 399). Scott has produced a tale "in which there is but little nature of any kind, little spirit, scarcely any feeling, and no historical truth" (400). Specifically, the reviewer accuses *Woodstock* of gross unfaithfulness to the events and persons of history. But reserved for special opprobrium are its pseudo-supernatural events: "The proper comment upon the whole story [of the supernatural] is implied in Cromwell's brief exclamation on detecting the miserable machinery that had been employed [to hide the putative Charles II from Parliamentary Commissioners],—'The simple fools!'" (409). Notably too, the sound-map of the tale receives a drubbing normally reserved for matters of content. The reviewer dislikes both the emulation and the quotation of Shakespeare, and abjures the use of Shakespeare by characters incapable of his greatness: "Shakspeare has occasionally been found a bore upon the stage, when abused by a dull performer; but who would have imagined it possible he should become one in the hands of the Author of Waverley" (418). He closes with a withering sarcasm that brings together the grounds of his critique: "Such is an HISTORICAL romance, by the author of Waverley" (457). The great historical novelist Walter Scott has produced a romance that is a resounding failure for its lack of historical accuracy and for its flawed performance of history through Radcliffean terrors and pseudo-Shakespearean overwriting. It is a bit of an embarrassment.

Neither Scott's supporters nor his detractors have any problem tracing the cause of his depleted genius. With the benefit of a hindsight that makes public Scott's financial embarrassment, the reviewer for the *Dublin and London Magazine* set a lasting critical discourse: "Sir Walter appears to be satiated with fame, and writes now, perhaps, only for profit" (June 1826: 271). His colleague in the *London Magazine* offers much the same interpretation, only in more picturesque terms: "There is a stratagem in old-clothes dealing called *duffing*. The practitioner—as we learn from those fountains of polite knowledge, the Police Reports—raises the scanty nap of a veteran garment, gives it a gloss with some preparation, and passes it off as new. Sir Walter Scott has taken to *duffing* in the novel trade" (June 1826: 173–81; 173). This reviewer ends: "Sir Walter should remember the fate of his own Hayraddin Maugrabin [in *Quentin Durward*], who played the Herald, and playing it ill, was found out and hanged" (181). The critics have laid Scott's apparent literary decline, his ramshackle performance in *Woodstock*, at the door of his recently public financial need.

Scott's early detractors all are quite correct. *Woodstock* is replete with historical error and stylistic infelicity. Furthermore, those false notes break the illusion of art; they point toward the fact of the text as performance, and to the inadequate herald who produces it. And these problems evolved under Scott's financial difficulties. After all, if *Woodstock* was begun before Scott's crash, it was produced while it loomed, and was finished after the fall. On 12 February 1826, Scott wrote in his journal: "Having ended the Second Vol of *Woodstock* last night I have to begin the Third this morning. Now I have not the slightest idea how the story is to be wound up to a catastrophe" (100).

However, *Woodstock*'s infelicities are not the product of a martyred intellect, as Scott's sympathetic editor, Andrew Lang, suggested.[7] Nor do they result from an uncritical mapping between Scott's circumstances and his text, as Philip Hobsbaum has insisted.[8] We know that the novel's supposed flaws arise in the face of what was by now a generation of criticism telling Scott to avoid Radcliffean supernaturalism and excessive plot machinery.[9] The critic for the *Westminster Review* understands that Scott knows better: "Deference to the understood taste of novel-readers, for it is not to be supposed that the great author himself has any pleasure in these frivolities, has disfigured most of his romances with some piece of idle mystery or of intricate machinery" (409). Scott himself had abjured such theatrics in his introductory chapter to his very first novel, *Waverley*. Now, the *Panoramic Miscellany* observed: "Sir Walter . . . suffers the author, more and more, to shine thro' the character; and the opinions and purposes of the writer become, occasionally, too nakedly apparent" (30 June 1826: 811–12). Precisely. Through *Woodstock*, Scott exposed the creaking machinery of text as problematic cultural performance—the machinery within which he, as Author of Waverley, the god in the machine, so long had lived.

This becomes clear in Scott's preface. Given the role of previous examples, the preface in *Woodstock* should serve as a guide for what follows. How does this one compare? Usually, Scott dramatizes his putative narrator here; in *Woodstock*, the narrator remains undramatized. Scott's narrators commonly assert the provenance of the tale they will tell; this narrator offers a history that calls the tale into question: "It is not my purpose to inform my readers how the manuscripts of that eminent antiquary, the Rev. J. A. ROCHECLIFFE, D. D., came into my possession" (1: Preface).[10] The speaker recommends these documents in solipsistic fashion: "As for the authenticity of the anecdotes which I have gleaned from the writings of this excellent person, and put together with my own unrivalled facility, the name of Doctor Rochecliffe will warrant accuracy, wherever that name happens to be known." What follows in a supposed attempt to establish the fictional and thus unknowable Rochecliffe's credibility merely compromises him further—Rochecliffe's "*Malleus Haeresis*, was considered as a knock-down blow by all except those who received it," and the doctor's reputation in the Royal Society rests on an experiment in which he was proved egregiously wrong. So it is highly ironic when the narrator concludes: "It is . . . to little purpose for me to strain my memory about ancient and imperfect recollections concerning the particulars of these fantastic disturbances at Woodstock, since Doctor Rochecliffe's papers give such a much more accurate narrative than could be obtained from any account in existence before their publication." Obviously, Scott's focus is on the process of narration, the circulations of story, and on the uncertain performance it entails.

Scott's concern is the more visible when we consider that he embeds prefatory matter to the same effect within his text. Ambushing any reader who, like Miss Primrose in the *Literary Coterie*'s parody of a perplexed *Woodstock* audience, "never read[s] prefaces; [for] not one in ten repays the trouble," Scott's narrator begins assertively (3rd S., 7 [June 1826]: 346). "There is a handsome parish church in the town of Woodstock," he declares; yet this certainty dwindles away as he adds: "I am told so, at least, for I never saw it" (1:1). Then the narrator cites a source for his description: "I had the church accurately described to me, with a view to this work." Again, he undercuts his supposed knowledge, this time with a Shandean flourish: "I have some reason to doubt whether my informant had ever seen the inside of it himself."[11] His description thoroughly compromised, he nonetheless proceeds to give it in some detail. Once more, Scott's aim seems not to provide a seamless narration, but to import into his text questions of its own construction.

The "Introduction" for the 1832 Magnum edition continues to dwell on textual performance as problem. Here, if anywhere, Scott could be assumed to give the data on which his tale is based. But while he offers sources, he stresses that some are unreliable, and others unobtainable. Most tellingly, he repeats the story of an exploding shrub that his narrator recounted in the preface's reference to the "bow-pot." Then he gives a comment that can only be tongue in cheek: "Nothing, indeed, is more certain, than that incidents which are real, preserve an infinite advantage in works of this nature over such as are fictitious. The tree, however, must remain where it has fallen." The fictive performance will remain unaltered. So it seems that Scott is largely self-conscious regarding his tale's construction, and that its construction is its theme. Thus, Scott's success, rather than his failure, can be tabulated according to the degree to which critics chide him for his inaccuracy, and expect that what is fictional should somehow be "real" and at the same time seamless. The critics respond to Scott's tissue of fabrication, while remaining unaware of its inherent critique—they are uncomfortably subject to a virtuoso performance of performance.

Throughout *Woodstock*, Scott foregrounds his concern that all tales and modes of telling, all truth or fiction, can achieve nothing more than clunky and temporary performance. His treatment of Charles brings this home. In the novel, Charles—yet to be II—appears at Woodstock on the run. Here, he participates in supernatural manifestations designed to terrorize his pursuers. Meanwhile, the English Lees protect him by substituting for a monarch revealed through his camouflaging but often disturbingly real performances as raw Scot or sexual predator. Repeatedly, Scott's reviewers abjured his dramatization of the monarch. The *Westminster Review*'s critic chided: "The real Charles . . . is in every respect so different a person from the author of Waverley's Charles, that it is exactly as if the attention were claimed by a new character abruptly intruded upon us in place of the old one" (428). That, however, is precisely Scott's point. His Charles, above all, stands forth as performance, and thus makes clear the impossibility of literary "reality."

In the course of the novel, Charles circulates in three roles: he plays a gypsy woman, then a face at the window, and finally Louis Kerneguy—he figures as everyone but "himself." And Scott exposes the problems in each of these equivalences. Through his performance as gypsy, Charles is figured as a "denaturalized [woman]," one whose class "with open profligacy and profanity . . . [or] the fraudful tone of fanaticism or hypocrisy, exercised . . . their talents for murder or plunder" (1:18). How very "denaturalized" he is becomes clear when, in the ill-fitting garb of ancient gypsy-woman, he flirts with Alice Lee. Further, in his appearance as face at the window, he neither originates the role nor plays a part of any great stature. He reprises a performance that the louche cavalier Wildrake, now masquerading as Parliament man, learned "from a French player, who could twist his jaws into a pair of nut-crackers," and has acted to the terror of Cromwell's Commissioners (1:5). Finally, in Louis Kerneguy, Charles shows himself not just as a

Scot, but as a distinctly stagy and unattractive one. With his tousled red wig, boorish manners, and coarse accent, the King of Scotland performs himself according to English conventions as Scottish untouchable.

Scott's problematizing of the King does not stop here, however. Charles's performances are not only inappropriate, and reflect badly on the figure of the king, they are also inadequate. Albert Lee points out that "there is a medium, if one could find it . . . so this morning, when you were in the woman's dress, you raised your petticoats rather unbecomingly high, as you waded through the first little stream; and when I told you of it, to mend the matter, you drag-gled through the next without raising them at all" (2:3/chapter 21). Of the King's performance as Scot, he comments, "your dialect [is] somewhat too coarse for a Scottish youth of high birth, and your behaviour perhaps a little too churlish." Charles's response on both counts proves disturbing. To the first he declares, unrepentantly: "I was a libel on womanhood." The young King of Scotland's response to the second, however, reflects not so much on his role-playing, as on his role as king. He counters Albert Lee's suggestion that "some of your Scottish sounded as if it were not genuine":

> Not genuine? . . . Why, who should speak genuine Scottish but myself?—Was I not their King for a matter of ten months? and if I did not get knowledge of their language, I wonder what else I got by it. Did not east country, and south country, and west country, and Highlands, caw, croak, and shriek about me, as the deep guttural, the broad drawl, and the high sharp yelp predominated by turns?—Oddsfish, man, have I not been speeched at by their orators, addressed by their senators, rebuked by their kirkmen? Have I not sat on the cutty stool, mon . . . and wilt thou tell me, after all, that I cannot speak Scottish enough to baffle an Oxon knight and his family?

Thus when subsequently, for his hosts' entertainment, Charles imitates and mocks his Scottish subjects, the proto-Jacobite monarch reveals the Scot who is supposed to give meaning to his subjects as a problematic performer—and only a performer—of Scottishness.

Yet all of these are mere roles. What matters, surely, is the reality of the king, the core of kingly truth that the role-playing protects or that Scott, as the moment's literary and cultural site of Scottish circulation and valu-ation, allows. The problem here, however, is that such truth does not reside in Charles. Scott demonstrates not Charles's greatness of soul as king, but his ability to put on the king. When Charles's motives regarding Alice Lee are justly suspected by her brother, the monarch icily responds: "And what does Colonel Albert Lee hope? . . . *I hope* that Colonel Lee does not see in a silly jest any thing offensive to the honour of his family, since methinks that were an indifferent compliment to his sister, his father, and himself, not to mention Charles Stewart, whom he calls his King" (2:3/chapter 21). Charles constantly constructs himself, even as King, according to his audience. In addition, when he considers once more the possibility of a liaison with Alice, he rejects it not as unworthy but because it would end in the wrong kind of stage production. It would lead not to the pageantry of Restoration, rather to a reprise of his father's last appearance before a London audience. He ponders: "The risk of reopening the fatal window at Whitehall, and renewing the tragedy of the Man in the Mask . . . and lovely though Alice Lee is, I cannot afford to intrigue at such a hazard" (2:5/chapter 23). In Charles, kingship— and perhaps Scott's role as the site of Scottish signification—stands revealed as mere performance.

Alice Lee gives the final twist to Scott's implication that there is a fundamental lack at the center of all performances of Scottishness. Unaware of the plainly inadequate monarch standing before her—who dishonorably listens to her sing his praises—Alice waxes lyrical.

> "I will try to paint an Alexander, such as I hope, and am determined to believe, exists in the person of our exiled sovereign, soon I trust to be restored. . . . He shall have all the chivalrous courage, all the warlike skill, of Henry of France, his grandfather. . . .
>
> "For the man . . . need I wish him more than the paternal virtues of his unhappy father. . . . Temperate, wise, and frugal, yet munificent in rewarding merit—a friend to letters and the muses, but a severe discourager of the misuse of such gifts—a worthy gentleman—a kind master—the best friend, the best father, the best Christian"— (1:4/chapter 22)

No king true to Alice's depiction exists, even at the heart of Charles's performance of himself. In Scott's circumstance as national author, the determinative Sign is a fraud upon Scotland, and her valuation thereby an impossibility.

So in *Woodstock*, Scott manifests the authoritative signification of Scottishness as an extremely obscure object of desire. Kingship is pointed to, as much as it is hidden, by the performances of the old gypsy, Louis Kerneguy, and their like, but it is unobtainable, even when grasped. The monarch, figured as love object within Rosamund's tower, upon his capture proves to be Albert Lee. In a chapter of confusions, Albert climbs the tower called Love's Ladder, but leaps to Rosamund's tower just before Love's Ladder is demolished. His leap topples a soldier from Rosamund's tower, who falls before and is buried by Love's Ladder. That soldier is mistaken for Charles in the moments before Charles/Albert is discovered (2:16, 17/chapters 34, 35). Neither can Albert Lee, that good, dull servant of monarchy be held as a marker for the King. Cromwell releases him only so he may fade to death at

Dunkirk, in a European war that featured English participants on both sides. Through such multi-layered and problematic performances of the king, Scott suggests that Scottishness, even in the proto-Jacobite Charles and certainly through the Eidolon or Author of Waverley, can only ever be a product of theatrics.

Scott drives home his point that Scotland subsists only in performance, and that nothing exists save performance, through those of his textual elements most subject to critique: his secondary characters, his style, and his plot mechanics. Nowhere in *Woodstock* can the reader lay hold of history; nowhere can s/he grasp unmediated truth, Scottish or English. For instance, the King is only *Woodstock*'s central performer. Albert Lee performs as monarch; Wildrake masquerades as Parliament man; Rochecliffe appears as his ghostly alter ego. Furthermore, no performance remains unproblematic. Wildrake experiences the utmost difficulty staying in character, and both Rochecliffe and Albert perform according to plots already compromised by the doctor's persistent inadequacies as stage manager. Nor are the performances limited to the Cavaliers. The Commissioners perform to one another and to Alice's cousin and love interest, the Parliament officer Markham Everard. Terrified by the supernatural appearances allowed by Woodstock's stage machinery, Bletson quavers to Everard: "'You see, my good Colonel . . . here are only you and I, and honest Desborough, left behind in garrison, while all the others are absent on a sally'" (1:12). In his moment of terror, Bletson portrays his comrades' ghost hunting as a military exercise, and performs his own fear as comradely courage. As for the erstwhile gamekeeper Phil Hazeldine, now performing as the Parliament's "Trusty Tompkins," he proves untrustworthy to both sides, and instead of manipulating the national discourse through the machinery of *Woodstock*, dies ignominiously in a romantic subplot.

Most interesting here is Sir Henry Lee's Shakespearean discourse. It, too, participates in Scott's problematizing of nationality as performance. As the *Westminster Review* understands, not only does Sir Henry speak in poor Shakespearean cadences, when he quotes Shakespeare, he does so with no feel for his source (5 [January–April 1826]: 418). In fact, Sir Henry's style and his quotations draw attention to themselves for their inappropriateness—especially given their context in his worshipful attitude to the bard. The narrator even comments that Sir Henry "was wont to quote [Shakespeare] from a sort of habit and respect, as a favourite of his unfortunate master [Charles I], without having either much real taste for his works, or great skill in applying the passages which he retained on his memory" (1:4). Moreover, Sir Henry frequently misquotes, with results the reader can only judge as cruel yet comical. The conscience-driven Markham Everard he characterizes as Rosencrantz and Guildenstern: "O, an you talk of conscience . . . I must have mine eye upon you, as Hamlet says"—and Hamlet has his eye on his two false friends (1:4; *Hamlet* II:ii:290). His faithful daughter Alice becomes Shakespeare's female two-headed monster: jealous of her feelings for Everard, Sir Henry rants "Soh, mistress! . . . you play lady paramount already; and who but you!—you would dictate to our train, I warrant, like Goneril and Regan!" (1:4).

In this circumstance, Charles's championing of D'Avenant as Shakespeare's son gains meaning. Sir Henry is horrified:

> "Will D'Avenant the son of Will Shakespeare!" said the knight, who had not yet recovered his surprise at the enormity of the pretension; "why, it reminds me of a verse in the puppetshow of Phaeton, where the hero complains to his mother—
> 'Besides, by all the village boys I'm sham'd;
> You the Sun's son, you rascal, you be d—d!'" (2:7/chapter 25)

Here, the usurper of Shakespeare through misquotation attacks D'Avenant's appropriation of Shakespearean authority by invoking language from Henry Fielding. If we turn to Scott's *Journal*, we find a gloss on this moment of seeming incompetence from the great literary historian. Scott writes:

> Read a few pages of Will D'Avenant who was fond of having it supposed that Shakespeare intrigued with his mother. I think the pretension can only be treated as Phaeton's was according to Fielding's farce.
> Besides by all the village boys I'm sham'd,
> You the Sun's son, you rascal?—you be damned.
> Egad I'll put that into *Woodstock*. It might come well from the old admirer of Shakspeare—then Fielding's lines were not written—what then it is an anachronism for some sly rogue to detect. Besides it is easy to swear they were written and that fielding adopted them from tradition. (*Journal*, 101–2)

Scott sets Shakespearean dialogue in play as self-reflexive farce. Here, Shakespeare serves not to police performance (Watson, 78), but to highlight its problems. To repeat even Shakespeare is inevitably to usurp, and what is usurped may be mere playful construction in the first place.

Evidently, Scott does not limit himself to exposing Scottishness as the product of performance. In *Woodstock*, the very fact of literary construction stands revealed and critiqued. As Judith Wilt points out, "[in this novel] . . . the comedy of historical interpretation . . . becomes farce" (161). What better evidence could we have than the house itself, with the secret passages and the latches and pulleys that allow the illusions of the Just Devil of Woodstock? Scott's reviewers bemoaned the false supernaturalism that emerged from Woodstock's labyrinthine architecture. To the *Monthly Review* it recalled "that species of pseudo-horrors, which have been hitherto confined to the Minerva press" (3rd S., 2 [May 1826]: 83). But Woodstock is the stage turned inside out; a space where performances reveal the machinery that produces them. What matters here is not the appearances the house allows, which are palpably false—consider, for example, the first apparition: Commissioner Harrison is terrorized by the supposed figure of a ham actor he murdered in battle, and who swaggers to the door resplendent in red velvet to play upon the feelings of a susceptible audience. What matters is that the house, as machine—and here it seems rather like Abbotsford when occupied by Scott—is seen to produce such illusions. It is not Scott's clumsiness that reveals this novel as artifice; rather *Woodstock* foregrounds itself as mere performance through its author's careful conceptualization of text as subject. This book thrusts to center stage the notion that all reality, however "historical," can only be farcical literary construction. And the house of fictive history is one of cards. At the crucial moment in the plot Love's Ladder, route to Fair Rosamund and thus to a counter narrative that always undermined the monarch's authority, crashes to the ground. The play of national signs can never be "for keeps."

Charles's restoration pageant caps Scott's critique of nation as constant performance. Into the moment of restoration rides a Charles we now recognize not just as amply fictionalized, but as inevitably fictional, and he encounters the thoroughly fictive Lees. Sir Henry quotes to him lines from *King John*. Charles can only catch: "Unthread the rude eye of rebellion, / And welcome home again discarded faith" (2:20/chapter 38; *King John* V: iv:11–12). The irony is multiple: King John is no hero; moreover by the end of the play, the King is dead, so allegiance to him can only be a gesture, not a reality. Further, the Stuarts' return, like Shakespeare's play, is a trick of performance, not a lasting fact—James II was ousted in 1688. The Scottish performance of Britishness (if I may be forgiven a term anachronistic to the seventeenth century), subsists only as stage play. Moreover, Scott suggests that reliance on such empty performances has deathly consequences for those subjected to them. Cromwell, this text's representative of assertive Britishness, has always closed down the play of discourse. "Do not answer," he forestalls Wildrake, "I know what thou wouldst say." "Nay, do not answer, my friend—I know what thou wouldst say" (1:8). Still, all performances fade. At the moment of the King's accession, Sir Henry, having given Charles his enigmatic Shakespearean blessing, dies. His trusty dog Bevis promptly follows him. As Sroka comments: "The ending of *Woodstock* hardly inspires confidence in the fortunes of the nation" (202). So much, then, for narrative circulation as an animating principle for Scotland. All remains to do again and again. Even if Scott achieves and directs meaning, as may have happened during George IV's visit to Edinburgh, even if he deconstructs nationhood as in *The Talisman*, tomorrow brings a new play of equivalences, a new competition for signification.

Thus, *Woodstock* manifests not Scott's maudlin self-dramatization or parlous literary control in the months of his tumble from financial and personal grace, so much as his growing awareness of national authorship's unproductive implications. Charles tells Wildrake, who has just thrown himself at the feet of his newly recognized monarch: "we have not privacy or safety to receive our subjects in King Cambyses' vein" (2:10/chapter 28). Now Scott adopts and makes obvious the ranting theatricality that lurks in every national text. The critic for the *Westminster Review* did not appreciate Scott's strategy, remarking on Sir Henry's excessive language, "Marry, this is King Cambyses' vein with a vengeance" (402). But King Cambyses's style stands central to Scott's critique of the literary ability that had brought Scotland to a pass he could not, as yet, negotiate. Exposed within the machine, the god demonstrates its motions and models its problematic constructive power to those he has previously subjected to its myths. Perhaps as he killed off Sir Henry and his faithful dog, and showed a Charles II heading into history, Scott pondered where, and how, Scotland could yet meaningfully be performed.

5

Telling Over

The Value of an Audience for Malachi Malagrowther and Chrystal Croftangry

We are no longer a poor, that is, so *very poor* a country and

people

In *The Talisman*, Scott worried that finding value through an English market produced a deformed Scotland. In *Woodstock*, he wondered whether his energetic reperformances of Scottishness remained simply performance. He anticipates N. T. Phillipson's critique that his Scotland is one of "noisy inaction" ("Nationalism," 186). *The Talisman* and *Woodstock* each show Scott's growing concern that his figuration as "Thomas the Rhymer" was meaningless at best, and actively damaging to self and Scotland at worst. Previously, Scott stressed the occulted author's prophetic abilities, his tendency to erupt within or alongside the romance that is history, and offer a site for the energetic production of nation as tale. He is "the Author of Waverley," the "Eidolon." In the persona of Walter Scott, Scotland's true teller haunts the domains of Abbotsford, producing and redirecting history through narrative at such moments as the King's Visit. But now?

"Hamako," the Saracens' inspired madman (otherwise known as Theodorick of Engaddi), certainly erupts into *The Talisman* (chapter 3). "The apparition" leaps at Saladin to bear down the infidel and his pagan song. In the wilderness, he produces mystic visions for Sir Kenneth. Theodorick resides at the center of international discourse, weaving together the usurping desires of Richard's fellow monarchs and the lives of gendered and racial others (Edith and Saladin). His voice seems at once national and prophetic. Yet it is wrong. When Kenneth retrieves his honor, and Richard would reward him with Edith, the King declares: "the wind of prophecy hath chopped about, and sits now in another corner." Prophecy is unpredictable. Or it is corrupted by the prophet. Theodorick laments: "The heavenly host write nothing but truth in their brilliant records—it is man's eyes which are too weak to read their characters aright. . . . I read in the stars that there rested under my roof a prince, the natural foe of Richard, with whom the fate of Edith Plantagenet was to be united. Could I doubt that this must be the Soldan . . . ?" (chapter 28). His own fate, too, he has read incorrectly: "I came hither the stern seer—the proud prophet—skilled, as I thought, to instruct princes, and gifted even with supernatural powers. . . . But . . . I go hence humble in mine ignorance, penitent" (chapter 28). Still, Saladin, a sort of Middle-Eastern Edie Ochiltree, maintains prophecy as an effect, at least. Moving freely in his many guises, he cuts through incorrect tales, suggests new combinations, and reworks the future. Thus, prophecy is queried, but not completely undone, in this novel written before the fall that made Scott question his personal status and national roles.

Woodstock, begun as financial clouds gathered, and continued through the deluge of Spring 1826, yields a bleaker picture. At the heart of the dramatic machinery that is the King's hunting lodge sits Doctor Rochecliffe, the stage manager. Taking pride in his title "Rochecliffe the Plotter," the reverend doctor produces the hauntings of Woodstock (2:4/chapter 22). He himself figures as one of Woodstock's ghosts when an old colleague recognizes him: "I saw him last night," whispers minister Holdenough. "Saw *him*—saw whom?" Markham Everard asks. "Whom I saw so ruthlessly slaughtered . . . Joseph Albany" (a.k.a. Doctor Rochecliffe) (1:17). But Rochecliffe is over-sanguine about his manipulations. Everard finds him amid the labyrinth that is Woodstock's backstage by the reek of his breakfast (2:4/chapter 22). Rochecliffe's setting reveals him as more worldly, and more caught by the world, than this inveterate mover around the margins of society imagines for himself:

> Around him were packages with arms . . . one small barrel, as it seemed, of gunpowder; many papers in different parcels, and several keys for correspondence in cipher; two or three scrolls covered with hieroglyphics . . . and various models of machinery. . . . There were also tools of various kinds, masks, cloaks, and a dark lantern, and a number of other indescribable trinkets belonging to the trade of a daring plotter in dangerous times. Last, there was a casket with gold and silver coin of different countries, which was left carelessly open. . . . Close by the divine's plate lay a Bible and Prayerbook, with some proof-sheets. . . . There was also within the reach of his hand a dirk, or Scottish poniard, a powder-horn, and a musketoon, or blunderbuss, with a pair of handsome pocket-pistols. (2:4/chapter 22)

The Doctor presides over a props department not unlike Scott's own; he sits "eating his breakfast with great appetite"; yet he is surrounded by "various implements of danger." Rochecliffe is as thoughtless as "a workman . . . when accustomed to the perils of a gunpowder manufactory." And he is singularly ineffective. He refutes Albert Lee's suggestion that "all these plots [were] unsuccessful" by comfortlessly insisting his co-conspirators were hanged "because they did not follow my advice implicitly" and protesting "You never heard that I was hanged myself." Ultimately, the Rochecliffe who would "put a patch on [an unreliable double-agent's] better eye" obscures only his own vision with "the patch which he probably wore for the purpose of disguise" (2:18/chapter 36). Rochecliffe does not see straight, either for himself or others. His agent, Tompkins, betrays him; Cromwell manipulates him. His plotting is not meaning making, and meaning happens despite and against him. Prophecy is a dangerous, and perhaps empty, art.

These two depressing views of an occulted author's role to perform a different nation appeared unfortunately prescient in 1826. As Scott renegotiated the relationships between England and Scotland, he had brokered a sweet deal for himself. Money poured north, along with status. Increasingly, he had become the value added to his texts. But now he found that all fell subject to fluctuation as England's interests shifted. The Author had disported as "a productive labourer," whose "works constitute as effectual a part of the public wealth, as that which is created by any other manufactor"; Scott was paid in cash—with what else did he build Abbotsford?—and in kind—with which he established personal and national reputation (*Nigel*, 14). But lacking cash, the British market was not kind.

The intertwined businesses of Ballantyne's printing house, in which Scott was the main partner, and Constable's publishing house, for which he was the main producer, depended for their daily workings on a system of "accommodations": writer, printer, and publisher each underwrote the other's debts. Through Constable and his agreements with Hurst, Robinson, and Company, this system of supports and obligations extended to London. Thus, although Scott made money by a network of relationships that reached through London and out into English and other markets, he also stood liable to pay monies he had in fact earned by his authorship—should money become scarce and the "discount bills," a kind of monetary futures, prove unpayable (Rowlinson, "Scott," 26). From 1825, this financial house of cards began to collapse. Hurst and Robinson went first. Like many others, the company had depended on the expansive power of a colonial economy, underpinning business with speculation. When the money supply tightened, such financial fictions drew in to ruin Constable, Ballantyne, and Walter Scott (Johnson, 2:941–87). The author who generated money for others stood to lose everything: money, property, even his books. Writings past and present now were dedicated to repaying debts incurred by way of London.

Most seriously, Scott lost his literary independence and national play. So long as British purposes had the leisure to support regional performance, Scott could remain anonymous, the "Author of Waverley." A god paid outside the machine, he could plot—and apparently replot even Britishness—with a free will. But when his books were devoted to debts generated elsewhere, Scott no longer seemed the transcendent Scottish subject within Britain's economic narrative. The "Author of Waverley" devolved into Walter Scott, and stood bound to tawdry business interests, his cultural capital subordinated to the maintenance of a British economy grounded in London. Kathryn Sutherland notes that in *Nigel*, "Scott presented the imagination itself as . . . a thriving commercial enterprise." For Scott, "the worlds of objective fact and representation . . . become . . . collapsible entities, their equivalence grounded in the purchasing power, or exchange value, of words" (110). In 1826, Scott learned that authorship might prove to be a labor unproductive—monetarily, personally, and nationally. It might run him into cultural debt.

If Scott's situation seemed bad, Scotland's was worse. From a London perspective, the panic arose because local banks irresponsibly circulated small notes. As a result, the government moved to regulate private banks (Phillipson, "Nationalism"). The legislation was aimed primarily at England: "Eighty country banks in England failed and the financial life of London was for a time paralysed" (179). Financially, Scotland survived better. Matthew Rowlinson reports that this crash "led to the failure or merger of only three small banks, all of whose notes were taken up by the others with no loss to the holders" ("Scott," 8). Nonetheless, the government proposed to extend their legislation to Scottish banks. This could undermine an economy with no substantial resources of capital and that had finally been growing by the circulation of promissory notes. Behind this problem lay one even more distressing. Scott feared that he had become grotesque through his own financial fall. When he first appeared again in public on 24 January 1826, "like the man with the large nose [I] thought everybody was thinking of me and my mishaps" (*Journal*, 80). Scotland, too, stood revealed as grotesquely other than herself when circulated through the markets of British money and reputation. Westminster's presumption that Scottish banking practices could be legislated in England's behalf showed Scottish protections embedded in the Treaty of Union were falling into abeyance. There was no separate space within which to perform things Scottish. From a British perspective, national desires, driven by England, restricted the different performance of Scottishness. Both Scott and the nation suddenly were revealed as plotted elsewhere, and as loss.

The play of culture as economics had been undermined by lack of actual funds. Valuation occurs through the circulation of equivalent signs (Goux, 9). Each sign is valued or devalued in the context of others. However, valuation by context is unreliable. One term can be constituted as a general equivalent and appear to fix meaning or worth, but that term, too, is merely a sign and subject to play. This is where money comes into operation (16). Gold, or *"the money form of value"* operates in all systems and trumps all other terms (17; 20–21). So money controls each stage of valuation, and constricts all other modes of finding worth. Thus, Walter Scott, having attempted the various phases of contingent valuation, in 1826 might see the play of signs in *The Antiquary*, the incorporation of devaluation in *Nigel*, the constitution of self as literary and national site of meaning at the King's visit, all as yielding to the ever present power of mere money. Scott's reputation succumbs to the pressure for cash; Scotland's system of equivalents in evaluative circulation (her promissory notes) gives way to coin.

Still money too is "metaphor," "symptom," "sign," "representation" (Goux, 9). The nation supported by cash payment is nonetheless subject to the play of its signs. It remains in performance, subject to the deconstructive and reconstructive contingencies of everyday life—the full constellation of its circulations. And Scott, at this most subjected of moments, discovers that different circumstances merely produce further modes of personal and national negotiation.

Malachi Malagrowther Reperforms the National Audience

> as we have increased in wealth, we have become somewhat
> poorer in spirit, and more loath to incur displeasure by con-
> tests upon mere etiquette or national prejudice.

Scott worried that his financial catastrophe had replotted his authorial trajectory. He was embarrassed by the publicity he suffered, remarking on "[a] foolish puff in the papers calling on men and gods to assist a popular author who having choused the public of many thousands had not the sense to keep wealth when he had it," and disliking "the affected gravity" of some acquaintances "which one sees and despises at a funeral" (*Journal*, 80). He felt delimited. Embracing his difficulties, he asserted his determination "to be their vassal for life and dig in the mine of my imagina[tion] to find diamonds (or what may sell for such) to make good my engagements, not to enrich myself" (81). "My own right hand shall do it," he affirmed on 22 January 1826 (77). He submitted to outside forces and mapped his restricted operations accordingly. Yet at the same moment, Scott worried that he might "break my magic wand in a fall from this elephant and lose my popularity with my fortune" (76). However earnest, he might prove unable to repeat previous performances and fulfill his confined role. The audience may prove wanting. But Scott found his popularity replotted by Scotland's fall from the national elephant. And the trajectory was upward.

Scott preferred his difficulties to remain unmentioned. Lacking anonymity, invisibility would serve. He appreciated the demeanor of those friends who "smiled as they wishd me good day as if to say 'Think nothing about it my lad; it is quite out of our thoughts,'" and noted "The best-bred . . . just shook hands and went on" (80). Nevertheless, he found himself thrust into the limelight by the national catastrophe. With Scotland's constitutive differences under attack, Scott could not remain a quiet toiler in a personal cause. The author became a conspicuous national performer renegotiating the modes of Scotland's valuation for an enthusiastic Scottish audience.

How come? Although money may seem "trumps," it remains substitutive. Matthew Rowlinson stresses not "the economic function of bills and notes [but] . . . their discursive structure": "As directions and promises to pay, bills and notes . . . depended on complex effects of address, signature, reference, and reception. They bore value constituted as travelling between subjects whom they represented as signifiers—signatory, addressee, bearer, and so forth—and situated it in a formally determinate though open-ended series of relations to one another. . . . [Paper money] constitutes social relations within which can be formed subjects identified by class, place, and nation" ("'The Scotch,'" 48–49). "When [Scott] sold his fiction," Rowlinson clarifies, his "encounters with capital were, like the fiction itself, mediated and hedged about with substitutes" ("Scott," 26). The Scott whose fall came by the play of relative valuation that operated through the circulation of discount bills surely was aware of this. In these circumstances, Scott's personal awareness became a national strength. The *Edinburgh Review* identified Scotland's problem in terms that explain the author's sudden, unlikely involvement in the monetary meaning of a nation. "A very considerable sensation has been excited in this part of the empire," the journal noted, by the Chancellor's "announcing that he means to propose the suppression of the small notes of the Scotch banks, and that no principle of circulation ought to be tolerated either in Scotland or Ireland that is not tolerated in England" (86 [February 1826]: 297). Leaving aside the nationally incendiary issue of who tolerates what from whom, this comment is remarkable for its insistence upon different principles of circulation. Scott, more than any man in Scotland, understood not just (anew) the devaluative properties of circulation, but its ability to make meaning and renegotiate value. As author circulating Scotlands through varied populations in search of cultural and monetary valuation, Scott appreciated not just how to make money, but how to perform national difference as worth by animating an international audience.

He now deployed his knowledge and talents on Scotland's behalf. Although the *Scotsman*, through the persona "Terence MacRosty," roundly objected that "to write poetry and tales is but a left-handed preparative for discussing questions of this kind," it was the preparation necessary (10:643 [8 March

1826]: 145). In Parliamentary debates, the discussion revolved around the direction of circulation. "What right had Scotland to be exempted?" asked Mr. Ellice (Hansard, 14: col. 1341). The Earl of Carnarvon queried of Lord Liverpool: "The noble earl had intimated his intention of imparting to Scotland the blessings of his proposed system; but . . . would [it] not be better to place the currency in this country upon the same footing as that of Scotland" (col. 1350)? The Scott who had directed Waverley north of the border, Jeanie Deans south, and guided George IV, knew all about relative circulation, its dynamics, and its evaluative audiences. In early 1826, having lost fortune and, he thought, reputation, he was waiting out the market, wishing to see how and where *Woodstock* would find its value. Threatened with "a lawsuit to reduce [Walter junior's] marriage settlement," and thereby the loss of Abbotsford, however, Scott saw no reason tamely to submit to market forces: "By assigning my whole property to trustees for behoof of Creditors, and therewith two works in progress and nigh publication, with all my future literary labours, I conceived . . . I was entitled to a corresponding degree of indulgence," he wrote on 16 February (*Journal*, 106–107). *Woodstock* was circulating through audiences not purely cultural but also financially motivated. Scott negotiated its way. He added on 19 February, "I am not very anxious to get on with *Woodstock*. I want to see what Constable's people mean to do when they have their Trustee" (*Journal*, 110). He manipulated literary and economic audiences. In the meantime, he felt "horribly tempted to interfere in this business of altering the system of Banks in Scotland" (17 February, *Journal*, 109). "It is making myself of too much importance after all," he concluded. Still, the next day, Scott extended his attention to the monetary system itself, and to the nation of Scotland (*Journal*, 109).

Just when Scott seemed out of circulation for good, or doomed to move in limited systems that exposed the lack of mystery in the gap that was the "Author of Waverley," he erupted at the heart of the nation's discourse on evaluation. Instead of money trumping all worth, he reproduced the nation as difference and himself as national hero. Indeed, he forced the nation, not just its literary signs, into energetic and culturally determinative circulation. Beginning on 18 February, Scott produced three letters bearing the signature "Malachi Malagrowther" that turned the tide of debate and staved off the proposed legislation. The first letter, written during 18–19 February, appeared in the *Edinburgh Weekly Journal* for 22 February, and went into a revised and extended pamphlet edition by 1 March; the second letter, written between 25 and 28 February, was published in the same magazine on 1 March and its first pamphlet edition circulated on 3 March; the third letter, written 4–6 March, appeared in the *Edinburgh Weekly Journal* on 8 March and went into pamphlet on 10 March ("Malachi," xvii–xxi). In slightly more than two weeks, Scott's aggressively voiced concerns circulated widely in multiple forms to popular, banking, and parliamentary audiences.

What did Scott talk about? He argued from precedent for Scottish notes and against specie, which he considered rare in Scotland and unlikely to make its way there by government fiat. He noted Scotland's advances: "The facility which [the current banking system] has afforded to the industrious and enterprising agriculturalist or manufacturer, as well as to the trustees of the public in executing national works, has converted Scotland, from a poor miserable, and barren country, into one, where, if Nature has done less, Art and Industry have done more, than in perhaps any country in Europe, England herself not excepted" (letter 1:21–22). The nation has achieved value through its separate system running alongside that of England. Scott also stressed—as the Author of Waverley well might—that England has recognized Scotland as worth: "It becomes every Scotsman to acknowledge explicitly and with gratitude, that whatever tenable claim of merit has been made by his countrymen for more than twenty years back, whether in politics, arts, arms, professional distinction, or the paths of literature, it has been admitted by the English, not only freely, but with partial favour" (letter 2:63–64). Scotland is the land of inherent value; England is the site of applause and—presumably—money. But England wishes to circulate outside its sphere: "the conduct of England towards us as a kingdom, whose crown was first united to theirs by our giving *them* a King, and whose dearest national rights were surrendered to them by an incorporating Union, has not been of late such as we were entitled to expect." He continues: "There has arisen gradually, on the part of England, a desire of engrossing the exclusive management of Scottish affairs" (letter 2:64–65). Scotland maintains England's worth, but on the national level, at least, England undermines Scotland. When valuation becomes relative, England seeks to dominate: "if the English statesman has a point of greater or lesser consequence to settle with Scotland *as a country* we find him and his friends at once seized with a jealous, tenacious, wrangling, overbearing humour. . . . We cease at once to be the Northern Athenians. . . . We have become the caterpillars of the island, instead of its pillars" (letter 2:66). National worth is entirely a matter of positioning. And the circulation of British concerns through Scotland produces it as grotesque. But since valuation depends on the flow of meaning making, the current can be redirected and value shifted.

Thus, Scott embraces Scotland's otherness.[1] English pressures "fret—gall—gangrene—the iron enters first into the flesh" (letter 2:76). Scotland "has been bled and purged . . . and *talked* into courses of physic" (letter 1:10). She is "a subject in a common dissecting-room, left to the scalpel of the junior students, with the degrading inscription,—*Fiat experimentum in corpore vili*" (letter 1:11). Moreover, as a disgusting body, revealing all the otherness that England's presumed value obscures for herself, Scotland circulates alongside other problematic bodies politic. In the summer of 1825, Scott had visited his son Walter, and traveled with the Miss Edgeworths, in Ireland. Hitherto as prone to racist comments as any mainland subject, Scott discovered the real indigence of many Irish people. His clear look at their poverty produced an appreciation for qualities unrelated to money: "I said their poverty was not exaggerated. Neither is their wit—nor their goodhumour—nor their whimsical absurdity—nor their courage" (*Journal*, 5). Consequently, for "Malachi," the circulations that motivate the British body politic also direct nationalist discourse by way of Ireland: "no component part of the empire can have sufferings, which do not extend to the others . . . but must reach England and Ireland also" (letter 2:20). The English have a tendency to trim the members of the extended body politic to maintain their own worth at its head. Ministers may "take . . . the opportunity of our torpidity to twitch out our fang-teeth, however necessary for eating our victuals, in case we should be inclined, at some unlucky moment, to make a different use of them" (letter 2:22). What is worse, they may adopt "a well-known operation . . . for taming the ferocity of such male animals as are intended for domestication" (letter 2:22–23). "Patrick, my warm-hearted and shrewd friend," Malachi asks, "how should you like this receipt for domestication, should it travel your way?" The deployment of discourse across the extended body politic animates the otherness that is Scotland, but also Ireland.

To what effect? In his second letter Scott remarks: "the iron enters first into the flesh," but he goes on "and then into the soul." English pressures that produce Scotland as Other also motivate opposition. Thus, "I speak out what more prudent men would keep silent" (letter 2:76). Scott energetically extends otherness through a wide range of audiences normally obscured and disempowered, motivating each in turn. Perhaps it is more than a coincidence that at a time when Parliament again debated the abolition of slavery, and considered "Scotch Representation," Scott pursues the "worth" of human beings (Hansard, vol. 14). He circulates othered bodies themselves—even to the Irish, the dead, the dissected, and the castrated. Scott animated the otherness of the body politic and set its members quarreling among themselves to produce a different valuation, and different direction for circulation, within the British Isles.

On 20 January, in the first moments of his fall, Scott braved to his journal, "publick favour is my only lottery" (*Journal*, 73). Through Malachi, he played and won, deploying the otherness of Britishness to evoke an audience invested in the nation's active difference. This was no small feat. The Scots, he knew, were almost impossible to shift. With forelock-tugging irony, Scott remarks in the second letter: "Saunders, if it please your honours, has been so long unused to stand erect in your honours' presence, that, if I would have him behave like a man, I must (like Sir Lucius O'Trigger backing Bob Acres) [in Sheridan's *The Rivals*] slap him on the shoulder, and throw a word in every now and then about his *honour*" (letter 2:29). Even when most successful at evoking response, he declared one Edinburgh committee with "a thousand names on the petition" "disconcerted and helpless" (*Journal,* 123). "The philosophical reviewers . . . hold off—avoid committing themselves" (124). "We have more sneakers after ministerial favour than men who love their country." Yet Scott stirred them all up.

N. T. Phillipson remarks that before the letters' publication, petitioning against the legislation "had been confined to politically experienced bodies." "By the end of March . . . [the letters] had become widely known. And . . . the petitions had begun to flow in from [a] plethora of tiny interests" ("Nationalism," 184). The *Scotsman's* Whig editors supported the Tory plan. On 8 February they considered "the measure for the suppression of the smaller notes of the country banks . . . is one which . . . cannot fail, in our view of the matter, to occasion a most material improvement in the currency of the country" (10, no. 635: 85). A month later, on 8 March, "Terence MacRosty" attacked "Friend Malachi"—well known as Walter Scott—for his "false position, where every word you utter libels your past life and conversation" (10, no. 643: 145). On 1 March, however, the paper had been compelled to admit that "Petitions continue to flow into Parliament from Scottish towns and counties against the meditated changes in our Banking System, and we doubt if any single city or corporation in the country will be found to raise its voice in their favour" (10, no. 641: 133). On 8 March, it had to quote from the *Times:* "Some of the principal managers of the great Scotch Banks . . . are arrived in town for the purpose of protesting against the measure for withdrawing the small notes from circulation in Scotland" (10, no. 643: 147). "An Old Merchant" claimed in his letter to be "one of your disciples so far as concerns your leading views as to currency," and also "friendly to the present administration," but he attacked: "they have surely acted *unwisely* in meddling at present with the system of banking in Scotland." Moreover, he invoked the notion of Scotland's different audience for economic change for his grounds: "The people in Scotland are not so easily panic-struck as their brethren of the south: and hence *their confidence* in their banks" (151). Then on 15 March, "Terence MacRosty" temporized: "though I think many of [Malachi's] arguments unsound, and not a few of your general views ludicrous, I concur to some extent in your conclusion" (161). Scott had speeded the circulation of bankers across Britain—the banks, incidentally, ordered multiple copies of his letters (*Journal,* 113); he had pushed a Tory "Old Merchant" into writing oppositely to his party newspaper; and he had forced the *Scotsman* to contradict itself, purveying Scott's differentiating arguments within the columns of its own anti-Scottish "MacRosty." Appealing to the local audience in ways that disturbed even the Whigs, Scott forced his nation into a movement that differentiated and energized it both internally and externally.

It is clear that while mercantile sentiment did run against the proposed change, Scott's voice broadened and lent terms to this opposition. Phillipson notes the letters "provided a *genre*. The idea of explosive letters about slights to national honour, written in a spirit of bitter but humorous grumpiness, caught on. 'Saunders Saunderson' of Prestonpans wrote on these lines in the broadest Scots" ("Nationalism," 184). Scott had insisted in his letters that Scotland must speak out. In particular, her Ministers must speak as (because of Malachi) required by her people: "I pledge myself, ere I am done, to give such a picture of the impending distress of this country, that a Scotsman . . . would need to take opium and mandragora, should he hope to slumber, after having been accessary to bringing it on. If the voice of the public in streets and highways did not cry shame on his degeneracy. . . . The stones of his ancient castle would speak" (letter 2:18–19). Publicity, once the devaluative force of Scott's broad literary circulation, here is recognized as Scotland's motivating power. Audience is everything. In this context: "A little indolence—a little indifference" (might I add, in-differentiation) "—may have spread itself among our young men of rank. . . . But the trumpet of war has always chased away such lethargic humours; and the cry of their common country . . . is a summons yet more imperious, and will be, I am confident, as promptly obeyed" (letter 2:19). The multiplicity of audience produces not a diffusion but a concentration of national desire. It requires an active participation in public discourse.

The discourse, too, is required. By 17 March, Scotland's representatives were repeating Malachi's terms in the House of Lords. The Earl of Aberdeen objected that an "experiment was about to be made for which he saw no necessity" (Hansard 14, col. 1393). The Earl of Lauderdale thought Scottish petitions would "furnish the noble earl [of Liverpool] with some useful hints how to new model the banking establishment of this country [broadly conceived]; instead of inducing him to cram down the throats of Scotchmen the system pursued here" (col. 1396). Scott's medicalized terms were adopted in Ireland, too. The Earl of Limerick thought that "Where there was no disease [in Ireland and Scotland], no remedy was required" (col. 1394). Maurice Fitzgerald, speaking for the government and on behalf of Ireland to the Commons, felt obliged to disavow Scott's terms. No doubt thinking of Scott's assertion that "the heather is on fire far and wide," and his hint that "claymores [have] edges" (letter 2:4; 1:9), Fitzgerald "did not participate in that spirit of resistance, or rather of rebellion, which had been raised against it from certain quarters. He did not mean rebellion in the usual sense; he meant a rebellion of paper against gold, which had broken out in Scotland [a laugh]" (col. 1386). The Earl of Limerick demonstrated that the discourse had indeed produced a type of Irish rebellion when, a month later and discussing a bill on bank note forgery, he aligned himself once again with Scotland: "Noble lords from his own part of the United Kingdom were not generally so united as those who owned Scotland for their birth-place. He should therefore feel inclined to enlist under [the Scottish] banners, and take ref-

uge behind the sanitary cordon which the latter had attempted to establish"
(Hansard, 15 col. 217). Scott's medical metaphor draws in the Irish audience
to define broadly the United Kingdom's body politic and produce it through
the play of difference.

Even England was written in. Lockhart gossiped from London: "the Ministers are sore beyond imagination" (Scott, *Journal*, 121). Scott interpreted:
"I conclude he means Canning is offended." Certainly, Canning responded
to Malachi's terms and recognized Scott as the prophet for his times. He told
the Commons on 13 March that "I can look without terror upon the flashing
of the Highland claymore, though evoked from its scabbard by the incanta-
tions of the first magician of the age" (Hansard 14, col. 1319–20). The Earl
of Grosvenor understood Scott controlled the debate, warning the Lords
that "all this [ongoing inquiry, rather than enacted legislation] originated in
the fears excited in the minds of ministers by a celebrated personage, no
other than Malachi Malagrowther," and he recommended "not . . . to yield
to those fears, or to enter into any discussion" (col. 1392). He applauded John
Wilson Croker, who did enter into discussion—but in his own pamphlet. Yet
Croker oddly contended entirely on Scott's terms. An Anglo-Irish representative of government, Croker adopted Scott's strategies, enacting a Scott
persona to query Malachi's resemblance to "our common parent" in *Two
Letters on Scottish Affairs, from Edward Bradwardine Waverley, Esq. to Malachi Malagrowther, Esq.* (Croker, letter 2). He invoked Scott, too, on changes to
the judiciary in 1808, to imply dissension within Scott's own discourse (14).
"I may be forgiven if," he says, "I agree with Sir Walter Scott rather than
with Malachi Malagrowther" (16). Despite his strong opposition, Croker's
best option still was to align himself with Scott. He tried to set Scott against
Scott, but all language belongs to that wizard, present in the past, erupting in
the moment, and performing the future.

Robert Saunders Dundas, 2d Viscount Melville, and currently First Lord
of the Admiralty, made particularly clear Scott's ability to renegotiate value
by shifting audiences through the careful circulation of signs. Scion of the
great Scottish family that had dominated eighteenth-century British politics, Melville served as an arm of government. He perversely responded to
opposition against the change in currency by asserting that "the people of
North Britain who have lately come forward have . . . thought, as a matter
of course, that England was bound to submit to every inconvenience and
loss which Scotland might think fit to impose upon her" (*Arniston*, 317).
A Scot in exile through British power, he viewed his home down the wrong
end of the telescope. During the brouhaha of February–March 1826, Melville may have instigated Croker, his underling at the Admiralty, to give the
Tory response to Scott. On 6 March, he wrote himself to Robert Dundas:
"I have perused within these few days two letters in the newspapers from a
certain Mr. Malachi Malagrowther, and I should not now have mentioned

them if I had not heard with sincere regret that they are from the pen of Sir Walter Scott. I know the people of Scotland as well as he does, and I also know full well how they ought to be dealt with. . . . I do quarrel with him, first for the inflammatory tendency of his letters, secondly for the gross misrepresentations which are to be found in every paragraph" (*Arniston*, 316–22; see 318). Melville declares Scott's argument "preposterous . . . it is impossible to receive these remarks as arguments addressed to reason and common sense: they are directed to the passions of the ignorant and the illiterate" (319). Scott is "dabbling in . . . an impure stream." He resists Scott's mode of appeal to an audience prone to "inflammation," and implicitly restricts that broad audience's play through his determination that this letter should be privately passed around among mutual friends.

But Scott, shown the letter yet required to return it, was not subdued. He continued to circulate his grotesque images through an audience Melville considered unhealthy. "I would not term a blister [a remarkably uncomfortable medical procedure involving hot glasses] inflammatory merely because it awakened the patient," he replied to Robert Dundas (*Arniston*, 322; *Letters*, 9:457–61). And critiquing Lord Melville's attempt to restrict circulation by politics and class, he noted the First Lord's letter as "a general annunciation to Lord Melville's friends that Malachi is under the ban of his party" (*Arniston*, 323; *Letters*, 9:459). Such a direct attack brought the letter's circulation to an end. In fact, valuation ran in reverse to Melville's intent, with Scott claiming his Lordship's audience, too. Robert Dundas "condemn[ed] Lord Melville and says he will not shew his letter to any one" (*Journal*, 127). Melville subsequently wrote to Scott stressing that "however strong Lord Melville's dissent from Malachi's views on the currency might be, it would not be allowed to interrupt his affectionate regard for the author" (*Arniston*, 325). Perhaps most notable is that his Lordship found his political practice altered by Malachi Malagrowther. On 14 April, when the Earl of Limerick aligned himself against further banking legislation, he sided with "the noble lord"—that same Lord Melville. The Scottish peer's perspective had been thoroughly adjusted. Belatedly, Melville declared: "all the banks in [Scotland] viewed the present bill with the utmost alarm. Their system might, perhaps, ultimately appear to be bad; but until that fact was established, he thought no alteration should be attempted" (Hansard, 15 col. 215). Indeed, Melville invokes "Scotchmen," a group popular to the extent that it at least includes bankers, and argues for Scotland against government. Trying to restrict Scott's discourse, he finds his own has changed.

Phillipson contends that Scott made a "fuss about nothing" ("Nationalism," 186). But Melville's experience shows that Scott had shifted Scotland and redefined the role of audience in the making of national meaning. Scott's appeal to the otherness inherent in the body politic had activated audiences often excluded from debate. He emphasized the multiplicity that produced a healthy Scotland, but also a dynamic Union. In the second letter, he asked: "would the British empire become stronger, were it possible to annul and dissolve all the distinctions and peculiarities, which . . . makes its relative parts still, in some respects, three separate nations?" (letter 2:80–81). And he asserted: "For God's sake, sir, let us remain as Nature made us, Englishmen, Irishmen, and Scotchmen" (81). He argued: "We would not become better subjects, or more valuable members of the common empire, if we all resembled each other like so many smooth shillings." Successful nationalism, on small and large scales, evolves through the circulation of active difference.

Scott's own successful deployment as difference is evident in the fact that he argued this case against his personal needs at the time and his friends' desires—and came out ahead. The author sought invisibility to survive the months of his fall, and time to work at his financial survival. Yet on 3 March he noted to his journal, "I was named one of a committee to encourage all sort of opposition. . . . So I have broken through two good and wise resolutions—one that I would not write on political controversy—another that I would not be named on public committees" (*Journal*, 121). The night he pondered getting involved at all, he wrote: "I am horribly tempted to interfere in this business of altering the system of Banks in Scotland and yet I know that if I can attract any notice I will offend my English friends without propitiating one man in Scotland" (*Journal*, 109). He thought the letters "may chance to light on some ingredients of national feeling and set folks' beards in a blaze and so much the better if it does—I mean better for Scotland," but he presumed "not a whit [the better] for me" (*Journal*, 111). Nevertheless, the effects of Scott's involvement make clear that again he had redirected the flow of national and personal valuation. Scott noted that opposition from Croker and Canning "would make a man proud" (*Journal*, 135). He might be more proud when those who opposed him changed their positions and, like Melville and Croker, lobbied to stay aligned with him. A contentious audience ratified the continuing worth of Walter Scott—and its increased national relevance.

Although Scott wrote that he was "glad of this bruilzie," for "people will not dare talk of me as an object of pity—no more 'poor manning,'" he could not have anticipated how far his recirculations of Scotland raised his own value (*Journal*, 120). The *Scotsman*'s "Terence MacRosty" admitted "your power over the spirits of men" (10, no. 643 [8 March]: 145). In its May issue, *Blackwood's* waxed lyrical (19, no. 112: 596–607). Scott is an "unaccountable person"; he is an "improvident person" who has cared not for money or reputation in sacrificing "personal interests and friendships to the good of his country and countrymen" (596). He has moved beyond the limits of specie or even of circulation in his worth. Abjuring "soft, measured, and philosophical language" that would have appeased government friends, or "newspaper fashion and phraseology" that would have coopted his political opposition, "misguided Malachi took the tone of dauntless independence" (597). Scott circulated oppositely to all established discourse. The result was much criticism in the press, yet "To say anything in his defence is what we cannot deign to do. It would be an unpardonable absurdity were we to assert, that his talents, heart, and life, will bear comparison with those of . . . his . . . slanderers" (597). For a moment—albeit in the biased *Blackwood's*—Scott had slipped the bonds of valuation.

It was here, too, that Rhymer-like, he escaped the constrictions of time. In 1979, Scotland attempted but failed to achieve even limited legislative devolution through referendum. Harvie and Jones stress, "The bill . . . was a bad bill. The Assembly was to be handed down its powers in a way which would have made constant conflict with Westminster inevitable. The Scotland Act wrote down definitions of everything that the Assembly could do; anything else was outside its power" (119). As Denver et al. point out, "The actual question on which Scots were asked to vote . . . appears almost abstruse . . . : 'Do you want the provisions of the Scotland Act 1978 to be put into effect?'" (23). The referendum covered more than the Assembly, but few understood what it covered, and the Assembly had little authority. This gesture toward Scottish power might be another "pig in a poke." So a Constitutional Steering Committee investigated modern Scotland's status within the Union, trying to bring clarity and purpose to the issue. On 6 July 1988, the committee presented its report to the Campaign for a Scottish Assembly. The document bore the title: *A Claim of Right for Scotland*. And at its head stood an epigraph from Scott's Malachi Malagrowther letters: "The Scottish Members of Parliament should therefore lose no time—not an instant—in uniting together in their national character of the Representatives of Scotland." A moment crucial in the movement toward Scotland's 1999 Parliament self-consciously repeated Scott's cry that representative Scots must remember they are participants in a Scottishness driven by difference and active in time. Scots do not have to succumb to the drone of Westminster jargon. All Scots together make up an audience of critics producing the nation through their energetic otherness. So the *Claim of Right* pushed Scots toward today's Parliament through Sir Walter's remembered and still powerful discourse.

An Audience for Sir Walter in The Chronicles of the Canongate

we have some merits to plead

James Ballantyne thought Scott neglected his literary responsibilities. "He reproaches me with having taken much more pains on this temporary pamphlet than on works which have a greater interest on my fortunes," Scott wrote on 24 February 1826—when only the first Malachi letter was complete (*Journal*, 113). Scott needed to work on his monetary fortune, whatever his reputation. Indeed, his personal fortunes seemed to plummet. In March, the intellectual hope of the family, young Charles, showed no good reports from Oxford. His tutor thought "he *might* try for a *second* class," and Charles wished to forego an honors degree (Johnson, 2:982). Johnson summarizes the ongoing exchange between an over-taxed Scott and his adolescent son: "The Army was out of the question; Scott had no money now to buy advancement. . . . The Scottish or the English bar would involve years of severe study and self-denial" (2:983). Scott, never indolent and recently not much concerned with formalities, on 10 May wrote irritatedly to Lockhart: "he is not so much impressd as I think he should be with the necessity of his qualifying himself to make his own way which can only be by much exertion and not by dwelling on decencies only" (*Letters*, 10:28). On 15 May, Scott's ailing wife died at Abbotsford in his absence (*Journal*, 166). Meanwhile, the bank seemed likely to seize Scott's home. In July, a Mr. Abud in London sought immediate payment of Scott's debt to him, threatening the trust (202). *Woodstock* remained in trust, with its ownership undetermined until July of the next year (377). Small wonder that Scott wrote to his journal: "these misfortunes come too close upon each other" (136). He really needed a success, for monetary purposes, but also simply to lift his spirits.

Still, Scott had enough sense of self-worth to refuse the suggestion that he might be made a Baron (judge) of Exchequer, with accompanying payment (*Journal*, 122). And he could easily resist when Sir John Sinclair—he who had been duped by Raspe—continued to act "the Caledonian bore" by recommending that Scott marry the Dowager Duchess of Roxburghe. Sir John wrote on 11 September: "she ought to marry (for so young and rich a widow, while she remains single, is very awkwardly situated)" (Partington, 130–31). He continued in telling terms: "She is really a most valuable woman, and would make any man happy who had the good fortune to obtain her hand." Declaring himself "absolutely mute and speechless," Scott responded derisively in his journal, "Marry hang him, brock!" and decided to "write to his present stye . . . that the Swine may if possible have warning not to continue—this absurdity" (*Journal*, 225). Yet Scott needed money.

"My own right hand shall do it" (*Journal*, 77). Now it would. Days after Charlotte's death, on 27 May, Scott wrote in his journal:

> A sleepless night—It is time I should be up and be doing and a sleepless night some times furnishes good ideas. Alas! I have no companion now with whom I can communicate to relieve the loneliness of these watches of the night. But I must not fail myself and my family and the necessity of exertion becomes apparent. I must try a *hors d'oeuvre*,

something that can go on between the necessary intervals of [*The Life of Napoleon*]. Mrs. M. K's tale of the Deserter with her interview with the lad's mother may be made most affecting. (172)

The next day he reported: "I wrote a few pages yesterday. . . . I believe the description of the old Scottish lady [Mrs. Bethune Baliol] may do. . . . I will go on to-day. . . . I intend the work as an *olla podrida* into which any species of narrative or discussion may be thrown" (173). With a real sense of his obligations and limited opportunities—his family's need, his own difficulty, and the pressures of *Napoleon*—Scott projected a kind of composition new to him. He imagined volumes formally stretched by a variety of short tales. Scott was working away at the first piece, "The Highland Widow," on 18 June: "This morning I wrote till 1/2 twelve, good day's work at *Canongate Chronicle*. Methinks I can make this work answer" (182). By 22 June, he had sent off one-third of the first volume for a work now marked by place—the Canongate—and form—the Chronicle.

He was also pondering how it would circulate. Always aware of the monetary and reputational relationships between author and reader, and perhaps stimulated by his recent experiences with Malachi, Scott worked through ideas on how to evoke an audience.

> Our plan [with his trustees and publishers] is that this same Miscellany or Chronicle shall be committed quietly to the public and we hope it will attract attention—If it does not we must turn public attention to it ourselves. This latter issue of the business will resemble the old woman at Carlisle who not doubting that the highlanders when they took the place in 1745 were to violate all the women shut herself up in a bedroom to await her fate with decency. But after a little time . . . she pop'd out her head and askd a Rorie who was passing 'Pray, Sir, is not the Ravishing going to begin?' (*Journal*, 189–90)

It is through the audience that value will come. The Wizard's magic still resides in the tale, but a further magic weaves around its reception and the ensuing, complex interaction between author/pleader and reader/ravisher. Given Scott's needy state, this could be no half-magic. *Malachi* showed he could create the audience as national. Could he regain it for himself?

Analysis of the *Chronicles* typically focuses on its tales. The first volume comprised "The Highland Widow," which Scott declared "in my bettermost manner"; "The Two Drovers," which he thought "interesting"; and "The Surgeon's Daughter," which depended on assistance for its Indian color and thus suffered a "patch" he suspected "too glaring to be pleasing," but which he hoped could compete against "one or two East Indian novels" that had recently appeared (*Journal*, 193; 372; 399).

All three tales seem products of Scott's circumstances. In the first, a young highlander seeks a way to survive in a changing world. He takes the tartan in the only form remaining to him—as a soldier. His mother, remembering a previous generation, tries to prevent him from returning to his regiment, with the result that he kills his officer and is executed. "The Two Drovers" traces two friends, a Scot and an Englishman, who herd cattle together, but compete for grazing. In an exchange of insults the Englishman considers friendly, the Scot kills his friend and suffers death through southern laws that cannot recognize his system of honor. In "The Surgeon's Daughter," the illegitimate son of an Englishman and his Jewish lover is abandoned to the care of a Scottish doctor. The boy grows in rivalry over the doctor's daughter with a fellow medical trainee from the north of England. Always in search of money and status, he leaves his Scottish opportunities for better prospects in India. There, he disgraces himself militarily and racially (after having killed his mother with unwitting unkindness as he sets out on the journey). He tempts the young woman abroad with promises of marriage, but with the intention of selling her to an Indian prince. For punishment, he gets squashed by an elephant! The young woman, rescued by her English admirer, returns to Scotland and a life of rich spinsterhood. These three tales seem to focus darkly on the prospects of material survival—never mind advancement—for Scots within a British discourse. Moreover, options from earlier novels seem undone here. The woman who renegotiated national forces by virtue of a gender that situated her outside politics—Jeanie Deans—has been replaced by a mother whose separation from the world kills her child in the present and prevents the future. The Waverley who meandered freely north, and the Nigel who circulated yet survived in the south, when shifted in class cancel one another out in the persons of the two drovers. And Flora McIvor, Rose Bradwardine, and Effie and Jeanie Deans, seem transmuted into unfortunate love objects valued only by their monetary and political market in a world far from home.

However, the intriguing aspect of Scott's *Chronicles* is not the tales but their telling—specifically, the ways in which this first series negotiate an audience. Frank Jordan has read Chrystal Croftangry, the tales' narrative persona, as "Scott's Last and Best Mask." But paradoxically, through Chrystal we can trace Scott's masking/unmasking relationship with his reader. Here, Scott removed the veil of anonymity and at last revealed the face all knew to lie beneath. As far back as *Waverley* (1814), Scott's authorship had been an open secret. The *Edinburgh Review* had implied it, and the *Critical Review* assumed it.[2] But the necessary disclosures attendant on Scott's fall and setting up the trust to manage his affairs made even the illusion of anonymity impossible. On 18 December 1825, Scott lamented to his journal: "the magic wand of the Unknown is shiverd in his grasp. He must henceforth be termd the Too well Known" (*Journal*, 48). Then in February 1827, Scott attended the Theatrical Fund dinner. Although all Britain now recognized Scott as the "Author of Waverley," and much more besides, the connection had never been publicly avowed by Scott himself. It happened by "mere accident," he told Lady Louisa Stuart on 8 March (*Letters*, 10:172–75). He admitted that "[t]he circumstances attending Constables Bankruptcy placed the secret such as it was in the hands of too many persons to suppose that a denial could any longer be taken at my hands." He was looking for "some decent opportunity to lay aside the mask which was grown as thin as my aunt Dinah's [in Sterne's *Tristram Shandy*]." So when, at the dinner, Lord Meadowbank asked Scott whether he cared any longer about his anonymity. "'Not I' I replied 'the secret is too generally known.'" And Meadowbank freed an old and familiar cat from the bag.

Scott's introduction to the *Chronicles* stands in response to this moment and the great publicity he now suffered. In April 1827, the *London Magazine* ungraciously reported the full state of Scott's financial affairs (533–35). Itemizing the "Value of Sir Walter Scott's Literary Property," the magazine declared that Ballantyne's accounts "lay open the precise state of Sir Walter's private affairs" (533; 535). Disingenuously, it remarked, "a hundred years hence they may be a great curiosity, and their publication may then be correct; at present it would certainly be indelicate and unhandsome" (535). It went on to decide that "[e]very thing belonging to a great national genius is public property." In the meantime, it remarked: "[a]s [Scott] was well aware that the circumstances would soon make their way through the press, he determined to catch at some little *eclat*, while yet there was time—some little credit for disclosing that himself, which all the world were soon to learn from others" (533). Scott's admission of authorship to the Theatrical Fund becomes the last grasp for "credit," or reputation. A genius, he loses control of his own circulation and, if the *London Magazine* is anything to go by, suffers devaluation. What, then, of money-making?

Not surprisingly, the introduction Scott produced on 3 July 1827 engaged directly the problem of the Great Unknown's circulation and evaluation at the hands of a now too-knowing audience. "Workd in the morning upon the Introduction to the *Chronicles:* it may be thought egotistical," he wrote (*Journal*, 367). He begins with the image of Arlechino, encouraged by an admiring audience to cavort without his mask, and thereby "considered on all hands as having made a total failure" (3). "He had lost the audacity which a sense of incognito bestowed, and with it all the reckless play of raillery which gave vivacity to his original acting. He cursed his advisers, and resumed his grotesque vizard; but, it is said, without ever being able to regain the careless and successful levity which the consciousness of the disguise had formerly bestowed." Harlequin changes his relationship to his audience—and loses it. Raillery and levity become impossible, and with them go reputation and money. "Perhaps the Author of Waverley is now about to incur a risk of the same kind," Scott worries (3). Then he concludes: "Hoping that the Courteous Reader will afford to a known and familiar acquaintance some portion of the favour which he extended to a disguised candidate for his applause, I beg leave to subscribe myself his obliged humble servant, / WALTER SCOTT" (11). Invoking Jedidiah's earlier, successful address to the reader in *The Heart of Mid-Lothian* (9), Scott names himself as the site for a new one. The performance of authorship must begin all over again, lacking the mystery and in the full glare of publicity. Without that returned public gaze, without audience, there can be no authorship.

In *Chronicles of the Canongate*, like Walter Scott, Chrystal searches for an audience. He struggles to re-establish relationships within which he, as author, can find meaning. Chrystal has enjoyed audiences in the past, marked by familial relationship and ancient friendship. But he has squandered his inheritances of money and reputation, alienating even his mother—perhaps driving her to death—and proving ungrateful to friends who try to save him. He is first bankrupted and committed to internal exile within the debtors' sanctuary in Holyrood, then released and exiled to a colonial existence (17). Returning home with "enough to support a decent appearance for the rest of my life," Chrystal imagines an audience of cousins who will be forced by his funds "to be civil," and gossips who will say, "I wonder who old Croft will make his heir" (17)? However, he finds no old friend who can pay attention to him. The man who exercised all his legal capacities to rescue Chrystal from his own irresponsibility has declined in mental faculties and faded into a past Chrystal can no longer occupy. Chrystal's home, sold to a manufacturer, has been razed to allow the construction of a *nouveau riche* monstrosity. But the manufacturer himself has died, the heir is bankrupt, and the mansion stands open for sale. The systems that once valued Chrystal are at multiple removes. Worse, they will not readmit him. Christie Steele, his mother's attendant who has no reason to remember Chrystal fondly, ejects him from his past. Latterly the landlady of the dower-house turned inn, and on the verge of a flit herself because of the Treddles' bankruptcy, she allows no return to Chrystal, and ruthlessly evicts him from his memories. "Dinna let him come here," she warns to a Chrystal masquerading as his own friend, the sole audience that makes him still existent for a new Scotland: "Dinna let him come here, to be looked down upon by ony that may be left of his auld reiving companions, and to have the decent folk that he looked ower his nose at lang syne look ower their noses at him" (43). "Stop there, goodwife, if you please," Chrystal pleads. There is no going home, no going back again. The audience that gave Chrystal meaning is dead or determined not to readmit him. His value is irretrievably lost.

Malachi Malagrowther had modeled the need and means to activate an audience, and suggested the type of audience that can motivate change, trumping politics, class, and perhaps even money. In *Chronicles*, Chrystal constructs an audience capable of recognizing him, but that gives him meaning through the reverse of the admiration first afforded to the Author of Waverley. This audience is remarkable for its unpredictable, assertive, jaundiced perspective. Scott would not beg favor: "I am sure I will neither hide myself to avoid applause which probably no one will think of conferring nor have the meanness to do anything which can indicate I had any desire of ravishment. I have seen when the late Lord Erskine enterd the Edinburgh [theatre] papers distributed in the boxes to mendicate a round of applause, the natural reward of a poor player" (*Journal*, 257). Instead, he would build an audience. And it would not be friendly.

Failing to negotiate his way back into past relationships, Chrystal locates himself elsewhere. He seeks out his erstwhile landlady—an outsider for her highland origins and social class. Years ago, released from the fear of prosecution for bankruptcy, Chrystal had "left my lodgings as hastily as if it had been a pest-house" (16). Now, Chrystal and his housekeeper settle into a place near his old Holyrood haunts. Chrystal cannot return to the past, but neither can he escape the formative moment in his monetary and social career. And here, Janet constitutes Chrystal's first audience. She recognizes this Chrystal, changed by his difficulties, but known to her through them: "The light, kind-hearted creature threw her napkin into the open door [she was cleaning], skipped down the stair like a fairy, three steps at once, seized me by the hands,—both hands,—jumped up, and actually kissed me" (46). Even better, she listens to his stories: "The dignity of being consulted delighted Janet" (54). Yet Chrystal cannot take his audience for granted. He admits that "I felt more delight than I ought to have done in my own composition, and read a little more oratorically than I would have ventured to do before an auditor, of whose applause I was not so secure" (54). But Chrystal is too sanguine: Janet is not knowing enough. She cannot grasp "the latter part of my introduction," connecting it to her own experience and missing the point: "the German philosopher who wrote upon Solitude . . . must be of the same descent with the Highland clan of McIntyre, which signifies Son of the Carpenter. 'And a fery honourable name too—Shanet's own mither was a McIntyre'" (54–55). She is also too knowing. "The Highland Widow" complete, and the printer's devil at the door, she complains: "I am sure you know a hundred tales better than that about Hamish MacTavish, for it was but about a young cateran and an auld carline, when all's done; and if they had burned the rudas quean for a witch, I am thinking, may be, they would not have tyned [wasted] their coals" (123). Chrystal has constructed Janet, his supposed ideal audience, as a resistant reader.

So he searches out other listeners. Mr. Fairscribe, his man of business, is not a promising audience. Although "[h]e gave me a most kind reception on my return," "[h]e was too much engaged in his profession for me to intrude on him often" (22). However, Chrystal must have readers to recognize him if he is to obtain value once more. Chrystal interrogates his own need:

> Frankly, I was ashamed to feel how childishly I felt on the occasion. No person could have said prettier things than myself upon the importance of stoicism concerning the opinion of others, when their applause or censure refers to literary character only; and I had determined to lay my work before the public, with the same unconcern with which the ostrich lays her eggs in the sand. . . . But though an ostrich in theory, I became in practice a poor hen, who has no sooner made her deposit, but she runs cackling about, to call the attention of every one to the wonderful work which she has performed. (147)

A literary "deposit" requires an audience to declare it brass, not muck, and validate the author's worth. Thus, Chrystal turns to Mr. Fairscribe—but the lawyer fails to respond. "This is very unlike my good friend's punctuality," Chrystal worries (148). And Chrystal pursues Fairscribe into his home, not once but twice, interrupting Sunday devotions and appearing unfashionably early for dinner, to extract a comment. Pressed for an opinion, Mr. Fairscribe proves no more faithful or easy an audience than Janet. He considers Chrystal's interest a "vanity" for which he can find little time (150). On the second visit, he forgets the manuscript (152–53). His praise is limited and qualified with unintentional irony: "I really think you have got over the ground very tolerably well," he remarks, and applauds Chrystal over Schiller, but for writing in a way that does not intrude upon his business (153-54). He comments on technical errors. Then he advises Chrystal to "[s]end [his muse] to India" (155). The ideal audience is hard to find.

But is it? Janet and Mr. Fairscribe make no allowances for past brilliance, pass over no careless expressions, are not at all polite about plots, hesitate not a moment to offer alternatives, and often fail to note what the author considers his texts' graces. This audience is not kind. At times it seems uneducated, even philistine. It is very "pass remarkable," as the Scots would say. That is, with all its business, its other interests, and its oppositional concerns, this is, importantly, an engaged audience. The most problematic of Chrystal's audiences makes the issues clear. Young Katie Fairscribe arranges a reading to her tea circle. Chrystal offers "The Surgeon's Daughter." Reading aloud, "I was feeling the chilling consciousness, that [the words] might have been, and ought to have been, a great deal better" (287). Chrystal himself opens the way to negative criticism. But as every author discovers, criticism always directs itself elsewhere than we expect: "We kindled up at last when we got to the East Indies" (287). However, "on the mention of tigers, an old lady . . . broke in with, 'I wonder if Mr Croftangry ever heard the story of Tiger

Tullideph'" (287)? She "nearly inserted the whole narrative as an episode in
my tale" (287). Although she is "brought to reason," "subsequent mention
of shawls, diamonds, turbans, and cummerbands, had their usual effect in
awakening the imaginations of the fair auditors." Nevertheless, there is an
obvious triumph: "At the extinction of the faithless lover in a way so horribly new . . . one Miss of fourteen actually screamed" (287). The audience's
oppositional criticism, its failures to grasp, and insistence on participation,
mark an active engagement between author and reader across text.

Kathryn Sutherland observes that "the reader was for Scott . . . a consumer whose good will and confidence, even complicity, were stimulants to
narration" (104). In *The Chronicles of the Canongate*, Scott learns to depend,
too, on the reader's philistine, oppositional readings. These readings grasp
the reality of author and text, make them fully present, and maintain them as
active in an ongoing, personal and political culture. The resistant reader gives
persistence to the work of authorial valuation.

And Scott was thoroughly revalued through these short stories. The magazines appreciated the stories themselves. The *Gentleman's Magazine* commented: "Elspat Mac Tavish . . . [is] the best of the author's creations. . . .
The Two Drovers, is [a tale] which the talents of Sir Walter Scott alone could
have redeemed from vulgarity; in his hands, however, it is full of absorbing
interest. . . . The third tale . . . is, perhaps . . . less interesting. . . . But . . .
'*Scott's lees is better than other men's wine!*'"[3] But the reviewer suggested that
the real story was Scott: "It is to [the] preface we would first direct the attention of our readers" (439). The *Literary Gazette* agreed: "No where do we
find the writer more happy than he is in all that relates to his assumed part
of the Chronicler; he seems to have transfused himself into this new and
original personage. He paints his anxieties of authorship as if this were really
his *debut*."[4] The sharp eyes of *Blackwood's* reviewer noted that what stood at
stake was Scott's relationship with the reader.

Scott had transcended evaluation, the magazine asserts.[5] "Of Sir Walter
Scott and his genius," it notes, "we have said little or nothing during the last
three or four years, for reasons sufficiently obvious to the meanest capacity. His works went on the wings of the wind to the uttermost corners of
the earth (22, no. 132:541). But *Blackwood's* can adopt this superior stance
because it has passed the test of audience set by Scott's anonymity and in
his texts. Everyone knew, the writer declares, that the Author was Scott:
"He, she, or it, that knew [it] not . . . was a fool of the first order." "Poor
creatures, indeed, who mumble that Sir Walter Scott will not be read a hundred years hence!" (543). They "don't seem to know the signification of the
monosyllable 'read.'" Rather overstating the case, it avers, "[w]hen any fault
is found with a story like this, it is not the story that is ill-constructed, but
the critic's cerebral organization" (554). In so arguing, *Blackwood's* performs
the critical work stimulated by Scott's tale of Chrystal Croftangry. It evokes

oppositional criticism—from the straw dogs it sets up as failed readers of Scott—and provides its own, over-the-top response. Together, these characterize Scott's *Chronicles* as no easy read soliciting shallow attention and polite favour. Rather, Scott's tales gain their value through the rowdy, interventionist attention of gloriously problematic readers.

Of course, *Chronicles* did not sell well. On 7 November, Scott began the second series, confident that the first had been "well approved" (*Journal*, 423). However, on 11 December, he received an ominous "formal communication from Ballantyne, enclosing a letter from Caddel [*sic*] of an unpleasant tenor. It seems Mr. Cadell is dissatisfied with the moderate success of the Ist Series of *Chronicles*" (442–43). Was the interest purely critical? Had Scott failed to stimulate the popular audience whose ongoing attention alone could support his monetary reputation? A three-way exchange between the *London Magazine*, the *Literary Gazette*, and the *London Weekly Review* hints at what happened. In its November 1827 issue, the *London Magazine* thanks "the Weekly Review, a sensible and industrious literary journal, for thus early gaining a sight of a part of the forthcoming work of Sir Walter Scott, which is expected with something like the old interest that used to attach to their publication. . . . We trust, however, that no short-sighted policy may induce the proprietors to complain of this apparent invasion of their copyright."[6] The magazine goes on to reprint "The Two Drovers." On page 409, however, the publishers retract. They were "not aware of the mode in which the periodical from which we copied it had procured the sheets of the original" and which they now consider "confers little honour on any party concerned." They do, incidentally, insist that "[Scott's] introduction all the world must read," and "take the liberty of quoting a considerable part of it" (410). The *London Weekly Review*, meanwhile, on 7 November responds to "the *Literary Gazette* [which] now pretends to consider it unfair and piratical to print an extract from a book, before publication, without the consent, we suppose, of author, printer, or publisher."[7] It clings to precedent against the *London Magazine*'s late accusations, which it reasonably notes as hypocritical. Certainly, it was common practice to publish long sections of novels within reviews. Still, in this case, the magazines were publishing whole stories. Thus, it may have been Scott's popularity that undermined his sales. Struggling against one another to stand forth as Scott's prior and appreciative audience, the journals showed how thoroughly he had constructed himself and his tales as valuable according to oppositional audience dynamics. Unfortunately, that competitive audience intensively valued Scott's tales, but likely cut his profits.

Scott worried that his diminished sales indicated a loss of power, money, and prestige. Contemplating Cadell's new edition, to comprise all his works, he could claim: "They cannot say but what I *had* the *crown*" (*Journal*, 427, 429; 443). Indicating how much he had focused in *Chronicles* on his audience evaluation, Scott blustered in response to Cadell's criticism: "I was not fool enough to suppose that my favour with the public could last for ever and was neither shockd nor alarmd to find that it had ceased now as cease it must one day soon. It might be inconvenient for me in some respects" (443). His trustees surely knew how inconvenient. He stated "no other receipt than lying lea for a little while taking a fallow-break to reli[e]ve my Imagination which may be esteemd nearly cropd out" (443). "I will not push the losing game of novel writing," he determined next day (443). However, the vagaries of play, with the London magazines competing for the best hand—all Scotts—indicate that the author already had discovered how, once more, to make the game a winning one. The trick lay in the appeal to the audience, to keep it current.

6

Making Meaning beyond the Ending

Castle Dangerous
and Walter Scott's Last Words

Before their eyes the Wizard Lay

Walter Scott has fallen out of currency. Over his career, Scott projected his nation into the future. Far from narrating Scotland into the past or outside of history, he voiced a range of different, differing, deferring possibilities— and let them play freely through the absence that is the Author of Waverley and the potentiality that is Scotland. Through Scott's texts, Scotland stands always in formation, not limited to any story of past or present, and gesturing toward its realization in the ever opening tomorrow that is history. But the future remains closed to the author himself. Walter Scott is dead.

Scott put a lot of effort into his dying. Then, after more than two years writing a series of avowedly "last" novels (*Count Robert of Paris, Castle Dangerous*, and the unpublished "Siege of Malta"), last tales (the incomplete "Bizarro"), last letters (a belated and discarded "Malachi Malagrowther" piece on the Reform Bill), and last words (in the introductions and epilogues for *Tales of My Landlord* Fourth and Last Series, which hosted the *Count* and the *Castle*), on 21 September 1832 Walter Scott finally died.[1] Of course, the "Author of Waverley" had been dead since the Theatrical Fund dinner of 23 February 1827 when the bankrupt Sir Walter showed his hand behind the pen.[2] And courtesy of Foucault, we might recognize that both Scott and the Author of Waverley were always and already "dead" in the moment of their first inscription.

So why have generations of Scots struggled to kill off Sir Walter? Why, a mere two weeks after Scott's death, did Hogg jostle for his prior right to inter his friend under the device of high-Tory Baronet? He declared, with a certainty seldom questioned, "[t]he Whig ascendency in the British cabinet killed Sir Walter."[3] This even though Scott "opposed the Reform Bill of 1832 not . . . because it would aid [the workers], but because it would give increased power to precisely those manufacturers who were responsible for their distress" (Johnson, 2:1253). Why did the author's much-loved son-in-law, John Gibson Lockhart, labor in his biography to bury Sir Walter under the bricks and debts of Abbotsford to the degree that strangers had to come to Scott's defense? It was left to Horace Smith to remember (in 1848) a fact still much forgotten: "Not strange was it, but perfectly natural, that Sir Walter, believing his pecuniary means to be fully equal to the attempt, should seek to realise the vision over which his mind had incessantly brooded. . . . Neither by his outlay at Abbotsford, nor by any indulgence in selfish profusion elsewhere, was his fortune dissipated" (Robertson, *Lives*, 290–99; 298). Why was Thomas Carlyle so keen to delimit Scott as the healthy body now no more (Carlyle; Hayden, 348–49)? The sage-in-progress damned Scott with praise: "he was, if no great man, then something much pleasanter to be, a robust, thoroughly healthy and withal very prosperous and victorious man. An eminently well-conditioned man, healthy in body, healthy in soul; we will call him one of the *healthiest* of men."[4] Why, to turn to Scott's more popular reputation, should successive articles in a 1932 celebration written by various hands and printed for the Scottish Motor Traction Company compete each to confine Scott within a different pinfold? Chapters by the great, the good, and the obscure read: "Sportsman and Country Gentleman," "Scott's Appeal to Youth," "A Treasure-House of Tradition," "Romantic Territory," "The Humanity of Scott." In this centenary volume, the author lies compressed into the gobbets of an overripe reputation. Finally, why can we hear the shout of the Jedburgh weavers against Scott at the reform elections echoing into our present moment from Murray Pittock? Pittock orients his important argument for a vibrant Scottish culture against a Scott whose ideas ultimately "invented Scotland as a museum of history and culture, denuded of the political dynamic which must keep such culture alive and developing" (*Invention*, 87). He typifies a phenomenon so extensive that Cairns Craig and Beveridge and Turnbull offer incisive descriptions of this imperative to center and silence the author as a first gesture in their arguments for a different dynamic in a new Scotland (*Out of History*, chapters 2 and 3; *Scotland*, chapter 4). Why do the considerations of Scotland's most interesting national critics—from Edwin Muir to Tom Nairn—resound with "Burke Sir Walter!"?

For the Scots, this dead author speaks. As Pittock puts it, Scott's "version of events became, and remains, highly influential" (*Invention*, 90). Scott has become the uncanny voicing within and around Scottish culture that must constantly be made away with quietly or, to use a contemporary Scottish term, "burked," if the nation is to function today.[5] But while the critical concern about the author's backward ideas and negative influence hangs on a handful of novels—most notably *Waverley* for Scots—I contend that the issue arises from anxiety about the nature of national authorship, and is founded in the problem of Scott's late works.[6] Are they last words, lost words, or living on in the narration of the nation? Does Scott somehow still perform the nation with a difference? The reason Scots work so hard to lay the ghost of Sir Walter—to stop the speaking of what is, after all, a silence—is that the absent author has become a condition of possibility in Scottish culture as necessary, as productive, and as problematic as Red Clydeside, the Stuart line, and the Highlands. He lurks within the counter-comedy of Glaswegian Billy Connolly and the strange complexity of Fettes College graduate Tony Blair. Scott stands forth as one of the figures by and against whom his countrymen negotiate their nationhood.

To understand how the dead author impossibly speaks from this non-position, we must consider Scott once more within the perplex of national valuation—that problem of Scotland's arguably "postcolonial" self-construction. Meaning is possible and worth recognizable—if only for a moment—within the circulation of equivalent terms. From this perspective, valuation is a potential and problem of articulation. And from *Waverley* to *Nigel*, Scott articulated varied tales of Scotland that through the process of exchange served to establish the nation as capable of, if also uncertainly subject to, valuation. He made Scotland a many-voiced subject moving among the variety that constituted nineteenth-century nationhood.

Further, meaning can appear stabilized by privileging one term that can then set the value of others. Scott made his nation a voice persistently heard, and a subject apparently valued, by establishing George IV as transcendent Sign. More than that, as the insistent absence that is the Author of Waverley, Scott himself functioned as a center around which texts, authors, Scots, and perhaps an English king could be seen in circulation in hope of a valuation that might prove national. By his manipulations of exchange, Scott was constituted as worth and his relative position spoke Scotland's apparent valuation.

Yet when the role to determine value is located in a mortal and unique individual, not a replaceable monarch or an ineffable Christ, it begs a question difficult to answer—the crucial question if we are to understand how Scott speaks today in the narrative of the nation. When the dominant term visibly tends toward collapse back into the sign, rather than being invisibly substituted from within the system, what happens? Specifically, when Scott began to intimate mortality insistently through his body and his texts, when approaching the moment of his demise he increasingly marked the boundary between life and death—the two equivalents that undo exchange and reduce all values to zero—what happened to the story of Scotland? Who now tells it, and from where?

This chapter will consider the interplay between Scott's "last" novels, his last words on his last novels in introductions and epilogues, the words exchanged by printer, publisher, author, and editor during the time when Scott suffered his five strokes, and Scott's last voyage—which preemptively analogized his voyage out of life for an anxious British public. We will ask whether Scott's last words are truly lost—whether the dead Scott is always and already "burked," the author completely silenced in the narration and valuation that is modern Scotland. But we will wonder whether Scott continues to speak within the nation precisely because he has nothing to say and no place to say it from that does not more appropriately belong in a given moment to others from that time such as Lockhart, the Motor Traction Company, or the pantheon of Scotland's recent critics.

From his first stroke, on 15 February 1830, Scott's already complicated position became for the author an unremitting perplex (*Journal*, 661). Certainly, he remained surrounded by evidence of his evaluative role. Scots, the English, Whigs, Tories, male, and female continued noisily to solicit recognition from Walter Scott, the Author of Waverley. The audience that validated the Author would not look away. Between 22 February and 7 March 1831, for instance, Scott responded to at least three approaches from fellow authors. Susan Ferrier thought to dedicate a novel to Scott; William Godwin and Robert Chambers wrote to ask Scott's help in valuing their work by writing to publishers and authoring reviews.[7] A host of publishers still sought his name to signify their projects as worthy—in February 1830, G. R. Gleig wanted a book—any book—for his proposed *National Library*: "to you we fondly look for that great support which the mere announcement of your name as connected with any literary scheme cannot fail to give" (Millgate, *Last*, 96). Even the King—and even William IV, not his Scottophile brother George—recognized Scott's continued worth and ability to confer value when he put the frigate *Barham* at the author's command for his recuperative voyage to Naples. As Johnson notes, "The entire country rang with applause of the generous offer; never had William IV been more popular" (2:1191). The very sailors fought to be on the crew that would ferry Walter Scott.[8]

Moreover, the author was aware of his apparent worth and relative function. He testily declared in his *Journal* after the unusually encroaching post of 5 May 1831: "A fleece of letters which must be answerd I suppose, all from persons my zealous admirer[s] of cours[e] and expecting a degree of gen[e]rosity which will put to rights all their maladies physical and mental, and expecting that I can put to rights whatever losses have been their lot, raise them to a desireable rank and [be] their protector and patron" (732).

Nevertheless, Scott took pleasure in his role when it brought a fishmonger across London to supply him with the cod his servant had unsuccessfully desired earlier in the day. He laughed to Captain Basil Hall: "if that is not substantial literary reputation, I know not what is!" (Robertson, *Lives*, 98–9). Strikingly, too, Scott deployed the power of valuation his position allowed over those who circulated themselves around him. He graciously thanked the kind and unobtrusive Susan Ferrier for her dedication, but refused Godwin, whose response indicates that the social critic felt his value fail in the context of Walter Scott's now exercised ineffable worth (*Letters*, 11:474; 476–78). Godwin complained: "The most obvious reason for your declining to recommend me is my unworthiness" (*Letters*, 11: 476 fn. 1). Basil Hall exaggerates when he declares of Scott in 1831 that he was "perhaps the foremost man of all the world," still the author stood positioned as an excess that spoke valuation—and he embraced the part (Robertson, *Lives*, 87).

However, after his first stroke, Scott gradually manifested the other truth of any system's dominant term—he was visibly collapsing into the vacancy that is the sign. Further, as a sign, he stood subject to the revaluation and potential devaluation of exchange. One by one, his strokes reduced the playful multiplicity that was Walter Scott, the Author of Waverley. Persistently, they diminished him into a circulable singularity expressible only through another. His voice failed, and his hand, so that writing became a stuttering process dependent on amanuenses.[9] Scott told Lockhart that in the winter of 1830–31, he "had more than once tried writing in his own hand, because he had no longer the same 'pith and birr' that formerly rendered dictation easy to him; but that the experiment failed. He was now sensible he could do nothing without Laidlaw to hold [the pen]" (Lockhart, 7:281–82). He continued, "Willie is a kind clerk—I see by his looks when I am pleasing him." On 11 January 1831, Scott had welcomed Laidlaw's return and his offer of secretarial help: "I tried to write before dinner but with drowsiness and pain in my ha[n]ds made little way. My friend Will Laidlaw came in to dinner and after dinner kindly offerd his services as amanuensis. Too happy was I and I immediatly plunged him into the depth of *Count Robert*" (*Journal*, 701–2). But on 13 April, Scott told his journal: "Laidlaw begins to smite the rock for not giving forth the water in quantity sufficient. I remarkd to him that this would not profit much" (727). As hand was substituted for voice and another hand for his own, Scott's words increasingly entered the realm of exchange and revaluation in the moment of their utterance.

Scott knew he was falling into circulation. He had long been aware that he risked being devalued by his imitators. Again and again he runs variations on the theme. In 1826, he noted that "like Captain Bobadil I have taught nearly a hundred gentlemen to fence very nearly if not altogether as well as myself." Yet always he could fall back on "something new" and remove himself from degrading comparison (*Journal*, 143). Now he was not sure he could. Thus we find him trying to assert a selfhood that could survive it. Just over a week after his third stroke, which he suffered on 17–18 April 1831, Scott declares, "I have been whistling on my wits like so many chickens and cannot miss any of them" (*Journal*, 728–29); three months later Lockhart found him "constantly setting tasks to his memory" (Lockhart, 7:291). And for the first time, the author who hid behind his texts at many removes, and who resisted naming until it was forced upon him, cared to be called aright. On 15 May 1831 he lambasted William Taylor for suggesting from bibliographic evidence that "William" (Scott as translator of "Lenore") had later taken the pseudonym "Walter" to become "the most extensively popular of the British writers." Either disingenuously, or in deep denial, the Author of Waverley objected: "to a native of Scotland there are few things accounted more dishonourable than abandoning his own name" (*Letters*, 12:16–17). He gripped tight to identity, terrified that he would become "an idiot and a show" like his father before him—a lack revealed in the cycle of exchange.[10]

Worse still, intimations of his own mortality pointed Scott toward the exchange that makes all circulation irrelevant. Thus, we find him choosing to memorize Dunbar's "Lament for the Makars," with its lists of poets all leveled by death and its drumbeat behind which no speech can be heard: "*Timor mortis conturbat me.*"[11] Notably, too, his major recuperative literary act of that year, Scott reprinted the *Trial of Duncan Terig* for the Bannatyne Club. In this report, a ghost indicts his murderers. Scott uses the introduction to consider the results of such cases. He invokes Foote's farce, *The Orators,* for the judge's declaration that a ghost using human means to intervene in human affairs "must consent to be tried in the ordinary manner," and he relates "a popular story" where the judge requires a ghost witness "must be sworn in usual form"—that is, it must appear in court (v–vi; vii). The dead are voiceless for the living. Even if their words may be heard, ghostly voicing undoes that which it speaks. On 31 March, Scott tellingly summed up the Terig case for Alexander Dyce: "The spirit did not carry his point, however; for the apparition, though it should seem the men were guilty, threw so much ridicule on the whole story, that they were acquitted" (Lockhart, 7:272–73). The author was wondering, but not optimistically, whether meaningful voicing remained possible from a position of absolute lack. The erstwhile determiner of value was anxiously falling through exchange and into a silence unbearable for a national author.

What Scott did not realize was that his voice already had been lost. The irony is that it was lost to those who circulated most anxiously around him for their valuation—those whose need it was to maintain Scott as dominant term and themselves as worth by the constant expression of his excess through his published works. Were it not for Scott, James Ballantyne and Robert Cadell might have remained figures of no account at all, and John Gibson Lockhart could never have been valued so high without his father-in-law's help.[12] In the 1830s, however, with Scott's health in decline and the lack that is the foundation of excess becoming visible as Scott subsided into the sign, these three began to assume themselves on a level with the Author of Waverley. Laidlaw registered alternately Scott's health and decline. On one distressing day, 6 September 1831, the amanuensis warned Cadell that "Sir Walter was dictating absolute nonsense," but almost immediately followed with the assurance that subsequently "Sir Walter had lighted up . . . and dictated what struck Laidlaw as very fine and very eloquent."[13] Yet despite repeated evidence of Scott's continued mental abilities, Ballantyne, Cadell, and Lockhart focused on his physical problems and read from them his decline. In words that should chill all messy eaters and circuitous thinkers, Cadell remarked on 9 August 1831: "However lively Sir Walter may be at times . . . there is settled languor over his spirits—he speaks but little—he slobbers when he eats— his hands do not write well . . . his memory is evidently confused in many respects—there is a want of clear perception about his mind—his speech is indistinct—he is evidently a broken down man."[14] With this justification, the cohort of printer, publisher, and editor had begun strenuously to intervene in Scott's authorial processes. Before, they had encouraged Scott's incessant productivity, for it ever-renewed the ineffable Author of Waverley and maintained him as the purveyor of meaning for his colleagues. In 1828, Cadell stressed Scott's power to coin value through writing:

> You do me much honor by asking in your last kind note what your next work is to be. . . . It is not for me to say what you may consider the best subject to try. . . . But I will say, *do not pause*. . . .
>
> At the present moment the enthusiasm in the public mind in favour of your writings, I do maintain is unabated, I see it as a Tradesman, and I hear it in all quarters; no sooner is one book done, than we receive orders for the next, altho' not named. (Partington, 361–62)

Even when he did suggest a revision to *Anne of Geierstein*, Cadell recommended that what was written merely should be rearranged. In 1829, he argued deferentially, "I cannot bear the idea of your rewriting any part." Scott should continue for "be assured [future novels] will sell" (Johnson, 2:1099). However, by 2 June 1831, Cadell was writing: "Mr Lockhart and I had a long confab about Sir Walter Count Robert &c. we agreed on every point and both see that the less Sir Walter writes after this, so much the better, indeed it would be better if he were to write no more Novels."[15] He rang the same changes with Laidlaw: "Mr Laidlaw and I are quite agreed that it would be a most fortunate circumstance if [Scott] were not to write any more—but this is too good to be at all likely."[16]

Ideally, *Count Robert* would never be published, but in case it should, Ballantyne and Cadell loaded Scott with recommendations about its style and substance (they feared the public response to a pregnant warrior, Effie Deans notwithstanding). Cadell provided lists of suggestions, marked excisable passages, and finally colluded to revise the text behind Scott's back.[17] As early as 23 September—on the day of Scott's departure for London—Cadell "agreed [with Lockhart] that I should send [Count Robert & Castle Dangerous] to him in London" but only "after Sir Walter had left for Portsmouth."[18] On 18 October, eleven days before Scott left the country, Cadell "made up and arranged Count Robert & Castle Dangerous for Mr Lockhart"; then on 4 November, with Scott gone, we read: "parcel from Mr Lockhart with Count Robert with his emendations."[19] This when Scott could not coax his proofs out of Ballantyne or Cadell. On 10 September— almost a fortnight before he left Scotland—he complained to the publisher: "I have not yet got the running copy which I now want very much. I must appeal to your authority. There is volumes I and II of Castle Dangerous wanted and all three volumes of Count Robert that I may see distinctly what I have been doing."[20] Ballantyne and Cadell already frequently criticized Scott's work. James Ballantyne disliked "The Two Drovers" (Johnson, 2:1022); Cadell, disappointed by the first series' sales, grumbled at the rest of *Chronicles of the Canongate* (2:1033); Ballantyne, soured by his wife's death, "totally condemned" *Anne of Geierstein* (2:1098). However, their comments reach a new extent and Cadell and Lockhart begin to supply major revisions with *Count Robert*. Now assuming Scott's equivalence with themselves, and asserting their own role in the construction of value, Ballantyne, Cadell, and Lockhart exchanged their hands for his.

Their concern was whether the author could yet make money for himself and for them. Their strategy, given Scott's apparent fall into the cycle of exchange, was to convert the playfulness that had been the Author of Waverley into the limited term "Walter Scott." Cadell twists and turns to make Scott produce *Count Robert* in a way that will render both author and the Magnum edition completed artifacts capable of successful—if restricted— circulation through the literary market. He insists (impossibly) to Scott "if Count Robert is . . . not received with applause—if it is not received with more applause than any of its precursors up to the Tales of the Crusaders it will injure the Magnum, and this injury will be done to 45 preceding volumes."[21] A poor novel will devalue the rest. Since the best way to maintain value is not to meddle with a current property, Cadell insinuates to Scott: "it has been said by good & fair judges that any addition to the Novels might impair what are gone before & create the question 'how long is this to go on[?]'" (ibid.). He tries to shut Scott up. Then, frustrated by Scott's continued authorship, Cadell substitutes the words of the author's colleagues and effective "joint stock" company to make an end to the Author of Waverley through a massively revised novel and extensively redirected introductions and epilogues—many of which insist that this is the last of Walter Scott.

For instance, Scott's involving farewell from his introduction, "the reader is now acquainted with the species of malady under which I have struggled," consolidates into Lockhart's trite epilogue: "The gentle reader is acquainted, that these are, in all probability, the last tales which it will be the lot of the Author to submit to the public."[22] On behalf of successful exchange, and through its processes, Cadell silences Scott to make "the Author of Waverley" a stable term, *Count Robert* a current coin, and the Magnum Robert Cadell's portable property.

Scott had always subsisted within exchange. At any time he ran the risk of being voiced through the play of terms he seemed to dominate. We should remind ourselves that more obviously than many authors, Scott wrote for money. Moreover, his texts always were corporate productions dependent on his critical printer, his commercial publisher, and the compositor and house stylist. Even as the apparently silenced author left Britain for his final voyage, he declared to Basil Hall: "Ah! if I had been in our excellent friend Cadell's hands during all the course of my writing . . . I should now undoubtedly have been worth a couple of hundred thousand pounds" (Robertson, *Lives*, 101). Further, Scott constantly flirted with exchange by parlaying his worth into value for others. For instance, on 27 May 1828 he enumerated nine separate profitable exchanges he had accomplished by a trip to London—including: "I have been able to place Lockhart on the right footing in the right quarter" (*Journal*, 541–42). Then, for his very last works, he actually invited editorial help from his son-in-law, telling Cadell that for "The Siege of Malta" he would have "the advantage of Lockhart's opinion."[23] Certainly, too, Scott recognized his interdependence with Ballantyne and Cadell following their mutual financial collapse.

But Scott also emphasized the difference between his role and theirs. On 12 April 1830 we find Scott dismissing yet another dispute between his printer and publisher in words that confirm his dominance through the productivity that is the condition of their valuation. He remarks of Cadell's desire to drop Ballantyne as publisher: "When we were all in distress we would not have been pleased that those who had the command in some degree of our destiny should [have] exerted their power rudely." Then he admonishes: "I am sure I may expect from my colleagues that they will give me as little of this species of trouble as possible since it interferes seriously with my labours" (*Letters*, 11:328–30). In fact, Scott maintained a delimited notion of their responsibilities. While he may invite their help, he characterizes their contribution as "management." Cadell is to manage the completed works as a money-making property; son Charles and Lockhart are to manage the copyrights.[24] Although in 1820 he trusted Lockhart to correct "inaccuracies," in 1831 he stresses Lockhart's inability to make substantive changes in his work, warning his son-in-law that if he died before completing the Magnum notes,

Lockhart "would naturally have to take up that job, and where could you get at all my old wives' stories" (*Letters*, 6:159–61; Lockhart, 7:284)? As Scott made clear in the Magnum preface for *Chronicles of the Canongate*, he did not care for a "literary picnic" (Scott, *Prefaces*, 230).

All indications are, that taking for granted Scott's decline, Cadell and Lockhart went disturbingly beyond their brief. Cadell told Scott's trustees that "Sir Walter had authorised him to apply to Mr Lockhart" for help with unfinished Magnum notes and introductions. But Scott's discussions of his Jedediah introduction suggest that at most, the author expected Cadell and Lockhart to make "verbal alterations" or minor rearrangements to his latest texts after he embarked for Naples—not substantive changes ("Jedediah" as spelled in proofs).[25] Significantly, on the eve of his departure, Scott rushed to complete his introductions and epilogues for the fourth series of *Tales of My Landlord* and retain it as his, and he sharply resisted Cadell's pressure to rewrite *Count Robert*, declaring, in Grierson's succinct paraphrase: "He sends the third volume of Count Robert. He cannot correct it as Cadell seems to think necessary. He cannot cut according to objections which he does not think necessary. He will take his chance and Cadell cannot expect him to do more."[26] Long before, Scott had boasted that "publick favour is my only lottery" (*Journal*, 73). Now, on 19 November, Ballantyne wrote to Cadell: "I will speak very honestly on this occasion. I think very much of the judgment and attention displayed by Mr. L[ockhart] in his alterations, and *quite as much* of your own. Without *both*, the thing would have been unproduceable. As it is—I will not deny that these works are the very worst that ever came from the author; but the best has undoubtedly been made of them, and a large sum of money saved out of the fire."[27] Scott had no conception that his work could be so altered and yet still take its chance under his name. In 1831, he was ever more anxiously working for reconstitution as his society's valu/able term—even as Ballantyne, Lockhart, and Cadell day by day effected "the death of the author."

Yet if these three now determined the work that made up "Walter Scott, the Author of Waverley," and controlled that term's circulation, why did they deploy strategies seeming to imply Scott's continued dominance? With unconscious irony, Cadell obsessively remarks on the responsibility Scott requires of them all to be truthful. He replies to the author's anguish over *Count Robert*: "Your letter is one which I can look upon only as testifying a confidence in me for which I am very grateful, and what my merits scarcely entitle me to. It calls upon me . . . to strain every faculty to benefit you, to conceal no one feeling."[28] He goes on interminably about his honesty and frankness. In one letter he covers both himself and Ballantyne: "I trust you will think no more of the frown of honest James," he cajoles, and continues, "there is one great good in speaking frankly to you, and it is, that you never take ill what is well intended."[29] Then, when piracy forced *Count Robert* out of literary dry dock and onto the high seas of exchange, the publisher wrote to Scott: "*Count Robert of Paris*. It will not do to be faint-hearted about this worthy Knight. The title is good—the public have long had it before them—the pillaged extract is fortunately a very happy bit—and will create an interest for the whole."[30] A couple of days later he added: "it is more prudent to sail the Count into the market." Cadell is the invisible pilot; Scott is the (supposedly reluctant) captain.[31]

Given that Scott was no longer supposed to have evaluative power, why did they work so hard to keep their distance? Cadell repeatedly hides behind someone else to criticize Scott's work. When *Count Robert* first appeared to be a problem, he wrote to Scott: "James Ballantyne has put a task upon me which he was much more able to undertake himself but as he is slightly indisposed I fancy I must indulge him."[32] And when Brenhilda seemed certain to go to battle *enceinte*, as Cadell coyly expresses it, he waited for Ballantyne to broach the subject—"having the wish now as heretofore to let [him] bear the brunt of these critical discussions."[33]

Most importantly, why did Cadell, Lockhart, and Ballantyne work so hard to keep the exchange they effect invisible even to themselves? Cadell softens his commercial negotiations. His Note Book reports, "Mr Lockhart and I had a long confab about Sir Walter Count Robert &c."[34] Rewritten proofs for *Castle Dangerous* bear his scribble: "C. Dangerous, as altered by Mr Lockhart," with "altered" struck through and "revised" inserted.[35] As for Lockhart, even when Scott had died, he used verbal sleight of hand to magic away the epilogue Scott wrote for Count Robert and that he had cut from the text, rather than admit his drastic editorial interventions. The "Advertisement" for the novel cavils: "Sir Walter Scott transmitted from Naples . . . an Introduction for *Castle Dangerous;* but if he ever wrote one for a second edition of ROBERT OF PARIS, it has not been discovered among his papers."[36] Lockhart knew of an epilogue for *Count Robert*'s first edition, so he truthfully finessed that there was no introduction for a second.[37] And by the time he wrote Scott's biography, Lockhart had convinced himself that his father-in-law implicitly desired his help: "Sir Walter's misgivings about himself, if I read him aright," he surmises, by summer 1831 "rendered him desirous of external support; but this novel inclination his spirit would fain suppress and disguise even from itself" (Lockhart, 7:290). Although Lockhart would meddle with Scott's texts, and though he would angrily assert to Hogg after the author's demise that "*we* [Lockhart and Cadell, his publisher for the *Memoirs*] now [stand] in the room of the dead," he revealed his unease in the position he had sought (Hogg, *Anecdotes*, 6–8). Did the supposedly voiceless Scott speak to his colleagues the truth of their own practice? Perhaps, even as they participated in it, they could not face the reality of exchange.

This would account for Cadell's response to the travelling Sir Walter's request for money. In terms that reveal the link between Scott's physical decline and his fall into devaluative exchange, Cadell obnoxiously talked about "doctoring" the author's later work.[38] When the author impinged from abroad on Cadell's newly quiet life managing Scott's apparently completed novels, the publisher wrote to Scott's son with a shocking insensitivity. Walter Scott, no longer actively authoring *Waverley*, through illness is figured as irrational and inarticulate to the degree of animality: "on getting to Naples [Scott] made so great a howling about money that I paid into Coutts & Co— 300—his howling, however, continued so great that I sent him farther & to Naples 500."[39] These words come from the man who, on 9 November 1830, celebrated Scott's refusal of a pension because "the pension best paid and sweetest when received is that flowing from your weary publisher" (Partington, 365). What could produce such inconsistency—such unkindness?

Cadell stood as Scott's banker. Typically, Scott received payment against work in progress, and Cadell made money from publishing Scott. At this point, he was eager to buy Scott's copyrights. When he finally gathered them in, Millgate observes, the man who had gone bankrupt alongside Scott, and whom the Trustees considered more to blame, became worth "at a conservative estimate, almost £121,000, virtually all of this accumulated from publishing Scott" (*Last*, 51). In 1832, Cadell was trying to silence Sir Walter and thus maintain the property of the Magnum, yet also to continue their relationship through finance because he could ultimately swap Scott's debts to him for copyrights. As Lockhart reports: "[in 1833] Mr Cadell [accepted] as his only security, the right to the profits accruing from Sir Walter Scott's copyright property and literary remains" (ibid. 50). And Millgate notes that later, Cadell "made permanent his exclusive title to Scott's works . . . by agreeing to write off the remaining portion of the debt to himself" (51). So Cadell's diction may mark the level of his disquiet with his own processes. By translating Scott's understandable requests for money and according to his usual practices into "howling," Cadell attempts to hide his motivation behind an unreasonable and inarticulate Sir Walter. But the indistinct voice of an author Cadell figures as disappearing into the distances of Europe and of senility may point us toward the truth. The issue was money. Two days after Scott's death, Cadell declared: "Money I love—I always avow it—I make it when I can." He even specified, "I have realized a fortune by Sir Walter Scott." Evidently, in the context of the declining author, he felt tainted by the reality of his exchange. The publisher worked to shift its degradations to the source of his success, the dying Sir Walter.[40]

Scott made the taint hard to avoid or ignore, for he actually forced a process of substitution on those (like Nigel) who would practice but obscure exchange. Consider *Count Robert*. When Ballantyne first complained about the text's Byzantine location and style, Scott's early submission to his opinion provoked from Cadell conflicted encouragement that Scott should keep writing. It even pressed reassurances out of him that *Count Robert* now looked good: "Ballantyne . . . is most high in his praise of Anna Comnena," one of the heroines; he himself is "Most happy to see Count Robert again on the way"; and he declares "Count Robert seems to get on most gallantly."[41] The effect is so striking that John Sutherland assumes Scott's devious intention despite his evidently depressed state. Although Scott wrote "[t]he blow [of Ballantyne's opinion] is a stunning one," Sutherland argues that "[i]t was a masterly power play by Scott" (*Journal*, 733; Sutherland, 341). Consider, too, *Count Robert* as Scott's last novel. Cadell, Lockhart, Ballantyne, and ultimately the kind Laidlaw all agreed that Scott should write no more. They got the author to concur. On 9 April 1831, a relieved Cadell reported "a most interesting conversation whether or not Sir Walter should write any more Novels after Count Robert—his own wish is not to write any more. . . . he seemed inclined to think that the L'Envoi [the wrap for the Magnum] would be all he should add after Count Robert."[42] However, on 3 July, with *Count Robert* still unfinished, Scott revealed: "I have put on the stocks a tale of arms love antiquities battle & so forth calld Castle Dangerous and the first volume is ready for press."[43] Three days later, Cadell penned a contract.[44] Scott even impinged from abroad upon this cohort worn out by the exigencies of exchange. Cadell received a Christmas note from Scott that celebrated: "have finishd since I have been here 30 close pages. . . . The title is the Siege of Malta. . . . I have quite recoverd the power of thinking for myself and must after all be my own best critic."[45] It threw Laidlaw into a guilty panic on the publisher's behalf. Part pleased by Scott's good humor, part distressed by the notion of yet another novel to consolidate into circulable property, he fluttered: "I had a long letter lately from Sir Walter with which I am but half satisfied although he evidently writes in great spirits, not to say glee—He is busy with a Romance he says, & he says moreover that he never wrote any thing *better in his life*. It is *possible* but . . . it would not only be a literary curiosity but next to a miracle."[46] Writing or promising to be silent, Scott marked the parameters within which his colleagues could speak. All—even Laidlaw—stood confined within exchange.[47]

Moreover, through his own hastening limitations, Scott exposed those of the colleagues who would convert him into a restricted currency. He does so most clearly in the Jedediah Cleishbotham "Introductory Address" for *Tales of My Landlord:* Fourth and Last Series.[48] Lockhart had suggested this introduction. Cadell, "expressing my fears as to Castle D ever appearing after Count Robert with any kind of success, [Lockhart] suggested making them into Tales of My Landlord, and getting Sir Walter to write a short Jedediah Cleishbottom Introduction."[49] The double irony of the introduction is that Lockhart also gave its reference to Cervantes. Just days before Scott's departure from Abbotsford, Lockhart countered Wordworth's lament that authors seem unhonored in their decline by citing the case of Cervantes and a student's "raptures on discovering that he had been riding all day with the author of Don Quixote" (Lockhart, 7:310). Lockhart was hinting the appropriate mode and content for belated literary exchange. A Jedediah introduction would consolidate *Count Robert* and *Castle Dangerous* with known properties by the Author of Waverley. A gesture through Cervantes toward an appreciative audience would maintain Scott's connection with a friendly and book-buying public. Scott, however, turned the tale to a purpose far from that Lockhart could have desired.

The "Introductory Address" seems to march with Cadell and Lockhart's concerns. It offers a disquisition on failing authorial power and a simultaneous attack on the pirates who had recently forced the publication of *Count Robert*—despite the fact that they had served Sir Walter. But through this introduction, the seemingly unwitting Scott effects a damning critique of the strategies being developed by Cadell and Lockhart. As Peter Pattieson's editor, Jedediah Cleishbotham has long obstructed yet allowed the speech of the dead—not unlike the interstitial Author of Waverley. Now, his own faculties are in decline. In addition, he finds himself competing with Pattieson's brother, Paul, for control of the author's literary remains. The upshot is that the text is stolen out from under his nose and pirated abroad. Thus, Scott opens a space for Jedediah to make a virtuoso argument for the failing author's particular circumstances. In Scott's own revised proof, the novel's flaws derive from "the rashness of . . . Paul Pattieson."[50] They are signs of an omission that cannot be blamed on Jedediah or Peter Pattieson. Yet they manifest a great authorial mind and test the greatness of its critics—as the case of Cervantes proves. Jedediah draws the parallel: "[Cervantes] rests upon the noble confidence that the merits of his labours were sufficient to call upon men to shut their eyes against a few casual errors; and that in filling up, during the perusal, such sketches as the carelessness of the author had suffered to remain loose, they will not do more than manifest becoming gratitude for the exquisite feast which has been spread to their imaginations in the adventures of the knight of La Mancha" (NLS MS 23052 3–4 with Scott's revisions). Also, Jedediah reminds us, Cervantes's errors, such as they are, often derive from the printer, or from envious critics or imitators who imported their own: "what chiefly called forth the complaint of the genuine author . . . was the conduct alike unfair and ungrateful of the author of a spurious second part . . . augmented by the malicious ingratitude which raked together and overcharged the trifling errors which had crept into the original, to which he was indebted" (3). Still Jedediah admits, "the difference is too great betwixt that great wit of Spain and ourselves, to permit us to use a buckler which was rendered sufficiently formidable only by the strenuous hand in which it was placed" (4). Too great for Jedediah, perhaps. But Scott opens a space for himself. Then he drops that "assumed buffoonery": the role of Jedediah (11). He steps through a door left ajar by careless editor Lockhart to specify the analogy between Cleishbotham, Cervantes—and Walter Scott. "The reader is now acquainted with the species of malady under which I have struggled," Scott says at last in his own voice, and he goes on to draw the authorial analogy directly: "I have mentioned the state of Cervantes struggling by turns with the imperious command of his disease" (11–12). Through illness, a sign Lockhart neglected in his reference to Cervantes, yet the ground of Scott's colleagues' critique and their guilty exchange, the author accepts his predecessor's greatness as his own and appropriates for himself Cervantes's stinging attack on printers and critics.

His whip stung those Scott had considered helpers. The joint-stock company's extensive revisions (mostly by Lockhart), performed once Scott was safely embarked for Naples, rip from the introduction its trenchant critiques and thus reveal the extent to which the now absent author evoked and spoke his colleagues as inadequate to criticize a Walter Scott. Lockhart's alterations enhance the awfulness that is Jedediah, making his diction ludicrously Latinate and consequently distinct from the voice of Scott. Jedediah's plain statement of Peter Pattieson's worth produces the riff: "These pages, I have said, were the *ultimus labor* of mine ingenious assistant"; "mistakes" becomes "*hiatus valdi deflendi*."[51] Jedediah's voice, and thus his criticism, must not be considered Sir Walter's. At the same time, Lockhart undermines the judgement and reputation that Scott manifests in the Author of Waverley even by the person of Jedediah. The schoolmaster's comment "I found these manuscripts, with all their faults, contained other passages, which seemed plainly to intimate, that disease itself had been unable to extinguish the brilliancy of that genius which had been made celebrated by the creations of Old Mortality," the editor translates into "I no question flattered myself that these manuscripts . . . contained here and there passages which . . . [intimated] . . . that fancy which the world had been pleased to acknowledge."[52] Scott's careful revaluation of Jedediah—who always has had the wit to appreciate Pattieson's work in large—and thus Scott's covert valuation of himself, is transmuted into Jedediah's self-denigrating self-aggrandizement. Indeed, this altered text actually exaggerates authorial problems. Lockhart converts Pattieson's "two manuscripts" into "certain woefully blurred" texts and inserts a description entirely his own.[53] They are "the last, and it is manifest never carefully revised or corrected handiwork of Mr. Peter Pattieson."[54] Clearly, they need his attention. This version goes so far as to remove Scott's attacks on printers, cutting the mordant remark: "This deeply experienced author flatly places such errors to the charge of the printer." Outrageously, Lockhart has Jedediah voice the apparently respectful determination not yet to

submit the manuscripts to "the Ballantynian ordeal."[55] And, maybe thinking of himself, he cuts Jedediah's sarcastic declaration that textual errors
"must unhappily now be imputed to the rashness of my worthy assistant,
Paul Pattison," and thus turns criticism away from the practice of editing
and toward the schoolmaster behind whom stands Walter Scott."[56] Lockhart is precisely the critic Scott feared. But such revisions, performed at
Scott's textual prompting, expose Lockhart and his cohort as self-servers
floundering in the morass of exchange.

Of course these changes also obscure the joint-stock company's collusion
to revise and silence Scott, for only this bowdlerized introduction made it
into print. Yet in that form, too, a text supposedly "stolen" and certainly
rewritten gestures toward its various authors and allows their circulation in
the moment of our reading. In fact, since Jedediah had been declared dead in
order to obviate another act of plagiary years before, and since Cervantes too
was long gone, despite Lockhart—yet also through him and his argument for
an introduction—Pattieson, Cleishbotham, Cervantes, and Scott together
spoke their critique across the bounds of death.[57] Their necessary silence
produced and disturbed the ongoing process of exchange between author
and editor, text and reader that is an inevitable condition of publication.

Castle Dangerous *and the Returns of True Thomas*

As if he had not been dead a day

Castle Dangerous, written while Scott pondered revising *Count Robert*, indicates how the absent author becomes the source of such complex unease.
For Lockhart and his colleagues, the question was: Should Scott continue to
speak once he had been converted into current coin through the Magnum?
For Scott, it was: Could he speak when he would circulate only in memory
and through the hands of editors? In *Castle Dangerous* (1831), numerous characters try to speak across the bounds of place and time—and even of life. The
English Lady Augusta cross dresses and travels from England to Scotland to
revise her words that challenged Sir John de Walton to demonstrate his hero-
ism by holding the Douglas's castle for one year. The Douglas tries to regain
his Scottish power and recreate the present from the past, The once-beauti-
ful Margaret de Hautlieu wants to express herself despite her body, bound
by injury to ugliness. And each must go the way of death. The Douglas can
move across land that should be his own only when obscured and manifested
by "the emblems of the King of Terrors himself"—his black armour with its
skeletal device.[58] The Lady Augusta must move in his company and through
"the vapours of a new-made grave" (4:234/chapter 17). Margaret must sub-

mit to the little death of a convent before reemerging to the world. Even the otherwise unimplicated young knight Sir Aymer de Valence must pursue the truth of Lady Augusta and the Douglas in a graveyard and with an ancient sexton who lives in and upon the things of the dead (4:93–100/chapter 9). The declining Sir Walter comes close to suggesting that communication can be achieved only by passing through the grave.

Worse, Scott implies that the one figure who can cross all bounds and who will create and disrupt all realities is the author. Bertram the minstrel ambles easily from England to Scotland (3:222–25; 241–46; 269–80/chapter 3). Moving freely through the place that is fiction, Bertram alone can speak the border wars into the timelessness of fame. Disturbingly, however, the individual tales he will tell are deathly. To Bertram, "There are . . . minstrels, and . . . even belted knights . . . who do not sufficiently value that renown which is acquired at the risk of life" (3:276/chapter 3). Those who live shall do so through Bertram's tale of death. Further, when Sir Aymer and Bertram debate the facts of the wars, the minstrel caps the soldier with the suggestion that one tale bears the death of another: "were you a Scot," he notes, "you would with patience hear me tell over what has been said of [the Douglas] by those who have known him, and whose account of his adventures shows how differently the same tale may be told" (3:287/chapter 4). Bertram implicates as he tells, too. When he recounts his objective view of the current strife, Sir Aymer interrupts hastily, "this is beyond bargain" (3:283/chapter 4). Bertram is suspected of consorting with the plague and bringing death, but his auditors fear words—which reveal the degraded reality of their moment as much as physical contagion. To tell is to communicate taint through the excess that is truth.

This authorial facility menaces the present from beyond time when the minstrel is dead. Bertram has come north, in part, to retrieve the lost manuscripts of Thomas the Rhymer. Thomas is long gone, but already has spoken into a future that is now the past. When a previous minstrel sought to save the writings from a fire predicted by the Rhymer—Douglas Castle repeatedly will fall and be rebuilt grander than before—Thomas himself appeared to intervene: "[the book was] slowly removed from the desk on which it lay by an invisible hand. . . . A tall thin form, attired in, or rather shaded with, a long flowing dusky robe, having a face and physiognomy so wild and overgrown with hair as to be hardly human, were the only marked outlines of the phantom" (3:303/chapter 5). Thomas, reminiscent of the indeterminate "Eidolon, or Representation, of the Author of Waverley," subjects the present to a future he will yet inhabit. "Begone!" he tells Hugonet. "The fated hour of removing this book is not yet come" (3:307/chapter 5). That hour is Bertram's, and the book defines and reveals the problem within the moment it reappears. When Sir John de Walton battles the Douglas for the

Castle in a combat that exposes all worldly endeavor as a matter of perpetual exchange—the Scots will win, then the English, ad infinitum—the book from the past projects Bertram back to a fight now in progress. Bertram predicts: "I could tell of these onslaughts did I know whereabouts is a place in these woods termed Bloody-Sykes (4:270/chapter 18). However, the fight has already begun (3:249/chapter 19). The absent Thomas the Rhymer bears the truth and taint that is the present exchange out of a future that the author strangely inhabits by way of his own death.

In fact, despite Scott's worries and his colleagues' efforts, the yet-living author already spoke from the far side of death. Derrida explains this impossibility.[59] In his terms, Scott and his works would constitute the gift that (disturbingly) keeps on giving. Derrida notes that we code even unsolicited donations through the delimiting discourse of exchange. This suggests that we fear the phenomenon of the gift, insofar as a gift requires no return. Giving seems to be the trace that haunts the idea of precise valuation by careful exchange. Why is it so? The act of giving constitutes a present as object and duration, and thus implies valuation. But if giving works to suggest the presence of the present, it is itself an absence. Moreover, the notion of presence depends on what no one possesses: time. So instead of conferring value, giving hints at the ultimate exchange between presence and absence. It invokes death in life, and its functioning requires life in the context of impossibility. Giving is a function of infinite differing and deferring, gesturing from the space of no-time. Thus giving undoes all equivalencies, and "only a *singular surviving* can give" (*Given Time*, 102). Which is perhaps to say that only across the double death of the Foucaultian author—dead to the text and the world, yet persisting in both—is the gift possible and the exchange of culture allowed and also undermined. We might consider, by way of example, True Thomas and his book. Out of time but active within it, they offer the gift of the present even as it becomes the irrecuperable past.

For Scots of the early nineteenth century, it was Sir Walter himself who manifested a "singular surviving." The conditions of Scott's later years constituted the author, about to be absent, as being and offering the gift, in all its complexity. He stood outside of yet crossed space and time, thus making possible while undercutting all exchange and valuation. Scott's work participated in exchange, but equally, the Author of Waverley stood inscribed as the function of giving—particularly as he appeared to collapse into the current coin of the Magnum. In his "General Preface" to the edition (1829), Scott asserted the Author of Waverley as always beyond exchange. "I had not the usual stimulus for desiring personal reputation, the desire, namely, to float amidst the conversation of men." "Of literary fame," he continues, "I had already as much as might have contented a mind more ambitious than mine" (Scott, *Prefaces*, 94). Indeed, he told R. P. Gillies that "[t]he man who writes well, generally has a pleasure in writing, which alone is a recompense; and with regard to obtaining the favour of booksellers, or of the public, it is a mere lottery" (Robertson, *Lives*, 163–89; 169). Scott writes with no need to no one.

Further, even as the Author of Waverley becomes visible, he stands recreated as an absence. At the Theatrical Fund Dinner, Vedder tells us, Scott declared: "[h]e was now before the bar of his country, and might be understood to be on trial . . . yet he was sure that every impartial jury would bring in a verdict of Not Proven" (Robertson, *Lives*, 37). And as Robertson notes, when Scott appears to connect himself to his works, "the desire for certainty is continually deflected by the narrative and its supporting wealth of annotation. The impression of solidity which it creates is false" (*Legitimate*, 151). We might argue the same for Scott's supposedly self-revelatory preface to *The Chronicles of the Canongate* (1827). In the introduction to this first major text after his financial collapse, Scott apparently discards his mask. But he immediately defines what is revealed through anecdotes about those who have given or populated his stories. No one writes.

Moreover, Scott writes a gap. As Robertson observes, "Scott has a habit of assuring the reader that his is an inferior version of a really good story" (*Legitimate*, 153). Patricia Gaston comments that as early as 1810, "Scott's stance . . . is to admit, to enumerate, and . . . even to relish in the description of [textual] flaws; to draw them clearly and emphatically to the reader's attention; and then to do nothing at all about them" (13). A discourse of worthlessness disappears the very texts Scott produces.

Yet Scott could not stop writing. To Cadell's distress, he responded to his doctor's advice: "a man can no more say to his mind 'dont think' than Molly can say to her Kettle 'dont boil'" ([25/26 April 1831], *Letters*, 12:14). He told Lockhart: "if I were to be idle I should go mad" (Lockhart, 7:245). But after the Theatrical Fund dinner, it appeared he wrote for banks and publishers and the audience—not for himself. The *London Magazine*, we may recall, exposed Scott's finances to the world, but it also stressed that "We find him yielding up every stiver or its worth he could command . . . actually pledging future labours ([April 1827]: 533). Scott was pouring absence into an excessive emptiness. His was the gift that could neither be given nor received. It implied and overran the bounds of giving, for it produced an equivalence in which Scott could have no part. Scott thus deconstructed any cozy notion of contemporary literary exchange.

As Scott neared his end, this discourse of abstracted giving entered the realm of impossibility. The "Advertisement" for the Magnum figures it as preemptively posthumous: the "improved and illustrated edition" was supposed to be "a posthumous publication" (Scott, *Prefaces*, 83). Scott will not alter "in the slightest degree, either the story or the mode of telling it" (84).

He will "give them to the press in a corrected and, he hopes, an improved form, while life and health permit the task" (83). The author is already stealing time to speak across the death of both text and teller. Then when Scott embarked in the Barham, any subsequent words were constituted as coming from the beyond not just of Italy, but of death. The *Border Maga-zine* laments: "That wonderful being, who for many years has continued to excite the admiration of the world by . . . an unparalleled number of publi-cations—the produce of one mind, which is apparently inexhaustible—. . . he, the mighty magician, oppressed by the burdens of age, is now seeking in a foreign and milder clime relief from pain, where perhaps he will find a stranger's grave" ([1 December 1831]: 90). Further, since *Count Robert* and *Castle Dangerous* appeared after Scott's departure and Britain's maud-lin farewell, even their declarations of "lastness" were already superceded. In a few lines of Scott's farewell that Lockhart retained, though displaced into an epilogue, the author bids goodbye: "a ship of war is commissioned by its Royal Master to carry the Author of Waverley."[60] But the ship had sailed; Scott was gone. And with these *Tales of My Landlord* designated "Fourth and Last Series," even the mild farewell Lockhart had allowed the revised Jedediah, with its gesture toward the vague "state of my health," is preempted by absence. To complete the confusion, Graham Tulloch's researches reveal that "Cadell et al. dated the [introduction] according to the date of publication even after Scott was completely incapable of writing after his stroke on the way back from Italy. However once he was actually dead they had, in all decency, to date [the introductions] from before his death and they actually reverted to using something like the real date of . . . composition."[61] The novels pointed to but appeared to speak from beyond Scott's final dissolution. On 16 March 1831, Scott wrote of the trouble-some *Count Robert*, "I will take time enough" (*Journal*, 718). Scott had long been—in the fullest sense—already out of time.

Hastening out of time, and yet beyond it, Scott constituted a problem for the joint-stock company, whose rush to convert the author into an exchange-able token was both allowed and exposed by Scott's incessant voicing from an unrecognizable and unassailable absence. Small wonder Lockhart busily revised to remove Scott's insistence on his extended passing, so that until the Edinburgh Edition publishes its version of the *Tales*, no reader beyond Laidlaw, Ballantyne, Cadell, and Lockhart will have heard the specificity of Scott's analogy between his own and Cervantes's infirmities; no reader can appreciate Scott audibly persisting on the cusp of life and death.[62] Nor is it surprising that as Lockhart wrote Scott's biography for Cadell, he strove to put his father-in-law permanently to bed. Scott is supposed to have saved his last words for Lockhart: "My dear, be a good man—be virtuous—be reli-gious—be a good man. Nothing else will give you any comfort when you come to lie here."[63] However, this bogus epilogue to a complex life constructs the finality of one of the nineteenth century's first sentimental deathbed scenes. It sublimates Lockhart's mounting desire that Scott, please, be over and done with.

Walter Scott and the Story of Tomorrow

> Loud sobs, and laughter louder, ran . . .
> Because these spells were brought to day

Because Scott is "out of time," he poses an even bigger problem for those who would narrate the nation. He declared in his Magnum preface to *The Abbot* that "the quality of readiness and profusion [has] a merit in itself, independent of the intrinsic value of the composition. . . . By . . . new efforts . . . errors [are] obliterated, [authors become] identified with the literature of their country, and after having long received law from the critics, [come] in some degree to impose it" (Scott, *Prefaces*, 164). Scott's prolific authorship had made him national. As he drew near to death, his illness disarmed criticism. The *Monthly Review* gave in before it began to assess this last volume of *Tales*. "Sir Walter Scott," the reviewer cautions, "has taken his departure . . . from our shores, in a state of health which almost forbids us to think of commenting on his new and 'last' series of the 'Tales of My Landlord'" (5 ser., 1 [January 1832]: 66). In death, Scott stood confirmed as a teller of the nation, the *London Literary Gazette* reminding its readers: "he has made his own land classical" (no. 776 [3 December 1831]: 770). But because his telling was silenced in the past it remained audible in the future. The *Edinburgh Literary Journal* lamented: "THE LAST! The last echo of the last Bard's harp—the farewell prophecy of the silenced oracle" (no. 160 [3 December 1831]: 317). In spite of—or perhaps because of—the invisible Lockhart, the journal found Scott's last published novels execrable, yet it declared they bore "traces of his genius" and constituted his "farewell gift." Joanna Baillie thought the dead Scott at once "[t]he cover'd treasure of a sacred spot" and "[t]he cherish'd, speaking friend of living men" (Robertson, *Lives*, 12–22). He is a present absence that animates the nation; his is a "singular surviving." Scott sounds one of those impossible voices outside of time—allowing, revealing, and undoing the moment of exchange that is Scotland.

The trouble with Scott—right into today—is that because his words were stolen away as he uttered them, he became a speaking silence before he died and continues to lurk although dead. Scott is the gift—unwanted yet unrecognizable; deconstructive yet essential; and operative in too many cases. From Lockhart's young manhood, Walter Scott figured as the uncanny in

Scottish culture. He manifested an ineluctable giving that discomfited even those involved in the normal exchange between day and night, work and pleasure. Lockhart recounted a party where the host complained: "there is a confounded hand in sight of me here, which has often bothered me before, and now it won't let me fill my glass with a good will. . . . it fascinates my eye—it never stops—page after page is finished and thrown on that heap of MS., and still it goes on unwearied. . . . It is the same every night—I can't stand the sight of it. . . . I well know what hand it is—'tis Walter Scott's" (Lockhart, 3:128). It is thus that Scott continues to haunt the work of Scotland's most thoughtful national critics.

Scott is a silence that surrounds any moment of national authorship and speaks the taint in the daily exchange out of which we construct the life that is Scottish culture. He spoke it loudly in what Cairns Craig calls the "Scotch Myths debate." For Craig, the 1980s bitter scholarly dislike of tartanry (supposedly founded in Walter Scott) exposed "the profound hatred of the intellectuals for the culture they inhabited, the profound embarrassment they suffered by being unable, any more, to identify themselves with some universalist truth that would redeem them from Scottishness. They did not want to carry the burden of the Scottish past; they did not want to negotiate with the actualities of Scottish culture: they wanted to abolish it and create it anew in their own image" (*Out of History*, 107). Scott produced and now reveals the barrenness of their exchange. Yet Scott speaks the taint of exchange even to those who want to negotiate Scotland both through and beyond its history. This is why we find authors from Hogg to Pittock formally reinterring Sir Walter at the start of their various projects—whether as Tory laird, Borders bourgeois, over-Enlightened historian, Jacobite manqué, or any other possible Scot. The assumption is that if we are to accomplish Scotland in our moment of exchange, we need to burke Sir Walter. The irony, of course, is that the more we work to silence Scott, the more we construct him as a speaking excess and make him live in the national unconscious.

Tom Nairn, one of Scotland's more radical critics, admits in 1997: "Our *auld claes*, Walter Scott's tartan romanticism, have been an . . . effective spiritual antidote against the least romantic, the most boring of bourgeois societies." But he goes on, "[this] also explains why . . . Scottish nationalism alone among European nationalist movements, has proved so remorselessly philistine" (Nairn *Faces*, 191). In 2000, with the new Scottish Parliament established, Nairn still cannot get away from Scott (*Faces*, 192). "Walter Scott," he writes disparagingly, "was the most influential literary representative of . . . the long facing-both-ways era" (*After Britain*, 230). Nairn's insistence on the "new" depends on an exchange against Walter Scott as the old. However, when Nairn goes on to note "All intelligent visitors to Scotland have been conscious of . . . a 'phoney' identity-claim to which perfectly unphoney people cling," he comes around to the potentiality of Scott's processes, which have always suggested the necessity to make a future through and beyond the contradictions of the past (251).

Scotland, Nairn sees through his wry eye, "manifests a fundamental wish: the will to continue 'being something,' and hence to go on presenting a new image both to the outside world and to oneself." Focusing not on Scott but, I would argue, on his effects, Nairn uncomfortably observes:

> the national society which had generated the staid, pure reason of 'civil society' also ended by creating a fantasy *alter ego* for itself. . . .
> The real purpose here was always the preservation of nationality— something which . . . civic institutionalism by itself would never have sufficiently achieved. . . . A modern nation has first and foremost to be a 'community of citizens.' . . . social survival and reproduction . . . demands it be simultaneously a 'felt' association resting upon deeper and longer-range motifs linked to culture, emotion and transmissible 'instincts.' (251–52)

Nairn observes the power of imagined communities, but remains suspicious both of them and of the habits of practical politics: "inbred institutionalism" and "fake Celticism" need to be disentangled and transcended (252). "Scotland has to be unmade by an eruption of democracy. . . . national 'deconstruction' should take over from 'nation-building'" (262). In so suggesting, Nairn shows Scott as his point of resistance, but also as a problematic source of cultural signs, and deploys his predecessor's method of deconstructive potentiality. That is, through the seams of his argument Nairn reveals how persistently and annoyingly present, but also how disruptive and thus creatively formative, Walter Scott may prove in a society always new.

As Cairns Craig asserts, after (he says) Walter Scott has forced Scots into the past or beyond history (progress), they must embrace the simultaneity that is culture: "not simply that events happen simultaneously in space around us, but are happening simultaneously in the space that is our own bodies" or, as I would offer, the body of Scotland (221). Scott declared in his unpublished afterword for *Count Robert*, "the romance, though perhaps the last which the Author of Waverley shall write, comes before the public like the elder Hamlet before his last Judge, 'With all its imperfections on its head'" (*Prefaces*, 244). The real difficulty with Hamlet the King was that he insisted on coming still before Denmark. Walter Scott continues to appear before us as we try to inscribe the nation. Like the elder Hamlet, he remains simultaneous with the moment. Yet just as the elder Hamlet suffers from a notoriously imprecise description, so Scott remains indeterminate. He haunts us not as one possible and deniable Scotland, or even as possible Scotlands, but as a condition that disrupts our processes and keeps them self-conscious. He reminds us that the way we perform Scotland resides within and suffers the taint of exchange.

Thus, Scott constitutes not a curse, but an opportunity. We are entering a new millennium with a new Scottish Parliament—a present that was the future for Walter Scott in his role of Thomas the Rhymer. What Scotlands will ensue? If the occasional Member of the Scottish Parliament registers a whisper from the literary beyond that there is not one Scotland, but many, and that theirs circulates for worse and for better in a system of exchange, perhaps Sir Walter will yet prove, for the Scotland of the twenty-first century, the gift that keeps on giving. After all, "'Twas thus the LATEST MIN-STREL sung."

NOTES

Chapter 1

Epigraph is from Ian Rankin, *Set in Darkness* (2000; rpt. New York: St. Martin's Press, 2001), 229, 231.

Section headings are from Scott's *The Lay of the Last Minstrel* (1805), reference Canto and verse: C 2. XIX.

1. Jan-Andrew Henderson, *The Town Below the Ground: Edinburgh's Legendary Underground City* (Edinburgh: Mainstream, 1999), 94–95, gives a colorful retelling. Rebus hears the tale at the start of *Set in Darkness* (9).

2. "Donald Dewar's Speech at the Opening of the Parliament" (London) *Times*, 2 July 1999. http://www.Sunday-times.co.uk/news/pages/tim/99/07/02/timnwsnws02007.html?999. Accessed 20 January 2000.

3. *Billy Connolly, World Tour of Scotland*, Episode 1, dir. Willy Smax, BBC Scotland, 1994 (distr. Polygram).

4. Tanya Thompson, "A Showpiece for Scotland or Home for the Blairs?" *Scotsman*, 6 July 1998. http://www.alba.org.uk/scottish/doverhouse.html. Accessed 17 December 2003. Susie Steiner, "MPs Book Time Off," *Guardian*, 22 August 2002. http://politics.guardian.co.uk/bookshelf/story/0,9061,779154,00.html. Accessed 1 January 2003.

5. Mike Watson, "Scotland: A Place for Culture and Culture in Place," Donald Dewar Lecture, 20 August 2002. http://www.scottishlabour.org.uk/pressrel/pr2002821101421.html. Accessed 20 January 2003.

6. See Mitchell, Kellas, and Harvie (*The Road to Home Rule*).

7. Anon, *"Waverley: or, 'Tis Sixty Years since,"* *Scots Magazine* 76 (July 1814): 524.

8. Harvie, "Scott and the Image of Scotland," 173, quotes Theodore Fontane, *Jenseits des Tweed*.

9. "Burns versus Scott: The Debate Today." http://www.members.aol.com/scots4paf/bvsws.htm. Accessed 14 February 2002. November 1996–February 1998 postings include letters from Paul Henderson Scott and Mark Calney, and refer to comments by Angus Calder.

10. References to Scott's novels are to the *Edinburgh Edition of the Waverley Novels*. When a specific text is not yet published in that series, I refer to the best recent edition. Failing that, I cite the Magnum Edition by volume and chapter, with the exception of *Castle Dangerous*. Walter Scott, *Waverley; or 'Tis Sixty Years Since*, 1814, ed. Claire Lamont (Oxford: Oxford University Press, 1986), 3–4/ch. 1.

11. See *The Betrothed* in the Magnum Edition (Edinburgh: Cadell, 1832), xxiii–xli.

12. See Goslee, 4–5, for the authoritative account.

13. *Sociology of Nationalism*, 59–60. See Scott's letter to Miss Clephane, 13 July 1813 (*Letters*, 3:301–303) for the source.

14. To John B. S. Morritt, [PM. 28 July 1814], *Letters*, 3:477–81; see 478.

15. Johnson references *Poetical Works*, VIII, *Lady of the Lake*, Pref. 10–11.

16. Byron, *English Bards and Scotch Reviewers*, 175–84.

17. To James Ballantyne, 30 [August 1813], *Letters*, 3:331–35. Johnson recounts the crisis, 1:407–25.

18. To Charles, Duke of Buccleuch, 24 August 1813, *Letters*, 3:322–25.

19. See To Robert Southey, 1 September [1813]; To Lady Abercorn, 3 September [1813]; To Charles Carpenter, 3 September 1813; To Matthew Weld Hartstonge, 4 September 1813; To John B. S. Morritt, 4 September [1813]; To Messers Longman, 5 September 1813; To Mrs. Walter Scott, 5 September [1813]; To Joanna Baillie, 12 September [1813]. (*Letters*, 3:335–36; 337–40; 340–42; 348–50; 350–52; 353; 353–54; 355–57).

20. Jane Millgate reviews Scott's experiment with anonymity in *The Bridal of Triermain* (*Walter Scott*, 59).

21. James Buzard rehearses Fergus's Scottish/French/political/personal allegiances in "Translation and Tourism" (47).

22. John Sutherland, "How Much English Blood (If Any) Does Waverley Spill?" in *Is Heathcliff a Murderer? Great Puzzles in Nineteenth-Century Literature* (Oxford: Oxford University Press, 1996), 10–13.

23. Popularly termed the "Malachi Malagrowther" letters, these are reprinted in facsimile as *Thoughts on the Proposed Change of Currency*.

Chapter 2

Epigraphs for this section come from *The Antiquary*, 309–11.

1. These novels appear under their individual titles in the Edinburgh Edition of the Waverley Novels.

2. Review of *The Antiquary*, *Monthly Review* 82 (January–April 1817): 38–52; see 39.

3. John Wilson Croker, review of *The Antiquary*, *Quarterly Review* 15 (April 1816): 125–39; see 126.

4. Scott told his friend Morritt: "I begin to get too old and stupid I think for poetry and will certainly never again adventure on a grand scale." To John B. S. Morritt, 31 January 1817, *Letters*, 4:383–85.

5. To Archibald Constable, Bookseller, Edinburgh, 26 October 1816, *Letters*, 4:279–81.

6. To Lady Louisa Stuart, Edinburgh, 14 November 1816, *Letters*, 4:291–5.

7. Review of *The Antiquary*, *Augustine Review* 3 (July–December 1816): 155–77; see 177. Croker, see earlier note, (3) 128–29.

8. Review of *The Antiquary*, *European Magazine and London Review* 70 (September 1816): 248–50; see 248.

9. Variants appear in *Folk Songs of England, Ireland, Scotland and Wales*, *The Saltire Scottish Song Book*, and *The Fireside Book of Children's Songs*. http://www.contemplator.com. Murray Pittock connects some of James Hogg's versions in his edition of *The Jacobite Relics of Scotland: Being the Songs, Airs, and Legends of the Adherents of the House of Stuart* [First Series] (Edinburgh: Edinburgh University Press, 2002), 451 n. Song XLVIII. A modern version where "his ears are made of chocolate-tomatoes" appears on the audiocassette *The Singing Kettle: 1* (Kingskettle, Fife: Kettle Records, n.d.).

10. *The Surprising Adventures of Baron Munchausen*, intro. Thomas Seccombe (London: Lawrence & Bullen, 1895), 135.

11. Review of *The Antiquary*, *Monthly Review* 82 (January–April 1817): 38–52; see 48–51; review of *The Antiquary*, *Quarterly Review* 15 (April 1816): 125–39; see 136.

12. To Daniel Terry, 12 November 1816, *Letters*, 4:287–91; see 288.

13. The Edinburgh Edition returns to the title *The Tale of Old Mortality*. I abbreviate by the more common *Old Mortality*.

14. To Lady Louisa Stuart, 14 November 1816, *Letters*, 4:291–95; see 292.

15. To Daniel Terry, 30 April 1818, *Letters*, 5:133–35; see 135.

16. McCracken-Flesher, "English Hegemony," ch. "Old Mortality"; Georg Lukács coins the "middle way" (32); Robert -J. Mewton remarks the "stable order" (57).

17. Lockhart, 4:37–39. Lockhart's version directed critical conversation until challenged by Johnson's milder and probably more accurate utterance (1:552).

18. See McCracken-Flesher, "A Wo/man," and "Narrating."

19. To Lady Louisa Stuart, 14 November 1816, *Letters*, 4:291–95; see 292–93.

20. To John Murray, 18 December 1816, *Letters*, 4:318–19.

21. McCrie's "Vindication of the Covenanters" ran first in the *Christian Instructor* then appeared in book form: *Vindication of the Covenanters in a Review of the "Tales of My Landlord."* Citations are to the book.

22. To Lady Louisa Stuart, 31 January 1817, *Letters*, 4:380–82.

23. To Charles Kirkpatrick Sharpe, [January 1817], *Letters*, 4:355–56.

24. To Charles Kirkpatrick Sharpe, [early February 1817], *Letters*, 4:385–87.

25. To His Grace the Duke of Buccleuch, [January 1816], *Letters*, 4:158–60; To Charles Kirkpatrick Sharpe, [1816], *Letters*, 4:151–53.

26. [Francis Jeffrey], Review of *Waverley, or 'Tis Sixty Years Since*, *Edinburgh Review* 24 (November 1814–February 1815): 208–43; see 243.

27. To Lady Abercorn, 29 November [1816], *Letters*, 4:307–309.

28. To Joseph Train, 21 December 1816, *Letters*, 4:323–24.

29. To Lady Abercorn, 28 December [1816], *Letters*, 4:340–44.

30. John Buchan, *Sir Walter Scott* (1932; London: Cassell, 1961), 171; Johnson, 1:586.

Chapter 3

Epigraphs for this section are drawn from *The Fortunes of Nigel*, 170.

1. *Letters*, 6:346 and n.1, 377–78; 7:11–12, 17, 18–22, 26–28, 114, 192–96, 204–206, 208–10.

2. Johnson, 2:773–74 and Grierson, *Sir Walter Scott, Bart.*, 195.

3. To John Gibson Lockhart, 23 March [postmarked 1819], *Letters*, 5:321–24.

4. The baronetcy was in process from 1818 until it was patented on March 30 and gazetted 1 April 1820. See Johnson, 1:616, 634–35, 702; Hutton, 136–37.

5. Scott mentions this possibility to his son, Walter Scott, 26 May [1821], *Letters*, 6:650–53.

6. "The Steam-Boat" No. VI Part III, *Blackwood's Magazine* 54, no. 10 (August [part 2] 1821): 14–26. See 22–24 for a comic account and a response from Glengarry.

7. References here are to the Edinburgh Edition of the Waverley Novels.

8. Jeanie Deans invokes this proverb (*Heart of Mid-Lothian*, 225).

9. Heriot purchases James's assistance by selling him on credit a salver embossed with the judgement of Solomon (68).

10. To Mr. Fitzgerald of Raith, 17 August 1822, quoted in Maxwell, 45.

11. [William Maginn], "The King's Visit to Ireland," *Blackwood's* 10, no. 55 (September 1821): 224–28; see 224. I owe the article's attribution to Strout, (85).

12. To John B. S. Morritt, 18 February 1822, *Letters*, 7:69–72; see 70. For Brummell's quip, see Hibbert, 25.

13. Quoted from a speech at Glasgow in 1836 in *A Full Account*, 42.

14. *Don Juan* canto XI v.78, 620–24 (McGann, 5: 489). Byron produced canto XI in September–October 1822 (McGann 5:xv).

15. The song appears in Hogg's *Jacobite Relics*, 39. An "Account of a Coronation-Dinner at Edinburgh" credits "a country-looking man, well advanced in life, with red whiskers"—likely Hogg—with a rendition that terms George the Stuarts' son and heir. See *Blackwood's* 10, no. 54 Part II (August 1821): 26–33, especially 28, 30–31. Hogg's draft to Neil Gow (27 July 1822), with slight variations, appears in NLS MS 1809 ff.79–80. Scott's song appeared in many versions around the visit. I refer to that printed in the appendix to *Hints*, 29–32.

16. "Letter from a Goth," *Blackwood's* 12, no. 68 (September 1822): 354–59; see 354–55.

17. [Sir] Arthur Mackenzie to the Duke of Atholl, n.d. [end of July], "4th Duke Correspondence," ACR 68/12:239.

18. In August, the *Scotsman* reported: "his Majesty . . . said to Sir Walter Scott, 'I have always heard that the Scotch were a proud nation, and they well may be so they seem to be a nation of gentlemen.'" See "The Peers' Ball," *Scotsman*, 24 August 1822: 268–69; 268. In October, the *Edinburgh Magazine* recalled that as the King left Holyrood, "he called Lord Lynedoch to him, and . . . stated . . . 'I have often heard the Scots called a proud nation—they may well be so—they appear to be a nation of gentlemen.'" See "British Chronicle. August. The King's Visit to Scotland," *Edinburgh Magazine and Literary Miscellany, Being a New Series of the Scots Magazine* October 1822: 499–513; see 505. Sixteen years later, *A Full Account* declares: "Well might he exclaim . . . 'BUT WHERE ARE THE WORKING PEOPLE?—THIS SEEMS A NATION OF GENTLEMEN!'" (38).

19. "His Majesty's Celtic toilette had been carefully watched and assisted by the gallant Laird of Garth, who was not a little proud of the result of his dexterous manipulations of the royal plaid, and pronounced the King 'a vera pretty man'" (Lockhart, 5:203).

20. Mary Stewart Mackenzie to Sir Walter Scott, 10 August 1822, "Letters to Sir Walter Scott (1822 July–December)," NLS MS 3895: 43.

21. Lord Melville to Baillie Macfie, 30 July 1822 and 13 August 1822, NAS GD51/5/749 vol. 2: 49–52 and 67–68.

22. *Full Account*, 48, and Marquis of Lothian to Sir Walter Scott, [n.d.], NLS MS 3895: 89.

23. James Loch to Sir Walter Scott, 31 July 1822, "Letters to Scott 1820–22," NLS MS 867: 187. See also 189–90. The Marchioness did not go to Edinburgh, because of her husband's illness. Her son carried the Sceptre. See Marchioness of Stafford and Countess of Sutherland, letter to Sir Walter Scott, 3 September 1822, NLS MS 3895: 75.

24. [Anon] to "Sir Walter Scott Bart.," 5 August 1822, NLS MS 867: 199.

25. James Spence to Sir Walter Scott, 5 August 1822, NLS MS 867: 197.

26. George Tough to Walter Scott, 26 September 1822, NLS MS 3895: 109.

27. Scott to Sir William Knighton, 18 November 1822, and footnote 1, Aspinall, 544.

28. James Loch to Sir Walter Scott Bart. and enclosure, 31 July 1822, NLS MS 867: 187 and 189–90.

29. Duke of Atholl, "4th Duke Journals," 1 August 1822, ACR 1026/34: 23–24.

30. Lord Melville draft letter to George IV, [24] July 1821, NAS GD51/1/214/45.

31. Sir A. M. Mackenzie to Duke of Atholl, 29 July [1822], ACR 68/12: 238.

32. "A Representation of the St. Andrew's Cross, Presented by the Ladies to His Majesty, on his Arrival in Scotland; with a Description," *Royal Visit 1822*: vol. 2 Miscellanies, NLS F.5.f.17 (1–6): 3–4.

33. For Glengarry's claim, see "Walter Scott to Alexander Macdonell of Glengarry," [March–April 1816], *Letters*, 4:198–99 and 198 fn.1.

34. "To the Editor of the Observer, Edinburgh 30th August, 1822," *Edinburgh Observer*, 2 September 1822: [3] and A. Rn. Macdonell, "To the Editor of the Observer (Continued from Monday's Paper)," *Edinburgh Observer*, 5 September 1822: [3]. See 5 September.

35. A [ ] Macdonell to Sir Walter Scott, 4 September 1822, NLS MS 3895: 77–78.

36. David Stewart of Garth to Sir Walter Scott, 9 October 1822, NLS MS 3895: 148.

37. Joseph Gordon, Colin Mackenzie to Sir Walter Scott, 20 August 1822, NLS MS 3895: 152, 154.

38. "Glengarry *versus* the Celtic Society," *Blackwood's* 12, no. 68: 359–68, see 360–62.

39. Duke of Atholl "4th Duke Journals," 17 August 1822, ACR 1026/35: 8. See also Atholl, 319.

40. "The King's Arrival in Auld Reekie," (London) *Examiner*, 1 September 1822: 549–50; refrain, vv. 2, 3, 11.

41. Walter Scott to Monsr. Lieutenant Walter Scott, [28 August 1822], *Letters*, 7:225–29, see 228. Walter Scott to Lady Abercorn, 13 September 1822, *Letters*, 7:239–43, see 241.

42. Walter Scott to James Ballantyne, [15 September 1822], *Letters*, 7:246–47.

43. Sir Walter Scott to Sir William Knighton, 12 September 1822, Aspinall, 2:539–44, see 540–41.

44. Harriet Scott, letter to Anne Scott, 17 August 1822, NAS GD157/2548/3.

45. J. L. Adolphus, letter to Walter Scott, 12 November 1822, NLS MS 3895: 222.

46. See Raymond Duncan, "Unofficial Queen of Scots Plan," *Herald* (Glasgow), 18 October 1999; http://www.theherald.co.uk/news/archive/18–10–1999–23–58–15.html (accessed 19 January 2000); and James Dixon, "Queen to Go on Scottish Public Relations Drive," *Guardian* 18 October 1999; http://www .guardianunlimited.co.uk/Archive/Article/0,4273,3913616,00.html (accessed 21 January 2000). For Prince Charles, see Chris Holme, "Hint of Kirk Role for Prince Charles," *Herald* (Glasgow), 15 November 1999; http://www.theherald. co.uk/news/archive/15–11–1999–23–40–21.html. Accessed 19 January 2000.

47. For Blair, see chapter 1, n. 4. For the Queen's remark, see "Passion and Colour Produce a Triumph," (London) *Times*, 2 July 1999; for Dewar see: "Today is a Proud Moment: A New Stage of a Journey Begun Long Ago," (London) *Times*, 2 July 1999. http://www.sunday-times.co.uk/news/pages/ tim/99/07/02/timnwsnws01005.html?999 (accessed 20 January 2000) and http://www.Sunday-times.co.uk/news/pages/tim/99/07/02/timnws-nws02007.html?999 (accessed 20 January 2000). For Braveheart, see Taylor, 113; *Scotland's Parliament*; Scotland Act 1998.

48. Peter Hetherington, "Old Border War Reaches New Pitch," *Guardian*, 13 November 1999; http://www.guardianunlimited.co.uk/Archive/0,4273,3929967 ,00.html. Accessed 21 January 2000.

Chapter 4

Epigraphs for this section are from *The Talisman*, ch. 23.

1. R. E. Raspe, perhaps Dousterswivel's model, worked with Matthew Boulton, Charlotte Scott's family friend, and James Watt's partner.

2. *Pontefract Castle* (1819) masqueraded as the fourth series of *Tales of My Landlord*, bearing Jedediah Cleishbotham's name for author. *Walladmor* (1824) appeared in German, purported to be translated from English, and bore Scott's name.

3. As we await the Edinburgh Edition of *The Talisman*, I refer to the Magnum version and give running chapter numbers common to other editions

4. An earlier version of my *Talisman* argument, "The Recuperation of Canon Fodder," critiques twentieth-century readings of this text as an organ of empire.

5. Tobias Smollett, *The Expedition of Humphry Clinker* (1771).

6. Review of *Woodstock*, *Literary Chronicle and Weekly Review* 363 (29 April 1826): 257–67 (see 257). See also review in *Gentleman's Magazine* May 1826: 434–37, and *Monthly Magazine* 2d S., 1 (June 1826): 626–27.

7. "[We] cannot expect [Scott] always to be at his best [in *Woodstock*]: we are watching the martyrdom of an intellect. Literary criticism gives place to human affection and regret" (Lang, xii).

8. Hobsbaum (150) follows Lockhart, who traces in Anne Scott after the financial crash "a change . . . exactly similar to that painted in poor Alice Lee" (6:309).

9. Typical is the critique of *The Monastery* in *The Lady's Monthly Museum* for May 1820 (Hayden, *Critical Heritage*, 185–87).

10. As we await the Edinburgh Edition of *Woodstock*, I refer to the Magnum version by volume and chapter number, and give running chapter numbers common to other editions.

11. In Laurence Sterne's *Tristram Shandy* (1759–67), Tristram describes Calais, a town he never saw (7: ch. 3–6).

Chapter 5

Epigraphs for this section are from the first "Malachi Malagrowther" letter, 46–47.

1. For a reading of the Scottish body politic as grotesque, see McCracken-Flesher, "Speaking."

2. *Edinburgh Review* 24 (November 1814–February 1815): 243; *Critical Review* 1, no. 3 (March 1815): 288, [294].

3. Review of *The Chronicles of the Canongate, Gentleman's Magazine* 97, no. 2 (November 1827): 439–45; see 444–45.

4. Review of *The Chronicles of the Canongate, Literary Gazette* (November 1827): 709–12; see 712.

5. "A Preface to a Review of *The Chronicles of the* Canongate," and the Review that follows, *Blackwood's* 22, no. 132 (November 1827): 531–70.

6. Review of *The Chronicles of the Canongate, London Magazine* (November 1827): 341–410.

7. Review of *The Chronicles of the Canongate, London Weekly Review and Journal* (3 November 1827): 340–43; see 340.

Chapter 6

Epigraphs for this section come from *The Lay of the Last Minstrel*.

For this chapter, I owe thanks to Graham Tulloch, Iain Brown, J. H. Alexander, and Jane Millgate for their advice on sources, to Murray Pittock and the Scots-Irish Research Network Seminar at the University of Strathclyde, and to Susan Manning for their thoughtful comments. The staff at the New York Society Library kindly facilitated my research on the *Castle Dangerous* MS, and Peter Henderson of The King's School, Canterbury, generously shared the *Count Robert* MS. Thanks, too, to the College of Arts and Sciences, University of Wyoming, for funds to obtain microfilm proofs from the NLS.

1. *Tales of My Landlord*, Fourth and Last Series, was published in late November 1831 and bore an 1832 imprint (Edinburgh: Robert Cadell, 1832). See Lockhart, 7:310 and Johnson, 2:1227. *Count Robert* was written from September 1830 (*Journal*, 688). It seems finished by 8 May 1831, but was kept on the stocks for revision until mid-September 1831. See Scott to James Ballantyne, 9 May 1831, in "Scott Letters 1829–32," NLS MS 1752 f.286. Also Scott to Robert Cadell, [13 September 1831], NLS MS 1752 f.377. The revision of *Count Robert* was interrupted by the composition of *Castle Dangerous* from July to early September of 1831. See Cadell's Notebook for 6 July, NLS MS 21043 f.99, and Scott to Cadell, [6 September 1831], NLS MS 1752 f.370. Scott likely produced the epilogue for *Count Robert* by 13 September 1831. See Cadell's Diary, 13 September 1831, NLS MS 21021 f.39v. The Jedediah Cleishbotham introduction for the combined volumes seems to have been completed in London before 7 October. See Scott to Cadell, 7 October 1831, NLS MS 1752 f.401–02. Scott composed "The Siege of Malta" during his travels of 1831–32 around the Mediterranean. See Scott to Cadell, [received] 25 December 1831, NLS MS 1752 f.442–43. The last "Malachi Malagrowther" letter Cadell proposed 22 December 1830, but advised against by 1 January. Scott produced but withheld it for an 11 March meeting in Selkirk (*Journal*, 693, 698, 705, 710, 714–15). For detailed accounts see Gammerschlag, Sultana, and Millgate's "The Limits of Editing."

2. Sources vary on the date of the dinner. Anderson and Johnson give 23 February (*Journal*, 319; Johnson, 2:1008). David Vedder's contemporary account, drawn from the *Edinburgh Weekly Journal*, gives 24 February (Robertson, *Lives*, 32).

3. "Familiar Anecdotes," 132. For Hogg's involvement, see Douglas S. Mack in *Anecdotes*, 1–16.

4. For a critique of Carlyle's reading, see my "Carlyle's 'Sovereign' Problem."

5. Burke and Hare murdered to supply Dr. Knox the Edinburgh anatomist in 1828–29. See Scott's *Journal* through January 1829 (esp. 565–67; 571–72; 576–77). "To burke" derives from Burke's practices (strangling) and his fate (hanging).

6. Britain focuses on *Ivanhoe*, and the remnants of empire on *The Talisman* (see Said).

7. See Scott to Susan Ferrier, [22 February ? 1831]; to William Godwin, 24 February 1831; to Robert Chamber[s], Bookseller, 7 March 1831, in *Letters*, 11:474; 476–78; 484–85.

8. See Basil Hall's 1834 comment in Robertson's *Lives*, 98.

9. See letter to Lockhart, [20 April 1831], which begins "I use Annes hand to write a few lines" (*Letters*, 12:12).

10. A discrepancy appears between Anderson's edition of the journal and Lockhart's transcription. Lockhart's version shows a more self-satisfied Scott and amends Scott's reference to Johnson's lines on Swift to quote more precisely, but also more detrimentally, "a driveller and a show" (*Journal*, 692; Lockhart, 7:250–51).

11. Lockhart, 7:295–96. The poem begins: "I that in heill wes and gladnes / Am trublit now with gret seiknes, / And feblit with infermite: / *Timor mortis conturbat me.*" Dunbar turns to poets: "I se that makaris, amang the laif, / Playis heir ther padȝanis, syne gois to graif. / Sparit is nought ther faculte: / *Timor mortis conturbat me.*" Subsequent verses catalog dead poets.

12. The Ballantynes' business owed its existence to Scott, and Scott intervened with Cadell on James's behalf as late as April 1830 (Scott's letters to Cadell, 8 [April 1830], *Letters*, 11:325–27). For Cadell's dealings with regard to the Magnum, see Millgate's chapter "Robert Cadell and the Ownership of the Magnum" (*Last*, 41–52). Lockhart owed his position at the *Quarterly* to Scott (Johnson, 2:943–45).

13. See Tuesday 6 September in Cadell's Note Book, NLS MS 21043 ff.114v–5.

14. Note Book Tuesday 9 August, NLS MS 21043 f.110.

15. Note Book 2 June 1831, NLS MS 21043 f.98.

16. Note Book 9 August 1831, see NLS MS 21043 f.110.

17. For Cadell's list, see "Criticisms and Translations," NLS MS 900 ff.42–43; for the group's marked-up proofs and recommended changes, see NLS MS 3776 and NLS MS 3777. See Gammerschlag for an extensive account.

18. Note Book, NLS MS 21043 f.123.

19. Diary entries for 18 October, 4 November 1831, NLS MS 21021 f.44v, f.47.

20. To Cadell, 10 September [1831], NLS MS 1752 f.373. On 9 May, Scott had written to Ballantyne, "I desire to have a Copy [of Count Robert's purged pages]. . . . I must say your people are different from every other printing house in their want of attention to this very necessary particular" (NLS MS 1752 f.286).

21. See Cadell's letter to Scott, 15 December 1830, in "Letters to Scott 1830" (4), NLS MS 3915 f.172-75.

22. NLS MS 23052, 11, and epilogue to *Castle Dangerous* in *Tales of My Landlord*, Fourth and Last Series, 4 vols.; vols. 3 and 4 (Edinburgh: Cadell, 1832) 4:328-30; see 328. I refer to materials in *Castle Dangerous* according to the first edition, but also by the chapter numbers commonly employed elsewhere. The epilogue appears in the Magnum Edition (1833) after *Castle Dangerous*, which shares a volume with "The Surgeon's Daughter."

23. See letter to Cadell, [received 25 December 1831], NLS MS 1752 f.442-43.

24. *Journal*, 665; Scott to Major Walter Scott, [circa 15 January 1831], *Letters*, 11:456-59.

25. Millgate, *Last*, 27. Letters to Cadell, [14 October, received 16 October], and [received 21 October 1831], NLS MS 1752, f.411, f.419. In one, Scott gives Cadell freedom for the specifically termed "verbal alterations"; in the other, he accedes to a rearrangement of the text to which he had already agreed and requests only "pray correct what is grossly wrong."

26. Letter to Cadell [13 September 1831], summarized by Grierson in NLS MS 1752 f.377.

27. Letter of 19 November 1831 (dated in Cadell's hand), in "Count Robert of Paris II," NLS MS 3777 f.1-2.

28. Letter of 15 December 1830, NLS MS 3915 f.172-75.

29. Letter to Scott, 10 December 1830, in NLS MS 3915 f.158-59.

30. Letter to Scott, 30 August 1831, in "Letters to Scott 1831" (4), NLS MS 3919 f.77-78.

31. Letter to Scott, 2 September 1831, NLS MS 3919 f.113-14.

32. Letter to Scott, 6 December 1830, NLS MS 3915 f.142-43.

33. Note Book 9 April 1831, NLS MS 21043 f.93v.

34. Note Book 2 June 1831, NLS MS 21043 f.98.

35. See "Castle Dangerous I," NLS MS 3778 f.315r.

36. See the "Advertisement" for *Count Robert* (Magnum Edition [London: Cadell, 1833], iii) and *Prefaces*, 239-44. See the manuscript, in Laidlaw's hand, "Scott Original Compositions," NLS MS 876 f.44-54; and proofs "Count Robert and Castle Dangerous," NLS MS 3780 f.13-18.

37. Scott did once refer to what stands as unpublished epilogue as introductory. He grouped "the Introductions of Robert of Paris & Castle Dangerous" in a letter to Cadell (received 21 October 1831), NLS MS 1752 f.419.

38. Copy letter to Sir Walter Scott care of Chas. Scott, in "Cadell," NLS MS 21003 f.31-2: "Mr Lockhart and I are a good deal puzzled about [*Seventeenth-Century Letters*] . . . Mr Lockharts acute views of Literature & my bookselling qualities cannot well doctor this little episode."

39. Copy letter to Major Scott, 30 April 1832, NLS MS 21003 f.43–44.

40. Letter to Thomas Thomson, 23 September 1832, NLS MS 786 f.114–15.

41. Letters to Scott, 10 January 1831; 13 January 1831; 28 February 1831, in "Letters to Scott 1831" (1), NLS MS 3916 f.29–30; f.43–44; f.214–15.

42. Note Book 9 April 1831, NLS MS 21043 f.93–94.

43. Letter to Cadell, [3 July 1831], in Grierson's transcription, NLS MS 1752 f.322–24.

44. Letter to Scott, 6 July 1831, in "Letters to Scott 1831" (3), NLS MS 3918 f.156–57.

45. Letter to Cadell, [received 25 December 1831], NLS MS 1752 f.442–43.

46. Copy letter from Laidlaw to Cadell 18 March 1832, NLS MS 21003 f.30.

47. Mildly complicit in the wish that Scott cease writing, after Scott's death Laidlaw sought to produce a memoir of the author. Lockhart, Cadell, and the new Sir Walter all worked to restrict its form and circulation. See Major Scott's letter to Cadell 29 July 1833, NLS MS 21003 f.164–65.

48. Scott's introduction was heavily revised. For Scott's text see his corrected proofs: NLS MS 23052. For the text revised by others, see NLS MS 3777 ff.124–48; ff.103–23; ff.76–101. Lockhart provided the most substantial revisions, ff.124–48. For the printed text I refer to *Tales of My Landlord*, Fourth and Last Series, vols. 1–3 (Edinburgh: Cadell, 1832). Introduction is 1:1–43.

49. 16 September 1831, Note Book, NLS MS 21043 f.116.

50. See Scott's MS revision, NLS MS 23052, 2; also the revision, NLS MS 3777 f.126v.

51. See for example NLS MS 3777 f.127r, f.133r.

52. See Scott's MS revision, NLS MS 23052, 4–5; NLS MS 3777 f.133r.

53. NLS MS 23052, 4 and NLS MS 3777 f.132v.

54. NLS MS 23052, 1 and NLS MS 3777 f.126v.

55. NLS MS 23052, 2 and NLS MS 3777 f.133r.

56. NLS MS 23052, 1–2 and NLS MS 3777 f.126v.

57. In response to the plagiary *Tales of My Landlord, New Series*, containing *Pontefract Castle* (London: William Fearman, 1820), Scott killed off Jedi/ediah. In *The Monastery*, he is reported dead. Scott details Jedediah's success as a lion with some fondness: "There he stood, surrounded by the little band . . . of Northern literati. . . . the alert, kind, benevolent old man." After remarking "I am sorry to observe my old acquaintance Jedediah Cleishbotham has misbehaved himself so far as to desert his original patron, and set up for himself," the Author of Waverley adds a footnote: "I am since more correctly informed, that Mr Cleishbotham died some months since at Gandercleugh, and that the person assuming his name is an impostor. The real Jedediah made a most Christian and edifying end. . . . Hard that the speculators in print and paper will not allow a good man to rest quiet in his grave!" See Johnson, 1:685; "Answer by 'The Author of Waverley' to the foregoing letter from Captain Clutterbuck," and footnote, *The Monastery*. I quote from the 1830 Magnum Edition.

58. Where the printed text does not differ from the proofs, I refer to *Castle Dangerous* in *Tales of My Landlord*, Fourth and Last Series, vols. 3 and 4 (Edinburgh: Cadell, 1832). I also cite the novel's chapter numbers from its one-volume manifestations. 4:208/ch. 14.

59. See *Given Time*, esp. 24, 37, 12–13, 41, 54, 91, 102.

60. Scott's revised proof runs: "A ship of war is commanded by its royal Master to carry the author of 'Waverley' to climates in which it is supposed he may possibly obtain such a restoration of health as may serve him to spin his thread to an end in his own country" (NLS MS 23052, 12). Editing displaces the text to an epilogue marked "Abbotsford, September 1831," which shows no substantial revisions to this particular utterance (*Tales of My Landlord*, Fourth and Last Series, 4:328–30).

61. My thanks to Graham Tulloch for sharing his research in an e-mail of 24 September 2003.

62. See Scott's revised proof, NLS MS 23052, 11–12; also the publisher's three proofs: NLS MS 3777 146–8v; 98r–101v; ff.122v-23. *Tales of My Landlord*, Fourth and Last Series, edited by J. H. Alexander, is forthcoming in the Edinburgh Edition (titled by its individual novels).

63. Lockhart, 7:393. For Grierson's convincing dismissal of this version, see *Sir Walter Scott*, 299–300.

BIBLIOGRAPHY

Scott: Printed Sources

Scott, Walter. *The Antiquary.* 1816. Ed. David Hewitt. Edinburgh Edition of the Waverley Novels, Vol. 3. Edinburgh: Edinburgh University Press, 1995.

———. *The Betrothed.* 1825. New Edition (Magnum). Edinburgh: Robert Cadell, 1832.

———. *The Black Dwarf.* 1816. Ed. Peter D. Garside. Edinburgh Edition of the Waverley Novels, Vol. 4a. Edinburgh: Edinburgh University Press, 1993.

———. *The Bride of Lammermoor.* 1819. Ed. J. H. Alexander. Edinburgh Edition of the Waverley Novels, Vol. 7a. Edinburgh: Edinburgh University Press, 1995.

———. *Castle Dangerous. Tales of My Landlord,* Fourth and Last Series. 1831 (1832 imprint) New Edition (Magnum). Edinburgh: Robert Cadell, 1832.

———. *Chronicles of the Canongate.* 1827. Ed. Claire Lamont. Edinburgh Edition of the Waverley Novels, Vol. 20. Edinburgh: Edinburgh University Press, 2000.

———. *The Fortunes of Nigel.* 1822. Ed. Frank Jordan. Edinburgh Edition of the Waverley Novels, Vol. 13. Edinburgh: Edinburgh University Press, 2004.

———. *Guy Mannering.* 1815. Ed. Peter D. Garside. Edinburgh Edition of the Waverley Novels, Vol. 2. Edinburgh: Edinburgh University Press, 1999.

———. *The Heart of Mid-Lothian.* 1818. Ed. David Hewitt & Alison Lumsden. Edinburgh Edition of the Waverley Novels, Vol. 6. Edinburgh: Edinburgh University Press, 2004.

———. *Ivanhoe.* 1820. Ed. Graham Tulloch. Edinburgh Edition of the Waverley Novels, Vol. 8. Edinburgh: Edinburgh University Press, 1998.

———. *The Journal of Sir Walter Scott.* Ed. W. E. K. Anderson, 1972; rpt. Edinburgh: Canongate, 1998.

———. *The Letters of Sir Walter Scott.* Ed. H. J. C. Grierson. 12 vols. 1932–37; rpt. New York: AMS Press, 1971.

———. ["Malachi Malagrowther" letters]. *Thoughts on the Proposed Change of Currency, and Other Late Alterations as they Affect, or are Intended to Affect, the Kingdom of Scotland.* (1826). *A Second Letter to the Editor of the Edinburgh Weekly Journal, from Malachi Malagrowther, Esq. On the Proposed Change of Currency, and Other Late Alterations, as they Affect, or are Intended to Affect, the*

Kingdom of Scotland. (1826). *A Third Letter to the Editor of the Edinburgh Weekly Journal, from Malachi Malagrowther, Esq. On the Proposed Change of Currency, and Other Late Alterations, as they Affect, or are Intended to Affect, the Kingdom of Scotland.* (1826). Rpt. Facsimile *Sir Walter Scott Thoughts on the Proposed Change of Currrncy & John Wilson Croker Two Letters on Scottish Affairs,* ed. David Simpson and Alastair Wood. New York: Barnes & Noble, 1972.

————. *The Prefaces to the Waverley Novels.* Ed. Mark A. Weinstein. Lincoln: University of Nebraska Press, 1978.

————. *Private Letters of the Seventeenth Century.* Ed. Douglas Grant. Oxford: Clarendon Press, 1947.

————. *The Tale of Old Mortality.* 1816. Ed. Douglas Mack. Edinburgh Edition of the Waverley Novels, Vol. 4b. Edinburgh: Edinburgh University Press, 1993.

————. *The Talisman.* 1825. New Edition (Magnum). Edinburgh: Robert Cadell, 1832.

————. *Waverley; or 'Tis Sixty Years Since.* 1814. Ed. Claire Lamont. Oxford: Oxford University Press, 1986.

————. *Woodstock.* 1826. New Edition (Magnum). 2 vols. Edinburgh: Robert Cadell, 1832.

[Scott, Walter]. Review of *The Secret and True History of the Church of Scotland, from the Restoration to the year 1678. By the Rev. Mr. James Kirkton, &c. With an Account of the Murder of Archbishop Sharp.* By James Russell, an actor therein. Edited from the MS. by Charles Kirkpatrick Sharpe, *Quarterly Review* 18, no. 36 (October 1817 and May 1818): 502–41.

[Scott, Walter]. *Hints Addressed to the Inhabitants of Edinburgh, and Others, in Prospect of His Majesty's Visit.* Edinburgh: Bell & Bradfute, 1822.

Scott, Walter, ed. *Trial of Duncan Terig Alias Clerk, and Alexander Bane Macdonald, for the Murder of Arthur Davis, Sergeant in General Guise's Regiment of Foot. June, A.D. M.DCC.LIV.* Edinburgh: Bannatyne Club, 1831.

[Scott, Walter and William Erskine]. Review of *Tales of My Landlord, Quarterly Review* 16 (October 1816 & January 1817): 430–80.

Manuscript Sources

Blair Castle, Atholl Charter Room, Perthshire (ACR)

ACR 68/12: 4th Duke Correspondence.
ACR 1026/34, 35: 4th Duke Journals/Notebooks 34, 35.

National Library of Scotland (NLS)

NLS F.5.f17 (1–6): Royal Visit 1822: vol. 2, *Miscellanies.*
NLS MS 786: Scott and his contemporaries: letters and papers.
NLS MS 867: Letters to Scott 1820–22.
NLS MS 876: Scott Original Compositions: f.44 unpublished conclusion to Count Robert in hand of William Laidlaw.

NLS MS 900: Cadell Criticisms and Translations.

NLS MS 1553: Abbotsford Collection, Letters 1828–41 (mostly Lockhart correspondence).

NLS MS 1752: Scott Letters, not in *Letters*, transcription and summary, H. J. C. Grierson.

NLS MS 2890: Scott of Raeburn Letters 1800–22.

NLS MS 3776: Count Robert of Paris, proofsheets.

NLS MS 3777: Count Robert of Paris II, proof sheets, with revisions; Castle Dangerous, Introductory Address.

NLS MS 3778: Castle Dangerous I, proofsheets.

NLS MS 3779: Castle Dangerous II, proofsheets.

NLS MS 3780: Count Robert of Paris and Castle Dangerous, partial first proofs, and Epilogue.

NLS MS 3813: Small collections and single letters (Scott and others).

NLS MS 3894: Letters to Scott 1822 (1).

NLS MS 3895: Letters to Walter Scott, July–December 1822.

NLS MS 3915: Letters to Scott 1830 (4).

NLS MS 3916: Letters to Scott 1831 (1).

NLS MS 3918: Letters to Scott 1831 (3).

NLS MS 3919: Letters to Scott 1831 (4).

NLS MS 5317: Scott Letters.

NLS MS 21003: Robert Cadell correspondence, 1832–34.

NLS MS 21020: Cadell's Diary 1830.

NLS MS 21021: Cadell's Diary 1831.

NLS MS 21043: Cadell's Note Book.

NLS MS 21056: Cadell's Account Book.

NLS MS 23052: *Tales of My Landlord*, Introductory Address (proof with Scott's revisions).

NLS MS 23140: Count Robert of Paris, proofs of unpublished matter.

National Archives of Scotland, formerly Scottish Record Office (NAS)

NAS GD46/17/61: Papers of the Mackenzie family, Earls of Seaforth. Letters and Papers 1815-1822.

NAS GD51/5/749: Papers of the Dundas Family of Melville, Vol. 2.

NAS GD51/1/214: Papers of the Dundas Family of Melville.

NAS GD157/2548: Papers of the Scott Family of Harden. Harriet Scott to Anne Scott, her daughter.

NAS GD46/4/187, 188, 189: Papers of the Mackenzie Family, Earls of Seaforth.

New York Society Library

Stack 10, Z-large, S431 C2: Manuscripts of Walter Scott XX, Novels, Vol. XII, Castle Dangerous, 1831.

Contemporary Bibliography

Anon. *A Full Account of King George the Fourth's Visit to Scotland in 1822; with a collection of The Loyal Songs which appeared on that memorable occasion.* Edinburgh: Macredie, 1838.

———. *A Narrative of the Visit of George IV. to Scotland, in August 1822. By an eye-witness of most of the scenes which were then exhibited.* Edinburgh: Macredie & Skelly, 1822.

———. *Kilts and Philibegs!! The Northern Excursion of Geordie, Emperor of Gotham: and Sir Willie Curt-his, the Court Buffoon, &c. &c.: A Serio-Tragico-Comico-Ludicro-Aquatico Burlesque Gallimaufry; interspersed with Humorous Glees, Sporting Catches, and Rum Chaunts, by the Male and Female Characters of the Piece.* London: John Fairburn, [1822].

———. *The Royal Scottish Minstrelsy: Being a collection of Loyal Effusions occasioned by the visit of His Most Gracious Majesty George IV. To Scotland, August 15, 1822.* Leith: James Burnet, 1824.

———. *Report relative to The Proceedings of the Royal Company of Archers, upon the Visit of His Majesty, King George the Fourth, to Scotland, August 1822.* Edinburgh: J. & C. Muirhead, 1822.

Arniston Memoirs: Three Centuries of a Scottish House 1571–1838. Ed. George W. T. Omond. Edinburgh: David Douglas, 1887.

Atholl, John, 7th Duke of, K. T., coll. and arr. *Chronicles of the Atholl and Tullinbardine Families.* 5 vols. See 1822. Edinburgh: [privately printed], 1908–91.

Carlyle, Thomas. *Reminiscences.* Ed. Charles Eliot Norton. London: J. M. Dent & Sons, 1972.

———. Review of *Memoirs of the Life of Sir Walter Scott, Baronet. Vol. I–VI*, *London and Westminster Review* 6 & 28 (October 1837–January 1838): 293–345.

Cockburn, Harry A., ed. *Some Letters of Lord Cockburn with pages omitted from the Memorials of His Time.* Edinburgh: Grant & Murray, 1932.

Conder, Josiah. Review of *Tales of my Landlord, Eclectic Review* n.s., 7 (April 1817): 309–36.

Crabbe, George. *Selected Letters and Journals of George Crabbe.* Ed. Thomas C. Faulkner. Oxford: Clarendon Press, 1985.

Croker, John Wilson. *Two Letters on Scottish Affairs, from Edward Bradwardine Waverley, Esq. to Malachi Malagrowther, Esq.* (1826). Rpt., facsimile *Sir Walter Scott Thoughts on the Proposed Change of Currency & John Wilson Croker Two Letters on Scottish Affairs*, ed. David Simpson & Alastair Wood. New York: Barnes & Noble, 1972.

Cunningham, Allan. *The Life of Sir David Wilkie.* Vol. 2. London: John Murray, 1843.

Galt, John. *The Literary Life and Miscellanies of John Galt.* Vol. 1. Edinburgh: William Blackwood, 1834.

Green, Sarah. *Scotch Novel Reading; or Modern Quackery. A Novel* Really *Founded on Facts*, "by a Cockney." 3 vols. London: A. K. Newman, 1824.

Hansard, T. C. *The Parliamentary Debates*. 14 (2 February–17 March 1826) and 15 (20 March–31 May 1826).

Hayden, John O. *Scott: The Critical Heritage*. London: Routledge & Kegan Paul, 1970.

Hogg, James. "Familiar Anecdotes of Sir Walter Scott." In *James Hogg: Memoirs of the Author's Life and Familiar Anecdotes of Sir Walter Scott*, ed. Douglas S. Mack, 93–135. Edinburgh: Scottish Academic Press, 1972.

———. *Anecdotes of Sir W. Scott*. Ed. Douglas S. Mack. Edinburgh: Scottish Academic Press, 1983.

———. *The Jacobite Relics of Scotland: being the Songs, Airs, and Legends, of the Adherents to the House of Stuart*. First Series (1819). Ed. Murray Pittock. Edinburgh: Edinburgh University Press, 2002.

———. *The Jacobite Relics of Scotland: being the Songs, Airs, and Legends, of the Adherents to the House of Stuart*. Second Series (1821). Edinburgh: Edinburgh University Press, 2003.

———. *The Royal Jubilee. A Scottish Mask*. 1822. Annotated Valentina Bold. *Studies in Hogg and His World* 5 (1994): 102–51.

Huish, Robert. *Memoirs of George the Fourth*. Vol. 2. London: Thomas Kelly, 1831.

Lockhart, J. G. *Memoirs of the Life of Sir Walter Scott, Bart.* 7 vols. Edinburgh: Robert Cadell, 1837–38.

Macaulay, Thomas Babington. *The History of England from the Accession of James II*. Vol. 3. New York: Harper & Brothers, 1856.

Maclean, James M., & Basil Skinner. *The Royal Visit of 1822*. Edinburgh: University of Edinburgh, 1972.

Maxwell, Sir Herbert, ed. *The Creevey Papers: A Selection from the Correspondence and Diaries of the Late Thomas Creevey, M.P.* Vol. 2. London: John Murray, 1903.

McCrie, Thomas. "Vindication of the Covenanters." *Christian Instructor* (January, February, March 1817): 41–73, 100–140, 170–201, respectively. Rpt. *Vindication of the Covenanters in a Review of the "Tales of My Landlord."* Edinburgh: William Whyte, 1845.

Mudie, Robert. *A Historical Account of His Majesty's Visit to Scotland*, 2d ed. Edinburgh: Oliver & Boyd, 1822.

Partington, Wilfred, ed. *Private Letter-Books of Sir Walter Scott*. London: Hodder & Stoughton, 1930.

Robertson, Fiona, ed. *Lives of the Great Romantics II: Keats, Coleridge & Scott by Their Contemporaries*. Vol. 3. London: Pickering & Chatto, 1997.

Rodger, Alexander, ed. *Stray Leaves from the Portfolios of Alisander the Seer, Andrew Whaup, and Humphrey Henkeckle*. Glasgow: Charles Rattray, 1842.

Simpson, James. *Letters to Sir Walter Scott, Bart. on the Moral and Political Character and Effects of the Visit to Scotland in August 1822, of His Majesty King George IV*. Edinburgh: Waugh & Innes, 1822.

Skinner, B. C. ed. "A Contemporary Account of the Royal Visit to Edinburgh, 1822." *The Book of the Old Edinburgh Club.* Vol. 31. Edinburgh: T. & A. Constable Ltd., 1962: 65–167.

"Thoughts on Banking." *Edinburgh Review* 86 (February 1826): 263–99.

Journals and Newspapers

Augustine Review
Blackwood's Edinburgh Magazine
Caledonian Mercury
Critical Review
Dublin and London Magazine
Eclectic Review
Edinburgh Advertiser
Edinburgh Magazine
Edinburgh Observer
Edinburgh Review
Edinburgh Weekly Journal
Examiner
Gentleman's Magazine
Glasgow Courier
Inverness Courier
Lady's Monthly Museum
Literary Chronicle and Weekly Review
Literary Coterie
Literary Gazette
London Magazine
London Weekly Review
Monthly Magazine
Monthly Review
Morning Paper
New Monthly Magazine
Panoramic Miscellany
Quarterly Review
Scots Magazine
Scotsman
Westminster Review

Critical Bibliography

Anderson, Benedict. *Imagined Communities: Reflections on the Origin and Spread of Nationalism.* Rev. ed. London: Verso, 1983.

Ash, Marinell. *The Strange Death of Scottish History.* Edinburgh: Ramsay Head Press, 1980.

Aspinall, A., ed. *The Letters of George IV, 1812–1830.* Vol. 2. Cambridge: Cambridge University Press, 1938.

Bambery, Chris, ed. *Scotland, Class and Nation.* London: Bookmarks, 1999.

Beiderwell, Bruce. *Power and Punishment in Scott's Novels.* Athens: University of Georgia Press, 1992.

Bennie, Lynn, Jack Brand, & James Mitchell. *How Scotland Votes: Scottish Parties and Elections.* Manchester: Manchester University Press, 1997.

Beveridge, Craig, & Ronald Turnbull. *Scotland After Enlightenment: Image and Tradition in Modern Scottish Culture.* Edinburgh: Polygon, 1997.

———. *The Eclipse of Scottish Culture: Inferiorism and the Intellectuals.* Edinburgh: Polygon, 1989.

Bhabha, Homi K., ed. *Nation and Narration.* London: Routledge, 1990.

———. *The Location of Culture.* New York: Routledge, 1994.

Bourdieu, Pierre. *Outline of a Theory of Practice.* Trans. Richard Nice. Cambridge: Cambridge University Press, 1977.

Breitenbach, Esther, & Fiona Mackay. *Women and Contemporary Scottish Politics: An Anthology.* Edinburgh: Polygon, 2001.

British Council. "Who do we think we are? Identity Politics in Modern Scotland." www.britcoun.de/e/education/studies/scot2993.htm. Accessed 7 January 2003.

Brown, Alice, David McCrone, & Lindsay Paterson, *Politics and Society in Scotland.* 2d ed. Houndsmills: Palgrave, 1998.

Broun, Dauvit, R. J. Finlay, & Michael Lynch, eds. *Image and Identity: The Making and Re-making of Scotland Through the Ages.* Edinburgh: John Donald, 1998.

Buchan, John. *Sir Walter Scott.* New York: Coward & McCann, 1932.

Burgess, Miranda J. *British Fiction and the Production of Social Order, 1740–1830.* Cambridge: Cambridge University Press, 2000.

Buzard, James. *The Beaten Track: European Tourism, Literature, and the Ways to Culture, 1800–1918.* Oxford: Clarendon Press, 1993.

———. "Translation and Tourism: Scott's *Waverley* and the Rendering of Culture." *Yale Journal of Criticism* 8, no. 2 (Fall 1995): 31–59.

Calder, Angus. "A Descriptive Model of Scottish Culture." *Scotlands* 2, no. 1 (1995): 1–14.

Claim of Right for Scotland, A. Ed. Owen Dudley Edwards. Edinburgh: Polygon, 1989.

Cocks, Joan. "Fetishizing Ethnicity, Locality, Nationality: the Curious Case of Tom Nairn." *Theory & Event* 1, no. 3 (1997). muse.jhu.edu/journals/theory_and_event/v001/1.3cocks.html. Accessed 7 January 2003.

Colley, Linda. *Britons: Forging the Nation 1707–1837.* New Haven, Conn.: Yale University Press, 1992.

Cooney, Seamus. "Scott and Progress: The Tragedy of 'The Highland Widow.'" *Studies in Short Fiction* 11, no. 1 (Winter 1974): 11–16.

———. "Scott and Cultural Relativism: 'The Two Drovers.'" *Studies in Short Fiction* 15, no. 1 (Winter 1978): 1–9.

Corson, James C. *Notes and Index to Sir Herbert Grierson's Edition of the Letters of Sir Walter Scott.* Oxford: Clarendon Press, 1979.

Craig, Cairns. *Out of History: Narrative Paradigms in Scottish and English Culture.* Edinburgh: Polygon, 1996.

———. *The Modern Scottish Novel: Narrative and the National Imagination.* Edinburgh: Edinburgh University Press, 1999.

Craig, David. *Scottish Literature and the Scottish People 1680–1830.* London: Chatto & Windus, 1961.

Crawford, Robert. *Devolving English Literature.* 2d ed. Edinburgh: Edinburgh University Press, 2000.

———. "The Crown." Caroline McCracken-Flesher, ed. *Culture, Nation, and the New Scottish Parliament.* Lewisburg, Pa.: Bucknell University Press, forthcoming.

Daiches, David. *Edinburgh.* London: Hamish Hamilton, 1978.

Davidson, Neil. "In Perspective: Tom Nairn." *International Socialism Journal* 82 (March 1999). pubs.socialistreviewindex.org.uk/isj82/davidson.htm. Accessed 7 January 2003.

Davis, Leith. *Acts of Union: Scotland and the Literary Negotiation of the British Nation, 1707–1830.* Stanford, Calif.: Stanford University Press, 1998.

Dennis, Ian. *Nationalism and Desire in Early Historical Fiction.* Houndsmills: Macmillan, 1997.

Denver, David, James Mitchell, Charles Pattie, & Hugh Bochel. *Scotland Decides: The Devolution Issue and the 1997 Referendum.* London: Frank Cass, 2000.

Derrida, Jacques. *Given Time: I. Counterfeit Money.* 1991. Trans. Peggy Kamuf. Chicago: University of Chicago Press, 1992.

Devine, T. M. *The Scottish Nation 1700–2000.* London: Penguin, 1999.

Dickinson, Tony, ed. *Scottish Capitalism: Class, State and Nation from before the Union to the Present.* London: Lawrence & Wishart, 1980.

Donnachie, Ian, & Christopher Whatley, eds. *The Manufacture of Scottish History.* Edinburgh: Polygon, 1992.

Duncan, Ian. *Modern Romance and Transformations of the Novel: The Gothic, Scott, Dickens.* Cambridge: Cambridge University Press, 1992.

Duncan, Ian, Ann Rowland, & Charles Snodgrass, eds. *Scott, Scotland, and Romantic Nationalism.* Special ed. *Studies in Romanticism* 40, no. 1 (Spring 2001).

Ellis, P. Berresford, & Seumas Mac A'Ghobhainn. *The Scottish Insurrection of 1820.* London: Victor Gollancz, 1970.

Fanon, Frantz. *The Wretched of the Earth.* Trans. Constance Farrington. New York: Grove Weidenfeld, 1963.

Farrell, John P. *Revolution as Tragedy: The Dilemma of the Moderate from Scott to Arnold.* Ithaca, N.Y.: Cornell University Press, 1980.

Ferris, Ina. *The Achievement of Literary Authority: Gender, History, and the Waverley Novels.* Ithaca, N.Y.: Cornell University Press, 1991.

Finlay, Richard J. "Controlling the Past: Scottish Historiography and Scottish Identity in the 19th and 20th Centuries." *Scottish Affairs* 9 (Autumn 1994): 127–42.

Forster, E. M. *Aspects of the Novel.* 1927. Harmondsworth: Penguin, 1974.

Fradenburg, Louise Olga. *City, Marriage, Tournament: Arts of Rule in Late Medieval Scotland.* Madison: University of Wisconsin Press, 1991.

Fry, Michael. *Patronage and Principle.* Aberdeen: Aberdeen University Press, 1987.

Gammerschlag, Kurt. "The Making and Un-Making of Sir Walter Scott's *Count Robert of Paris.*" *Studies in Scottish Literature* 5 (1980): 95–123.

Garside, P. D. "Dating *Waverley*'s Early Chapters." *Bibliotheck* 13, no. 3 (1986): 61–81.

Gaston, Patricia. *Prefacing the Waverley Prefaces: A Reading of Sir Walter Scott's Prefaces to the Waverley Novels.* New York: Peter Lang, 1991.

Glendening, John. *The High Road: Romantic Tourism, Scotland, and Literature, 1720–1820.* New York: St. Martin's, 1997.

Gold, John R., & Margaret M. *Imagining Scotland: Tradition, Representation and Promotion in Scottish Tourism Since 1750.* Aldershot: Scolar, 1995.

Gordon, Jan B. "'Liquidating the Sublime': Gossip in Scott's Novels." In *At the Limits of Romanticism: Essays in Cultural, Feminist, and Materialist Criticism,* ed. Mary A. Favret and Nicola J. Watson, 246–68. Bloomington: Indiana University Press, 1994.

Gordon, Robert C. *Under Which King? A Study of the Scottish Waverley Novels.* Edinburgh: Oliver & Boyd, 1969.

Goslee, Nancy. *Scott the Rhymer.* Lexington: University Press of Kentucky, 1988.

Goux, Jean-Joseph. *Symbolic Economies: After Marx and Freud.* Trans. Jennifer Curtiss Gage. Ithaca, N.Y.: Cornell University Press, 1990.

Grierson, H. J. C. *Sir Walter Scott, Bart. A New Life Supplementary to, and Corrective of, Lockhart's Biography.* London: Constable, 1938.

Grieve, C. M. [MacDiarmid, Hugh]. *Albyn.* London: Kegan Paul, Trench, Trubner, 1927.

Guibernau, Montserrat. *Nations without States: Political Communities in a Global Age.* Cambridge: Polity Press, 1999.

Hart, Francis Russell. *The Scottish Novel from Smollett to Spark.* Cambridge, Mass.: Harvard University Press, 1978.

Harvie, Christopher. *No Gods and Precious Few Heroes: Scotland 1914–1980.* Toronto: University of Toronto Press, 1981.

———. "Scott and the Image of Scotland." 1983. Rpt. *Patriotism: The Making and Unmaking of British National Identity,* Vol. 2, ed. Raphael Samuel, 173–92. London: Routledge, 1989.

———. *Scotland and Nationalism: Scottish Society and Politics 1707 to the Present.* 3d ed. London: Routledge, 1998.

Harvie, Christopher, & Peter Jones. *The Road to Home Rule: Images of Scotland's Cause.* Edinburgh: Polygon, 2000.

Hearn, Jonathan. *Claiming Scotland: National Identity and Liberal Culture.* Edinburgh: Polygon, 2000.

Hibbert, Christopher. *George IV: Regent and King 1811–1830.* New York: Harper & Row, 1973.

Hobsbaum, Philip. "Scott's 'Apoplectic' Novels." J. H. Alexander and David Hewitt, eds. *Scott and His Influence,* 149–56. Aberdeen: Association for Scottish Literary Studies.

Hobsbawm, E. J. *Nations and Nationalism since 1780.* Cambridge: Cambridge University Press, 1990.

Hosking, Geoffrey, & George Schöpflin, eds. *Myths and Nationhood.* New York: Routledge, 1997.

Howe, Irving. "Falling Out of the Canon: The Strange Fate of Walter Scott." *New Republic* 207, nos. 8–9 (August 17, 1992).

Humes, Walter M., & Hamish M. Paterson, eds. *Scottish Culture and Scottish Education 1800–1980.* Edinburgh: John Donald, 1983.

Hunter, S. Leslie. *The Scottish Educational System.* Oxford: Pergamon, 1968.

Hutchinson, John, & Anthony D. Smith. *Nationalism.* Oxford: Oxford University Press, 1994.

Hutton, Richard H. *Sir Walter Scott.* New York: Harper & Brothers, 1887.

Johnson, Edgar. *Sir Walter Scott: The Great Unknown.* 2 vols. New York: Macmillan, 1970.

Jones, Catherine. *Literary Memory: Scott's Waverley Novels and the Psychology of Narrative.* Lewisburg, Pa.: Bucknell University Press, 2003.

Jordan, Frank. "Chrystal Croftangry, Scott's Last and Best Mask." *Scottish Literary Journal* 7 (1980): 185–92.

Kellas, James. *Modern Scotland: The Nation Since 1870.* New York: Praeger, 1968.

———. *The Scottish Political System.* 3d ed. Cambridge: Cambridge University Press, 1984.

———. *The Politics of Nationalism and Ethnicity.* 2d ed. New York: St. Martins, 1998.

Kerr, James. *Fiction Against History: Scott as Storyteller.* Cambridge: Cambridge University Press, 1989.

Kidd, Colin. *Subverting Scotland's Past: Scottish Whig Historians and the Creation of an Anglo-British Identity, 1689–c. 1830.* Cambridge: Cambridge University Press, 1993.

Krieger, Joel. *British Politics in the Global Age: Can Social Democracy Survive?* Oxford: Oxford University Press, 1999.

Kuppner, Frank. "Shall We Not Be Moved?" *Cencrastus* 31 (Autumn 1988): 45–46.

Lang, Andrew. "Editor's Introduction to Woodstock." *Woodstock.* London: Macmillan, 1912.

Lee, Yoon Sun. "A Divided Inheritance: Scott's Antiquarian Novel and the British Nation." *English Literary History* 64 (1997): 571–601.

Levy, Roger. *Scottish Nationalism at the Crossroads.* Edinburgh: Scottish Academic Press, 1990.

Lukács, Georg. *The Historical Novel*. New York: Humanities Press, 1965.

Malley, Shawn. "Walter Scott's Romantic Archaeology: New/Old Abbotsford and *The Antiquary*." *Studies in Romanticism* 40, no. 2 (Summer 2001): 233–51.

Manning, Susan. *Fragments of Union: Making Connections in Scottish and American Writing*. Basingstoke: Palgrave, 2002.

Mason, Roger, & Norman Macdougall, eds. *People and Power in Scotland: Essays in Honour of T. C. Smout*. Edinburgh: John Donald, 1992.

Mayhead, Robin. "The Problem of Coherence in *The Antiquary*." In *Scott Bicentenary Essays: Selected Papers Read at the Sir Walter Scott Bicentenary Conference*, ed. Alan Bell, 134–46. New York: Harper & Row, 1973.

MacArthur, Colin. "Breaking the Signs: 'Scotch Myths' as Cultural Struggle." *Cencrastus* 7 (Winter 1981–82): 21–25.

McCracken-Flesher, Caroline. "English Hegemony/Scottish Subjectivity: Calvinism and Cultural Resistance in the Nineteenth-Century 'North British' Novel." Ph.D. diss., Brown University, 1989.

———. "Thinking Nationally/Writing Colonially? Scott, Stevenson, and England." *Novel* 24, no. 3 (Spring 1991): 296–318.

———. "A Wo/man for a' that? Subverted Sex and Perverted Politics in *The Heart of Midlothian*." In *Scott in Carnival*, ed. J. H. Alexander and David Hewitt, 232–44. Aberdeen: Association for Scottish Literary Studies, 1993.

———. "Speaking the Colonized Subject in Walter Scott's *Malachi Malagrowther* Letters." *Studies in Scottish Literature* 29 (1995/6): 73–84.

———. "The Recuperation of Canon Fodder: Walter Scott's *The Talisman*." In *No Small World: Visions and Revisions of World Literature*, ed. Michael Thomas Carroll, 160–78. Urbana, Ill.: National Council of Teachers of English, 1996. Rpt. *Critical Essays on Sir Walter Scott: The Waverley Novels*, ed. Harry E. Shaw, 202–17. New York: G. K. Hall, 1996.

———. "'The Great Disturber of the age': James Hogg at the King's Visit, 1822." *Studies in Hogg and His World* 9 (1998): 64–83.

———. "Narrating the (Gendered) Nation in Walter Scott's *The Heart of Midlothian*." *Nineteenth-Century Contexts* 24, no. 3 (September 2002): 291–316.

———. "A Tartan Politics? *Couture* and National Creativity in the New Scottish Parliament." *Scottish Studies Review* 3, no. 1 (Spring 2002): 110–121.

———. "Carlyle's 'Sovereign' Problem: the Health and Wealth of Walter Scott."

McCrone, David. *Understanding Scotland: The Sociology of a Stateless Nation*. London: Routledge, 1992.

———. *The Sociology of Nationalism: Tomorrow's Ancestors*. London: Routledge, 1998.

———. "A Matter of Identity." *Edit* 3, no. 1 (Winter 2003): 22–23.

McCrone, David, Angela Morris, & Richard Kiely. *Scotland—the Brand: The Making of Scottish Heritage*. Edinburgh: Edinburgh University Press, 1995.

MacDiarmid, Hugh (C. M. Grieve). *A Drunk Man Looks at the Thistle*. 1926. Ed. Kenneth Buthlay. Edinburgh: Scottish Academic Press, 1987.

McGann, Jerome, ed. *Lord Byron: The Complete Poetical Works*. Vol. 5. Oxford: Clarendon Press, 1986.

Mewton, Robert-J. "Scott and a Romantic Difficulty, as illustrated by the Function of Power in the Fictional Development of Three of the Waverley Novels." *Le Pouvoir dans la litterature et la pensée anglaises*, ed. N. J. Rigaud, 57–69. Marseilles: Centre Aixois de Recherches Anglaises Université de Provence, 1981.

Midwinter, Arthur, Michael Keating, & James Mitchell. *Politics and Public Policy in Scotland*. London: Macmillan, 1991.

Miller, Delia. *Queen Victoria's Life in the Scottish Highlands Depicted by Her Watercolour Artists*. London: Philip Wilson, 1985.

Miller, Hugh. "The Centenary of the 'Forty Five." *Essays, Historical and Biographical, Political and Social, Literary and Scientific*. Edinburgh: A. & C. Black, 1862.

Millgate, Jane. "The Limits of Editing: the Problems of Scott's *The Siege of Malta*." *Bulletin of Research in the Humanities* 82, no. 2 (Summer 1979): 190–212.

―――. *Walter Scott: The Making of the Novelist*. Toronto: University of Toronto Press, 1984.

―――. *Scott's Last Edition: A Study in Publishing History*. Edinburgh: Edinburgh University Press, 1987.

Mitchell, James. *Strategies for Self-Government: The Campaign for a Scottish Parliament*. Edinburgh: Polygon, 1996.

Mitchison, Rosalind. *The Roots of Nationalism: Studies in Northern Europe*. Edinburgh: John Donald, 1980.

Mortimer, Edward, with Robert Fine. *People, Nation and State: The Meaning of Ethnicity and Nationalism*. London: I. B. Tauris, 1999.

Muir, Edwin. *Scott and Scotland: The Predicament of the Scottish Writer*. 1936; Rpt. Edinburgh: Polygon, 1982.

Murphy, Peter. "Scott's Disappointments: Reading *The Heart of Midlothian*." *Modern Philology* 92, no. 2 (November 1994): 179–98.

Nairn, Tom. "The Three Dreams of Scottish Nationalism." 1970. Rpt. *A Diverse Assembly: The Debate on the Scottish Parliament*, ed. Lindsay Paterson, 31–39. Edinburgh: Edinburgh University Press, 1998.

―――. *The Break-Up of Britain: Crisis and Neo-Nationalism*. London: Verso, 1981.

―――. *The Enchanted Glass: Britain and its Monarchy*. London: Hutchison Radius, 1988.

―――. *Faces of Nationalism: Janus Revisited*. London: Verso, 1997.

―――. *After Britain*. London: Granta Books, 2000.

Noble, Andrew. "Highland History and Narrative Form in Scott and Stevenson." *Robert Louis Stevenson*, ed. Andrew Noble, 134–87. Totowa, N.J.: Barnes & Noble, 1983.

Orr, Marilyn. "Public and Private I: Walter Scott and the Anxiety of Authorship." *English Studies in Canada* 22, no. 1 (March 1996): 45–58.

Overton, W. J. "Scott, the Short Story and History: 'The Two Drovers.'" *Studies in Scottish Literature* 21 (1986): 210–25.

Özkirimli, Umut. *Theories of Nationalism: A Critical Introduction*. New York: St. Martins, 2000.

Paterson, Lindsay. *A Diverse Assembly: The Debate on A Scottish Parliament*. Edinburgh: Edinburgh University Press, 1998.

———. "Scottish Democracy and Scottish Utopias: The First Year of the Scottish Parliament." *Scottish Affairs* 33 (Autumn 2000): 45–61. http://www.scottishaffairs .org/onlinepub/sa/paterson_sa33_autoo.html. Accessed 7 January 2003.

Paterson, Lindsay, et al. *New Scotland, New Politics?* Edinburgh: Polygon, 2001.

Phillipson, N. T. "Nationalism and Ideology." In *Government and Nationalism in Scotland. An Enquiry by Members of the University of Edinburgh*, ed. J. N. Wolfe, 167–88. Edinburgh: Edinburgh University Press, 1969.

———. "Scottish Public Opinion and the Union in the Age of the Association." In *Scotland in the Age of Improvement*, ed. N. T. Phillipson and Rosalind Mitchison, 125–47. Edinburgh: Edinburgh University Press, 1970.

Pittock, Murray G. H. *The Invention of Scotland: The Stuart Myth and the Scottish Identity, 1638 to the Present*. London: Routledge, 1991.

———. *Inventing and Resisting Britain: Cultural Identities in Britain and Ireland 1685–1789*. New York: St. Martin's, 1997.

———. *Celtic Identity and the British Image*. Manchester: Manchester University Press, 1999.

Plumb, J. H. *Royal Heritage: The Treasures of the British Crown*. New York: Harcourt Brace Jovanovich, 1977.

Pottinger, George. *The Secretaries of State for Scotland 1926–76: Fifty Years of the Scottish Office*. Edinburgh: Scottish Academic Press, 1979.

Prebble, John. *The King's Jaunt: George IV in Scotland, August 1822 'One and twenty daft days.'* London: Collins, 1988.

Punter, David. "Introduction." In Walter Scott, *The Antiquary*, ed. David Hewitt, xiii–xxx. London: Penguin, 1998.

Ragaz, Sharon. "'The Truth in Masquerade': Byron's *Don Juan* and Walter Scott's *The Antiquary*." *Keats-Shelley Journal* 48 (1999): 30–34.

Ritchie, Murray. *Scotland Reclaimed: The Inside Story of Scotland's First Democratic Parliamentary Election*. Edinburgh: Saltire Society, 2000.

Robertson, Fiona. *Legitimate Histories: Scott, Gothic, and the Authorities of Fiction*. Oxford: Clarendon Press, 1994.

———. ed. *Lives of the Great Romantics II: Keats, Coleridge & Scott by their Contemporaries*. Vol. 3. London: Pickering & Chatto, 1997.

Robertson, John, ed. *A Union for Empire: Political Thought and the British Union of 1707*. Cambridge: Cambridge University Press, 1995.

Rowlinson, Matthew. "'The Scotch Hate Gold': British Identity and Paper Money." In *Nation-States and Money: The Past, Present and Future of National Currencies*, ed. Emily Gilbert & Eric Helleiner, 47–67. London: Routledge, 1999.

————. "Scott Incorporated."

Said, Edward W. *Orientalism*. New York: Vintage, 1979.

————. *The World, the Text, and the Critic*. Cambridge, Mass.: Harvard University Press, 1983.

Schoene, Berthold. "A Passage to Scotland: Scottish Literature and the Postcolonial British Tradition." *Scotlands* 2, no. 1 (1995): 107–22.

Scotland Act 1998. Chapter 46.

Scott, Paul Henderson. *Walter Scott and Scotland*. 1991. Rpt. Edinburgh: Saltire Society, 1994.

————. *Still in Bed with an Elephant*. 1985. Rev. ed. Edinburgh: Saltire Society, 1998.

————. *Scotland Resurgent: Comments on the Cultural and Political Revival of Scotland*. Edinburgh: Saltire Society, 2003.

Scottish Motor Traction Company. *The Romance of Scott: His Home: His Work: His Country: Sir Walter Scott Centenary 1832–1932*. Edinburgh: Travel Press & Publicity, [1932].

Shaw, Harry. *The Forms of Historical Fiction: Sir Walter Scott and His Successors*. Ithaca, N.Y.: Cornell University Press, 1983.

Simpson, Kenneth. *The Protean Scot: The Crisis of Identity in Eighteenth Century Scottish Literature*. Aberdeen: Aberdeen University Press, 1988.

Smith, Anthony D. *Nationalism and Modernism: A Critical Survey of Recent Theories of Nations and Nationalism*. London: Routledge, 1998.

Smith, E. A. *A Queen on Trial: The Affair of Queen Caroline*. Stroud: Alan Sutton, 1993.

Smith, Gregory. *Scottish Literature: Character and Influence*. London: Macmillan, 1919.

Smout, T. C. *A History of the Scottish People, 1560–1830*. London: Collins, 1969.

————. *A Century of the Scottish People, 1830–1950*. New Haven, Conn.: Yale University Press, 1986.

————. "Perspectives on the Scottish Identity." *Scottish Affairs* 6 (Winter 1994): 101–13.

Sorensen, Janet. *The Grammar of Empire in Eighteenth-Century British Writing*. Cambridge: Cambridge University Press, 2000.

Spoto, Donald. *The Decline and Fall of the House of Windsor*. New York: Pocket Books, 1995.

Sroka, Kenneth. "Fairy Castles and Character in *Woodstock*." *Essays in Literature* 14, no. 2 (Fall 1987): 189–205.

Stein, Richard L. "Historical Fiction and the Implied Reader: Scott and Iser." *Novel* 14, no. 3 (Spring 1981): 213–31.

Strout, Alan Lang. *A Bibliography of Articles in* Blackwood's Magazine *1817–1825*. Lubbock: Texas Technological College, 1959.

Sultana, Donald E. *The* Siege of Malta *Rediscovered: An Account of Sir Walter Scott's Mediterranean Journey and his Last Novel*. Edinburgh: Scottish Academic Press, 1977.

Sutherland, John. *The Life of Walter Scott: A Critical Biography*. Oxford: Blackwell, 1995.

Sutherland, Kathryn. "Fictional Economies: Adam Smith, Walter Scott and the Nineteenth-Century Novel," *English Literary History* 54, no. 1 (Spring 1987): 97–127.

Taylor, Brian. *The Scottish Parliament*. Edinburgh: Polygon, 1999.

Thomson, Christopher. "The Anglicisation of Scots Law." *Cencrastus* 12 (Spring 1983): 2–5.

Tiryakin, Edward A., & Ronald Rogowski, eds. *New Nationalism of the Developed West: Toward Explanation*. Boston: Allen & Unwin, 1985.

Trumpener, Katie. *Bardic Nationalism: the Romantic Novel and the British Empire*. Princeton, N.J.: Princeton University Press, 1997.

Tulloch, Graham. "Imagery in *The Highland Widow*." *Studies in Scottish Literature* 21 (1986): 147–57.

Turnbull, Ronald, & Craig Beveridge. "Scottish Nationalist, British Marxist: the Strange Case of Tom Nairn." *Cencrastus* 13 (Summer 1983): 2–5.

United Kingdom Parliament. *Scotland's Parliament*. Scottish Office Cm 3658. July 1997.

Valente, Joseph. "Upon the Braes: History and Hermeneutics in *Waverley*." *Studies in Romanticism* 25, no. 2 (Summer 1986): 251–76.

Watkin, David. *The Life and Work of C. R. Cockerell*. London: A. Zwemmer, 1974.

Watson, Mike. *Year Zero: An Inside View of the Scottish Parliament*. Edinburgh: Polygon, 2001.

Watson, Nicola J. "Kemble, Scott, and the Mantle of the Bard." In *The Appropriation of Shakespeare: Post-Renaissance Reconstructions of the Works and the Myth*, ed. Jean I. Marsden, 73–92. New York: Harvester, 1991.

Watson, Murray. *Being English in Scotland*. Edinburgh: Edinburgh University Press, 2003.

Welsh, Alexander. *The Hero of the Waverley Novels*. New Haven, Conn.: Yale University Press, 1963.

White, Hayden. *Metahistory: The Historical Imagination in Nineteenth-Century Fiction*. Baltimore, Md.: Johns Hopkins University Press, 1973.

Whitmore, Daniel. "Bibliolatry and the Rule of the Word: A Study of Scott's *Old Mortality*." *Philological Quarterly* 65, no. 2 (Spring 1986): 243–62.

Williamson, Arthur H. *Scottish National Consciousness in the Age of James VI: The Apocalypse, the Union and the Shaping of Scotland's Public Culture*. Edinburgh: John Donald, 1979.

Wilt, Judith. *Secret Leaves: The Novels of Sir Walter Scott*. Chicago: University of Chicago Press, 1985.

Withers, Charles W. J. *Geography, Science and National Identity: Scotland since 1520*. Cambridge: Cambridge University Press, 2001.

Woolf, Virginia. "Sir Walter Scott." *The Moment and Other Essays*, 56–68. New York: Harcourt, Brace, 1948.

Wormald, Jenny. "James VI and I: Two Kings or One?" *History* 68 (June 1983): 187–209.

Youngkin, Molly. "'Into the woof, a little Thibet wool': Orientalism and Representing 'Reality' in *The Surgeon's Daughter. Scottish Studies Review* 3, no. 1 (Spring 2002): 33–57.

INDEX